INTERNATIONAL POLITICAL ECONO

General Editor: Timothy M. Shaw, Prof
national Development Studies, and Direc
Studies, Dalhousie University, Nova Scotia,

Recent titles include:

Pradeep Agrawal, Subir V. Gokarn, Veena Mishra, Kirit S. Parikh and Kunal Sen
ECONOMIC RESTRUCTURING IN EAST ASIA AND INDIA: Perspectives
on Policy Reform

Solon L. Barraclough and Krishna B. Ghimire
FORESTS AND LIVELIHOODS: The Social Dynamics of Deforestation in
Developing Countries

Kathleen Barry (*editor*)
VIETNAM'S WOMEN IN TRANSITION

Ruud Buitelaar and Pitou van Dijck (*editors*)
LATIN AMERICA'S NEW INSERTION IN THE WORLD ECONOMY:
Towards Systemic Competitiveness in Small Economies

William D. Coleman
FINANCIAL SERVICES, GLOBALIZATION AND DOMESTIC POLICY
CHANGE: A Comparison of North America and the European Union

Paul Cook and Frederick Nixson (*editors*)
THE MOVE TO THE MARKET? Trade and Industry Policy Reform in
Transitional Economies

Mark E. Denham and Mark Owen Lombardi (*editors*)
PERSPECTIVES ON THIRD-WORLD SOVEREIGNTY: The Postmodern
Paradox

John Healey and William Tordoff (*editors*)
VOTES AND BUDGETS: Comparative Studies in Accountable Governance in
the South

Noeleen Heyzer, James V. Riker and Antonio B. Quizon (*editors*)
GOVERNMENT–NGO RELATIONS IN ASIA: Prospects and Challenges for
People-Centred Development

George Kent
CHILDREN IN THE INTERNATIONAL POLITICAL ECONOMY

David Kowalewski
GLOBAL ESTABLISHMENT: The Political Economy of North/Asian Networks

George Kent
CHILDREN IN THE INTERNATIONAL POLITICAL ECONOMY

David Kowalewski
GLOBAL ESTABLISHMENT: The Political Economy of North/Asian Networks

Laura Macdonald
SUPPORTING CIVIL SOCIETY: The Political Role of Non-Governmental
Organizations in Central America

Gary McMahon (*editor*)
LESSONS IN ECONOMIC POLICY FOR EASTERN EUROPE FROM
LATIN AMERICA

David B. Moore and Gerald J. Schmitz (*editors*)
DEBATING DEVELOPMENT DISCOURSE: Institutional and Popular
Perspectives

Juan Antonio Morales and Gary McMahon (*editors*)
ECONOMIC POLICY AND THE TRANSITION TO DEMOCRACY: The Latin
American Experience

Paul J. Nelson
THE WORLD BANK AND NON-GOVERNMENTAL ORGANIZATIONS:
The Limits of Apolitical Development

Archibald R. M. Ritter and John M. Kirk (*editors*)
CUBA IN THE INTERNATIONAL SYSTEM: Normalization and Integration

John Sorenson (*editor*)
DISASTER AND DEVELOPMENT IN THE HORN OF AFRICA

Howard Stein (*editor*)
ASIAN INDUSTRIALIZATION AND AFRICA: Studies in Policy Alternatives
to Structural Adjustment

Geoffrey D. Underhill (*editor*)
THE NEW WORLD ORDER IN INTERNATIONAL FINANCE

Sandra Whitworth
FEMINISM AND INTERNATIONAL RELATIONS

David Wurfel and Bruce Burton (*editors*)
SOUTHEAST ASIA IN THE NEW WORLD ORDER: The Political Economy
of a Dynamic Region

NGOs, States and Donors

Too Close for Comfort?

Edited by

David Hulme
*Professor of Development Studies and
Director of the Institute for Development Policy and Management
University of Manchester*

and

Michael Edwards
*Head of Information and Research
The Save the Children Fund*

in association with

Save the Children

First published 1997 by
MACMILLAN PRESS LTD
Houndmills, Basingstoke, Hampshire RG21 6XS
and London
Companies and representatives
throughout the world

ISBN 0–333–66581–3 hardcover
ISBN 0–333–66582–1 paperback

A catalogue record for this book is available
from the British Library.

This book is printed on paper suitable for recycling and
made from fully managed and sustained forest sources.

10   9   8   7   6   5   4   3   2   1
06   05   04   03   02   01   00   99   98   97

Printed and bound in Great Britain by
Antony Rowe Ltd, Chippenham, Wiltshire

Published in the United States of America by
ST. MARTIN'S PRESS, INC.,
Scholarly and Reference Division
175 Fifth Avenue, New York, N.Y. 10010

ISBN 0–312–16190–5 (cloth)
ISBN 0–312–16191–3 (paperback)

Contents

List of Tables

List of Figures

Preface

Back in 1992 we edited a volume under the title *Making a Difference: NGOs and Development in a Changing World* (Earthscan). This was derived from an international workshop convened by the Institute for Development Policy and Management (IDPM) and Save the Children Fund (UK) at the University of Manchester. The debates that arose in the workshop and the book have stimulated much interest and, in parallel, both of us have become increasingly concerned about the causes and consequences of NGO growth, and what appears to be a closer relationship between NGOs (both Northern and Southern) and official aid agencies. To further investigate these concerns IDPM and SCF–UK organised a second international workshop in Manchester in June 1994 entitled 'NGOs and Development: Performance and Accountability in the New World Order', which provided the basis for this volume.

When we re-read the papers which were presented to the second Manchester workshop, it became clear that there were two particular themes of concern, albeit overlapping. The first concerned issues of NGO performance and accountability, and how these processes were being re-shaped by changing roles and funding arrangements. Papers on this topic have been published in *NGO Performance and Accountability: Beyond the Magic Bullet* (eds Edwards and Hulme, Earthscan and Kumarian Press). That book provides a detailed review of these concerns and explores practical ways of dealing with them. The second theme concerned the broader relationships between NGOs, governments and official donor agencies, and how these changing relationships were affecting state–society relations, the future of development cooperation, and the interests of poor people. These concerns are explored in the present volume.

Inevitably, both works are the result of contributions from a large number of people, not all of whom are credited in the text. In particular, we should like to acknowledge the contributions of all the participants at the second Manchester workshop who presented papers and took part in plenaries and discussion groups. These have helped to shape our own thinking, and the thinking of other contributors to the two books. We should also stress that none of the contributors speak 'on behalf of' or represent a constituency in their writing: all write as individuals with their own personal point of view. No collection of essays can claim to be truly comprehensive, but we have endeavoured to include as wide a range of views and experiences as possible, from different regions of the world, alternative viewpoints, and contrasting organisations. We apologise to Christy Cannon whose workshop paper 'Dancing with the State: the Role of NGOs in Gap-filling' (forthcoming in the *Journal of International Development*) would have been included in this volume but for our editorial incompetence. Amukowa Anangwe, at the University of Nairobi, also prepared a paper for this volume which could not be included because of space limitations.

We should also like to acknowledge the financial support of a number of institutions that helped to make the workshop and the resulting publications possible. These include the NGO Unit of the Swedish International Development Authority (SIDA), the Government and Institutions Department and ESCOR in the UK Overseas Development Administration (ODA), Save the Children Fund-UK, and the Institute for Development Policy and Management at the University of Manchester. A large number of other NGOs also sponsored participants at the workshop, and our thanks go to them, especially to SCF Field Offices in Sudan, Uganda, Bangladesh, Peru, India, Pakistan, Thailand, Ghana, Colombia and Honduras.

At the University of Manchester especial thanks go to Debra Whitehead and Jayne Hindle for their exceptional efforts which made the workshop such a success; Catherine Williams and Marcia Doyle undertook similar responsibilities for Save the Children (UK). The same teams spent long hours hunched over computer screens in order to prepare the manuscripts for the two books and encourage the editors to meet their deadlines! Our sincere thanks go to them and to all the other individuals and agencies who have helped us to see these books through to a successful conclusion. A final mention must go to our partners (Georgina and Cora) and children (Edward, Jasmine and Saffron) for tolerating our neglect of family duties and outings while preparing this book.

DAVID HULME
MICHAEL EDWARDS

List of Abbreviations

ABONG	Brazilian NGO Association
AKF	Aga Khan Foundation
AKRSP	Aga Khan Rural Support Programme (Pakistan)
ANGOC	Asian NGO Coalition
AUSAID	Australian International Development Assistance Bureau
BINGOs	Big International NGOs
BRAC	Bangladesh Rural Advancement Committee
BRI	Bank Rakyat Indonesia (state-controlled bank)
BS1	Basic Strategy 1: system reform
BS2	Basic Strategy 2: sectoral agendas
BSSs	Assetless People's Cooperatives (Bangladesh)
CBO	Community-based Organisation
CBR	Community-based Rehabilitation
CCH	Child and Community Health Project (Bolivia)
CCP	Chinese Communist Party
CCSS	Central Council of Social Services (Sri Lanka)
CENDHEC	Centro Dom Helder Camara (Brazil)
CGAP	Consultative Group to Assist the Poorest
CIDA	Canadian International Development Agency
CSO	Civil Society Organisation
DAC	Development Assistance Committee (OECD)
DANIDA	Danish International Development Agency
DES	Division of Environmental Sanitation (Bolivia)
DINGOs	Dying International NGOs
DONGOs	Donor Organised NGOs
DRDAs	District Rural Development Agencies (India)
DSS	Department of Social Services (Sri Lanka)
ESF	Emergency Social Fund (Bolivia)
FAO	Food and Agriculture Organisation (UN)
FNS	Friedrich Naumann Stiftung (Germany)
GAO	General Accounting Office (USA)
GATT	General Agreement on Tariffs and Trade
GDP	Gross Domestic Product
GONGOs	Governmental-oriented NGOs
GoSL	Government of Sri Lanka

GoU	Government of Uganda
GROs	Grassroots Organisations
GSOs	Grassroots support organisations
IAF	Inter-American Foundation (USA)
IDPM	Institute for Development Policy and Management, University of Manchester
IDRC	International Development Research Centre (Canada)
IDS	Institute of Development Studies (Sussex, UK)
IFAD	International Fund for Agricultural Development
IIED	International Institute for the Environment and Development (London)
INDAP	Institute for Agricultural Development (Chile)
INGO	International NGO
IPPF	International Planned Parenthood Federation
ITDG	Intermediate Technology Development Group (UK)
JTF	*Janasaviya* Trust Fund (Sri Lanka)
KfW	Kreditanstalt fHr Wiederaufbau (Germany)
KREP	Kenya Rural Enterprise Programme
KSSs	Farmers' Cooperatives (Bangladesh)
LGEB	Local Government Engineering Board (Bangladesh)
MOs	Membership Organisations
MoPH	Ministry of Public Health (Thailand)
MoU	Memorandum of Understanding
MPCSs	Multi-purpose Cooperative Societies (Sri Lanka)
MSOs	Membership Support Organisations
NGOs	Non-governmental Organisations
NICs	Newly Industrialising Countries
NNGOs	Northern NGOs
NNGOC	National NGO Council (Sri Lanka)
NORAD	Norwegian Development Assistance Agency
NOVIB	Dutch NGO
NPA	New Policy Agenda
ODA	Overseas Development Administration (UK)
ODI	Overseas Development Institute (UK)
OECD	Organisation for Economic Cooperation and Development
PAPSCA	Programme for the Alleviation of Poverty and the Social Costs of Adjustment (Uganda)
PEP	Primary Education Programme (Bangladesh)
PRA	Participatory Rural Appraisal
PSC	Public Service Contractor
QUANGOs	Quasi-NGO (sometimes a parastatal)

RDSs	Rural Development Societies (Sri Lanka)
SANASA	Federation of Thrift and Credit Cooperative Societies (Sri Lanka)
SCF-UK	Save the Children Fund (UK)
SDM	Savings Development Movement (Zimbabwe)
SEEDS	Sarvodaya Economic Enterprises Development Services (Sri Lanka)
SIDA	Swedish International Development Authority
SLPAP	The Sri Lanka Poverty Alleviation Project
SNGO	Southern NGO
SSM	Sarvodaya Shramadana Movement (Sri Lanka)
UNDP	United Nations Development Programme
UNFPA	United Nations Family Planning Association
UNRISD	United Nations Research Institute for Social Development
USAID	United States Agency for International Development
VOs	Village Organisations (of BRAC in Bangladesh)
WHO	World Health Organisation (UN)
WV	World Vision
WVC	World Vision Canada
WVI	World Vision International
WVUK	World Vision UK
WVUS	World Vision USA

Notes on the Contributors

Anthony Bebbington Lectures at the Department of Geography and Institute of Behavioral Sciences at the University of Colorado, Balder. Formerly, he was is a Research Associate with the International Institute of Environment and Development, the Overseas Development Institute (ODI) and Cambridge University. His recent work has dealt with the shifting roles of NGOs, states and markets in Latin America, the links between the development and political activities of Andean and Amazonian peasant organisations, and donor NGO support programmes. Recent publications include *NGOs and the State in Latin America* (with Graham Thiele), *Reluctant Partners? NGOs, the State and Sustainable Agricultural Development* (with John Farrington) and *Los Actores de Una Decada Ganada: campesions, comunidades y tribus en la modernidad* (with Galo Ramon and others).

Harry Blair is Professor of Political Science at Bucknell University. He has also held academic appointments at Colgate, Columbia, Cornell and Yale Universities. On leave from Bucknell during 1992–94, he served as senior social science analyst with the Centre for Development Information and Evaluation at the United States Agency for International Development. While with USAID, Professor Blair worked on assessing donor experience in assisting democratisation, looking primarily at judicial reform and civil society.

Margarita Bosch is Executive Director of the Brazilian NGO CENDHEC. She also sits on the Coordination Committee of the National Association of Defence Centres, and the National Forum for the Defence of the Rights of Children and Adolescents. Since 1967 she has worked as an adviser to grassroots organisations, especially on popular education for citizenship.

John Clark is in the Operations Policy Group at the World Bank, where he has lead responsibility for the Bank's relations with NGOs. During his 20 years in the development field, he has focused on bridging the gap between grassroots organisations and government and official aid agencies. His current role at the Bank includes fostering increased and higher quality operational collaboration between the Bank and NGOs, coordinating the Bank's dialogue on policy issues with NGOs, and working with Country Department staff to encourage governments to foster a more enabling environment for NGOs. From 1979 to 1992, John Clark worked with OXFAM UK as Campaigns Manager and Development Policy Advisor. He is the author of three books, including *Democratising Development*, as well as several published articles.

Steven Commins is Director of Policy and Planning at World Vision International. He is a member of the editorial advisory board of *Development in Practice* and has edited several collections on African development. He is Visiting Professor at the Department of Urban Planning at UCLA and the School of International Relations at USC.

Thomas W. Dichter is an anthropologist who has been working in international development since the 1960s, mostly with and for NGOs. Since the early 1980s he has specialised in small and microenterprise development. He is currently a consultant to the World Bank's 'Sustainable Banking with the Poor' project.

Michael Edwards has spent the last decade and a half working for development NGOs. From 1984 to 1988 he was OXFAM-UK's Regional Representative in Lusaka, and for the last five years he has been Head of Information and Research for Save the Children Fund-UK, based in London. He is currently on sabbatical from his SCF post, exploring the 'Future of International Cooperation in Development' with Fellowships from the Leverhulme Trust (London) and Simon Fund (University of Manchester). He is the co-editor (with David Hulme) of *Making a Difference* (1992) and *NGO Performance and Accountability: Beyond the Magic Bullet* (1995).

Roland Hodson was for 10 years Chief Executive of the British NGO, ACTIONAID. He was a Visiting Fellow at the Centre for Voluntary Organisations at the London School of Economics and worked for the World Bank as an advisor to the Sri Lanka Poverty Alleviation Project. He is at present Humanitarian Advisor to the United Nations in Sri Lanka.

Jude Howell is a senior lecturer at the School of Development Studies, University of East Anglia. She is author of *China Opens Its Doors: the Politics of Economic Transition* (1993), and co-author of a forthcoming book on civil society in China.

David Hulme is Professor of Development Studies at the University of Manchester and Director of the Institute for Development Policy and Management. His main interests are in rural development and poverty-reduction strategies and he has worked and researched in Papua New Guinea, Sri Lanka, Bangladesh and Kenya. He is co-editor (with Michael Edwards) of *Making a Difference* (1992) and *NGO Performance and*

Accountability: Beyond the Magic Bullet (1995), co-author (with Paul Mosley) of *Finance Against Poverty* (1996) and co-author (with Mark Turner) of *Governance, Administration and Development: Making the State Work* (1997).

Mohsen Marzouk is a Tunisian sociologist and a specialist in Arab social and political movements. He has undertaken studies of the student movement in Tunisia and of Maghreb political systems in general. Currently, he is the Director of a four-year comparative study across seven countries on 'NGOs and Civil Society in the Arab World', based at the El Taller Foundation, an NGO research and networking centre in Tunis.

Richard Mawer is Save the Children Fund UK Field Director in Uganda. Prior to this appointment he had many years experience with Save the Children Fund's Southeast Asian programmes.

Horacio Morales has for many years been the Director of PRRM, the Philippines Rural Reconstruction Movement, and has spent a lifetime in the struggle for democratic development in his home country. He was also one of the founders of El Taller, an NGO research and networking centre based in Tunis, and for a time was its acting Executive Secretary. He helped to found CIVICUS, the World Alliance for Citizen Participation. He has published many books and articles on development and democracy, including a selection of his speeches.

Jenny Pearce is a lecturer in the Department of Peace Studies, University of Bradford. She has researched extensively in a number of Latin American countries and has worked closely with NGOs and popular organisations in the region. She has been consultant/advisor to a number of British development NGOs including OXFAM, CAFOD and Christian Aid, and to the Project Counselling Service based in Costa Rica.

Jehan Perera is Director of the Sarvodaya Legal Service, a Director of the National Peace Council of Sri Lanka and a weekly political columnist for the Sunday Island newspaper in Colombo. He has a Doctorate of Law from Harvard Law School.

Roger Riddell has been a Research Fellow at the Overseas Development Institute, London since 1984. His recent publications include *Non-Governmental Organisations and Rural Poverty Alleviation* (1995, with Mark Robinson), *Promoting Development by Proxy: an Evaluation of the Development Impact of Government Support to Swedish NGOs* (1995, joint author), *Foreign Aid Reconsidered* (1987), *Manufacturing Africa* (1990, joint author), *Foreign Direct Investment in sub-Saharan Africa*

(World Bank 1991, with L Cockcroft), and *Zimbabwe to 1996: Prospects for Growth* (Economist Intelligence Unit/Business International (1992). Current research interests include a new role for foreign aid, and the growth, development and impact of NGOs in the development process.

Mark Robinson is a Fellow of the Institute of Development Studies at the University of Sussex. His current research interests are on the role of NGOs in civil society, foreign aid and democratisation in Africa, and on new approaches to public management in developing countries.

Isagani Serrano is a well-known writer, activist and development worker in the Philippines. He is currently the Deputy Director of PRRM, the Philippines Rural Reconstruction Movement, and was part of the delegation of Philippine NGOs to the World Summit on Social Development in Copenhagen. He has published many books and articles on development, including *Civil Society in the Asia-Pacific Region* (1994).

Ranjith Wanigaratne is Director of the Planning and Monitoring Unit of the Mahaweli Authority of Sri Lanka. He formerly worked as a researcher at the Agrarian Research and Training Institute (ARTI) in Colombo.

Geof Wood is Reader and Director of the Centre for Development Studies in the School of Social Sciences at the University of Bath. He has worked extensively in India and Bangladesh on agrarian change and with large NGOs as an adviser and research collaborator. He has recently published *Bangladesh: Whose Ideas, Whose Interests* (1994), as well as co-authoring *The Water-Sellers*, *Breaking the Chains* and *Trading the Silver Seed*.

Part I

NGOs, States and Donors:
An Overview and Key Issues

1 NGOs, States and Donors: An Overview

David Hulme and Michael Edwards

INTRODUCTION

Non-governmental organisations (NGOs)[1] involved in economic and social development have prospered with the 'associational revolution' (Salamon, 1993:1) sweeping the globe in the late twentieth century. Their numbers have grown exponentially; the size of some makes them significant players in social welfare and employment markets at the national level; the funding they attract has increased enormously; and their visibility in policy-making fora, the media, and with the general public, has never been higher. And yet, many NGO personnel and analysts have major concerns about the contribution that NGOs are making to development and about the ways in which 'success' has changed and is changing them (Edwards and Hulme, 1992 and 1995).

This concern is reflected in the title of the present volume, which raises the question of whether NGOs are getting so close (in terms of interests, values, methods, priorities and other factors) to Northern-government donors[2] and, to a lesser degree, developing-country states,[3] that important elements of their potential contribution to development have been lost or weakened. Popularity is pleasant, but does it reflect genuine recognition or does it accrue because NGOs have now been socialised into the establishment – the 'development industry'? Are NGOs being valued because of the different questions they ask and approaches they adopt? Or are they valued because they now have the social grace not to persist with awkward questions and the organisational capacity to divert the poor and disadvantaged from more radical ideas about how to overcome poverty? Are NGOs losing the 'special relationship' with the poor, with radical ideas, and with alternatives to the orthodoxies of the rich and powerful, that they have claimed in the past?

In this volume we examine the ways in which the relationships between NGOs, states and donors have and are evolving and their implications for poverty reduction. The reader should be aware that this is difficult terrain in which to make rapid progress: there is no consensus on the specification of where the limits of the NGO world lie; theoretical frameworks for analysing such relationships are only partially developed; within the NGO, donor and state categories there is enormous diversity; the associational cultures and contexts of NGOs vary greatly from country to country; the empirical study of such relationships has received little attention (though we believe that many of the chapters in this book strengthen the empirical base substantially); and individual NGOs, donor agencies and states are far from monolithic – different individuals and groups within each have differing interests and viewpoints which can make the identification of a precise agency 'position' difficult.

However, it is essential for NGO strategists and researchers to explore this complex and messy terrain if our understanding is to move beyond the public cheeriness of donors about the 'marvellous' work of NGOs and the quiet complaints of senior officials in developing countries about the continued propagation of the NGO 'myth'.

THE RISE AND RISE OF NGOs: BOTH PRINCE AND MERCHANT?

The number of development NGOs registered in the OECD countries of the industrialised 'North' has grown from 1600 in 1980 to 2970 in 1993 (Smillie and Helmich, 1993), and over the same period the total spending of these NGOs has risen from US$2.8 billion to US$5.7 billion in current prices (OECD, 1994). The 176 'International NGOs' of 1909 had blossomed into 28 900 by 1993 (Commission on Global Governance, 1995)! Similar figures have been reported in many countries in the 'South' with a particularly rapid increase over the last five years. For example, the number of NGOs registered with the government in Nepal rose from 220 in 1990 to 1210 in 1993 (Rademacher and Tamang, 1993:34); in Bolivia the figure increased from around 100 in 1980 to 530 twelve years later (Arellano-Lopez and Petras, 1994:562): and in Tunisia there were 5186 NGOs registered in 1991 compared with only 1886 in 1988 (Marzouk, in this volume).

Parallel to this increase in overall numbers has been the growth of some individual NGOs to cover the provision of health, education and credit services to millions of people in thousands of communities, especially in South Asia. For example, the Bangladesh Rural Advancement Committee (BRAC) now has more than 12 000 staff and has plans to work with over three million people (AKF/NOVIB, 1993) – it operates a field office in East Africa; in India, the Self-Employed Womens' Association (SEWA) has over one million clients in its credit programmes; Sarvodaya in Sri Lanka works in 7000 villages (Perera, in this volume). The access of NGOs to decision-makers in both North and South is greater than ever before, as their advocacy role continues to expand and they are courted in debates over policy and practice. Grassroots organisations (GROs) have a lower public profile, but they have also experienced considerable growth over the last decade and are beginning to organise themselves much more at the national and international levels (Korten, 1990; CIVICUS, 1994). Clearly, something significant is happening in the world of international development.

Beyond these figures the public image of NGOs and GROs has amplified in recent years. Their high visibility at the 1992 UN Earth Summit at Rio was eclipsed by events at Beijing in 1995 where the NGO forum got greater news coverage than the official UN Women's Conference. For the general public in countries such as the UK development is what OXFAM, Save the Children Fund and the like do – who has ever heard of the Overseas Development Administration?[4] On the television when a snatch of development or relief footage is required it is an NGO project we see, a tired Concern or Médecin Sans Frontières worker who tells us what is happening or a small-scale project which is used to illustrate 'successful' development.

The rise of NGOs and GROs on the world scene is an important phenomenon which has implications for the development prospects of poor people, for the future of these organisations themselves, and for the wider political economy of which they form a small but growing part. But what lies behind these trends? The rise of NGOs is not an accident; nor is it solely a response to local initiative and voluntary action. Equally important is the increasing popularity of NGOs with governments and official aid agencies, which is itself a response to recent developments in economic and political thinking. Over the last fifteen years, and particularly since the end of the Cold War, development policy and aid transfers have come to be dominated by what Robinson (1993) calls a 'New Policy Agenda'. This Agenda is not monolithic: its details vary from one official aid agency to another, but in all cases it is driven by beliefs organised around the twin poles of neo-liberal economics and liberal democratic theory (Moore, 1993).

First, markets and private initiative are seen as the most efficient mechanisms for achieving economic growth and providing most services to most people (Colclough and Manor, 1991). Governments 'enable' private provision but should minimise their direct role in the economy; because of their supposed cost-effectiveness in reaching the poorest, official agencies support NGOs in providing welfare services to those who cannot be reached through markets (Fowler, 1988; Meyer, 1992). Of course, NGOs have a long history of providing welfare services to poor people in countries where governments lacked the resources to ensure universal coverage in health and education; the difference is that now they are seen as the preferred channel for service-provision in deliberate substitution for the state.

Second, under the New Policy Agenda NGOs and GROs are seen as vehicles for 'democratisation' and essential components of a thriving 'civil society', which in turn are seen as essential to the success of the Agenda's economic dimension (Moore, 1993). NGOs and GROs are supposed to act as a counterweight to state power by opening up channels of communication and participation, providing training grounds for activists promoting pluralism and by protecting human rights. The rise of citizens' movements around the world documented by Korten (1990) and crystallised most recently in the establishment of CIVICUS (1994), the 'World Alliance for Citizen Participation', may not be a result of developments in official aid, but it cannot be separated entirely from the economic and political ideals that underpin the New Policy Agenda.

This context has fostered increased volumes of official aid being made available to NGOs and, to a lesser degree GROs. They are seen as one means for operationalising the New Policy Agenda's economic and political goals. Nerfin (1987) may have got it wrong – for some donors, NGOs are seen as being both 'prince and merchant'! Their relationship with the 'people' is seen as giving them greater public legitimacy than government while their managerial features are seen as permitting private sector levels of cost control and efficiency.

Published OECD data indicate that the volume of its members' aid going to NGOs increased from 0.7 per cent of the total in 1975 to 3.6 per cent in 1985 and 5.0 per cent in 1993/94. However, these published figures grossly underestimate the true volume (Overseas Development Institute 1995:1) as they exclude NGO funding from the US government (perhaps US$1 to US$2 billion in 1993/94), multilateral donors[5] such as the World Bank, European Union, UN agencies and the like, and official aid projects that are implemented by NGOs (estimated at US$640 million in 1994). The OECD estimate of US$5.7 billion for 1993, mentioned earlier, is certainly an underestimate, perhaps by as much as US$3 billion according to one World Bank estimate. Channelling funds to NGOs is big business!

This growth in official support has transformed the composition of NGO finances. The World Bank estimates that in the early 1970s about 1.5 per cent of total income for development NGOs derived from donors:

by the mid-1990s this had risen to around 30 per cent (Overseas Development Institute, 1995:1). In the UK, the five largest development NGOs are all increasingly dependent on government funding, with ratios varying from 20 to 55 per cent in the mid-1990s. Figures vary greatly from country to country, however, depending upon bilateral aid agency policy.[6] In Austria around 10 per cent of NGO income is from official sources. The figure increases to 34 per cent for Australia, 66 per cent for the USA and 70 per cent for Canada. For Sweden the figure reaches a staggering 85 per cent (ibid.: 2). If Canadian NGOs reach for the Vitamin C when CIDA (the Canadian International Development Agency) sneezes (Smillie, 1995) then Swedish NGOs are likely to be admitted into intensive care units when SIDA (the Swedish International Development Authority) has a snuffle! Of course, the Swedes may never catch a cold, but the potential havoc that can be wrought to dependent NGOs if government policy changes, is clear.

Comparative figures for Southern NGOs are not available, but all the evidence points to even higher rates of dependency on official funds, particularly for the larger NGOs in the South. As mentioned already, NGOs in Nepal, Bolivia and Tunisia have grown rapidly in numbers in the early 1990s because of a donor 'spending spree' (Rademacher and Tamang, 1993). In Bangladesh, BRAC and Proshika have negotiated aid packages with donor consortia in excess of US$50 million at a time, and the Working Women's Forum in India is funded mainly by UNFPA (Ramesh, 1995). The recently-announced 'Consultative Group to Assist the Poorest' (CGAP), housed in the World Bank, will provide US$200 million or more from bilateral and multilateral donors to NGO microfinance programmes in the South. Our personal experience in Bangladesh, Sri Lanka, Kenya and Nepal indicates that a dependency of 80 to 95 per cent on official funds is common, though often at second or third-hand as funds are channelled via Northern NGOs or other institutions.

WHAT DO WE KNOW ABOUT NGO, STATE AND DONOR RELATIONSHIPS?

The relationships outlined in the previous section have and are being reshaped by the New Policy Agenda and other forces. The promises that this holds out for NGOs, in terms of finance and seats at important fora, might indicate that this is a time of unbridled opportunity. However, as the sub-title of this volume indicates, we also perceive that the contribution of NGOs to development is under threat. Increased organisational scale and influence for NGOs can only be valued when it contributes to the achievement of developmental goals. If expansion and recognition mean diverting an agency from its mission, then there may be a higher price to pay. While the empirical evidence shows that the influences of the New Policy Agenda on NGOs are many and various, we concur with Smillie (1995) that the 'alms bazaar' of which NGOs are now a part increases the likelihood that they are becoming the implementers of donor policies.

The most obvious pressures for co-option arise from the availability of aid finance: 'he who pays the piper calls the tune'. While funds are important it must be recognised that the influence of utilising such funds goes well beyond simple finance. The acceptance of increasing volumes of foreign aid involves entering into agreements about what is done, and how it is to be reported and accounted for. This fosters an emphasis on certain forms of activity at the expense of others, on upward accountability (rather than downward accountability to members or beneficiaries), and on particular techniques and donor definitions of 'achievement' throughout the organisation (Edwards and Hulme, 1995). Not surprisingly, as NGOs get closer to donors they become more like donors (see Jorgensen *et al.*, 1993 for a discussion of the ways in which Danish NGOs have become a reflection of DANIDA). Unit costs, quantifiable outputs, logical frameworks and detailed specifications of what 'partners' are to do, become organisational norms. In themselves there is nothing inherently wrong with such approaches, but they are quite inconsistent with the operations of organisations that claim to be promoting qualitative change, who believe that development planning and management are a learning process rather than a blueprint and who claim to treat their 'partners' as equals. Even more importantly, donor approaches to beneficiary participation remain instrumentalist (see ODA, 1995; Bhatnagar and Williams, 1992): this is incompatible with the proclaimed vision of the vast majority of NGOs who conceptualise participation as a means to empower the poor and disadvantaged, not simply to achieve short-term project goals.

The absorption of donor ideas and norms has implications not only for methods but also for personnel. As NGOs adopt these approaches then English-speaking graduates with financial skills become increasingly important. Again, there is nothing inherently wrong with such people and the skills they bring, but there is often a downside as vernacular-speaking field management specialists see their importance waning in the organisation. Donor conceptualisations also have important implications for 'who' NGOs are seeking to help. Poor people, as in the case of many credit-delivering NGOs, are usually viewed by donors as those currently below an arbitrarily defined 'poverty line', disaggregated only by gender (Hulme and Mosley, 1996). Distinctions between the poor, core poor and vulnerable become irrelevant when you are judged by donors who believe that the poverty line is also the finishing tape for social welfare provision. Almost all women are viewed as 'poor', regardless of class, caste, ethnicity and other factors. Much of the fine tuning that NGOs have sought in their earlier work is gone.

While NGOs remain diverse, there is clear evidence that this diversity is being reduced by donor policies. Supplying increasing volumes of funds to SNGOs is encouraging them to pursue activities and take on structural forms that enhance the likelihood of access to funds. Nowhere is this clearer than in Bangladesh where NGOs increasingly converge on the provision of group-based credit for micro-enterprise as their main activity (Montgomery, Bhattacharya and Hulme, 1996). Many donors identify with this model of poverty-alleviation by 'promotion' (that is, individual enterprise and self-employment) rather than 'protection' (that is, public provision of basic needs); it promises to be financially sustainable (see Dichter in this volume); it can be scaled-up quickly, satisfying the donors' needs for high-volume, rapid disbursement; it upsets no-one; and it provides excellent opportunities for profile and public relations. Most major NGOs in the country have moved to accommodate this model. In recent years even the Association for Social Advancement has shifted 'from rural revolutionaries to village development bankers' (Rutherford, 1995:1). The impact of donor-financed NGO credit schemes is now so pervasive that society itself has changed: villagers expect NGOs to deliver credits as part of their programme and supply has shaped demand! No-one doubts that better financial intermediation to poor people is critical, nor that the achievements of the Grameen Bank and others in showing that 'the poor are bankable' have been tremendously important. But development is about much more than credit. The case against the current donor preoccupation with micro-finance is not about what is *included*, but about what is *excluded* by this model, and particularly its impact on the capacity of poor people to organise themselves independently to confront vested interests and structural inequalities.

Within the institutional triangle (see Wood in this volume) of state, community and market it is clear from the available record (Edwards and Hulme, 1992 and 1995; Farrington and Bebbington, 1993) that NGOs have made a contribution, albeit minor in comparison to other actors, to the rolling back of the state. What is unclear is whether this rolling back has strengthened the role of communities as citizens to influence state actions, as is commonly assumed by those who view NGOs as based exclusively in civil society; or whether it has contributed more to the identification of the private sector as the main provider of essential goods and services for the entire population (including the poor and disadvantaged). This latter position views the poor as consumers whose needs can be most efficiently met by the private sector. NGOs are analysed as non-profit private agencies accountable through the forces of competition in an open market. Beneficiaries and members become 'customers' (as BRAC in Bangladesh now terms the poor) and claims to be strengthening civil society become redundant. As with the private sector, 'empowerment' in such organisations is confined to leaders and managers.

There is of course a counter-case to all this. NGOs can claim to use their increasing closeness to donors to expand effective operations and influence official approaches and concepts. In terms of the recognition of the influence of gender on development interventions and outcomes there may be substance to such claims, although the independent influence of the feminist movement in the west was also very important. At the present time, however, claims for a counterflow of ideas back to donors focus on participation. Increasingly donors claim to be integrating participation into their methodologies, through the involvement of 'stakeholders' (ODA, 1995) in planning and the use of participatory rural appraisal (PRA). Detailed empirical research is needed to elaborate whether such approaches lead to changed interventions and whether such changes lead to improved outcomes. However, at the very least, the theoretical incompatibilities between donor rhetoric and donor practice must point to the improbability of donors treating participation seriously. Can participation be achieved by limited consultations about strategies that are already well formulated and that must fit into three-year time frames? Can citizens really participate in the activities of donors who disenfranchise them by attaching externally set conditionalities to loans? And, can we seriously believe that the participation of stakeholders in planning leads to consensus and harmony about how to proceed? Unfortunately the adoption of 'NGOspeak' by donors may have more to do with the need for aid agencies to improve their public image than change their practice.

Claims that donor funding can be used to expand effective NGO operations without compromising quality rest on the degree to which large organisations can manage growth successfully, and on the impact that scaling-up the size of NGO programmes has on other aspects of performance (such as local institutional development) and accountability (including downwards to the grassroots). There are few independent accounts which have tested these claims, though the picture from the large NGOs themselves is unsurprisingly rosy (AKF/NOVIB, 1993). Those studies which do exist conclude that it is certainly possible to avoid undesirable side-effects, but that this requires very well-developed managerial capacities, a favourable context, and a quality of relationships with donors, that are rare in practice (Howes and Sattar, 1992; Wils, 1995). It is also possible for NGOs to balance large-scale service provision with institution building and advocacy so that each supports and feeds off the other. However, the most comprehensive review of these dilemmas to date concludes that such an ideal scenario is much more difficult to achieve than the theory suggests (Edwards and Hulme, 1995).

In part, this debate turns on a confusion (or difference of view) over the position and function of NGOs in society. Paradoxically, however, the lack of clarity about whether NGOs are best viewed as civil-society or market-based institutions does provide some positive indicators for the future. It reveals that NGOs still have strategic choices open to them: depending on context they have room for manoeuvre to decide how close they get to donors and to examine how extensively they are promoting market-based or society-based strategies for development goals. The chapters that follow shed light, though often in a contradictory fashion, on these important issues.

CONCEPTUALISING NGO, STATE AND DONOR RELATIONSHIPS

At the heart of the present volume lie questions about the relationships between NGOs, developing-country states and donors, and in particular about the control or influence that each of these parties might have over the others. The relationships between the actors central to the present volume can be represented schematically (Figure 1.1). Such an approach risks oversimplifying complex linkages, but it facilitates the discussion of the key elements of these relationships and permits the reader to identify the particular emphases, and omissions, in this volume.

This conceptualisation views relationships between NGOs, states and donors in terms of bargaining and negotiation, although at times coercion is a possible strategy. While one actor may dominate any particular bilateral relationship it recognises that each actor will attempt to influence the behaviour of the others. Relationships are seen as having two main dimensions. The first concerns the particular objectives that an actor seeks to achieve through interacting with others. These are likely to be a combination of officially stated goals (for example, assisting the people of poorer nations, promoting national economic development) and hidden objectives (for example, opening up new export markets, staying in government). The second dimension relates to the levers that an actor may use to control or influence other actors: these range from persuading by argument, through offering financial inducements, to direct coercion. Such mechanisms may be formal (financial transfers, accounting, contracts, reporting systems and registration) or informal (information flows, staff exchanges, patronage, and seminars or discussions).

Central to this volume is the argument that both donors and developing-country states are taking a much greater interest in NGO activity, and are making greater efforts to influence it directly and indirectly. For donors

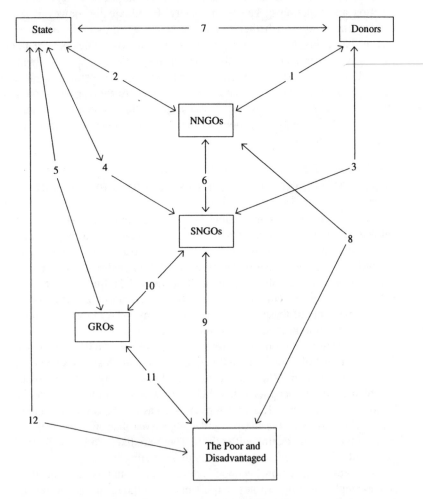

Figure 1.1 NGO, state and donor relationships: a schematic representation

this interest derives from the New Policy Agenda and the principles that underpin it. For developing country states it derives from a response to donor initiatives and a desire to ensure that state (and often regime) legitimacy is not weakened. The initial focus for such activity was on NNGOs through donor finance (relationship 1 in Figure 1.1) and state oversight of NNGOs (relationship 2) because of concerns that they might impinge on national sovereignty (for example, see Howell in this volume). For their part, NNGOs sought to influence donor and southern-state policies through operational collaboration, lobbying and advocacy (for an example see Mawer in this volume). Times have moved on, however, with donors shifting their attention to SNGOs (relationship 3: see Bebbington and Riddell in this volume) and developing-country states increasingly focusing on the role of indigenous NGOs (relationship 4) and GROs (relationship 5) in development. The main donor lever has been the incentive of direct access to increased volumes of foreign aid. For developing country states a range of interventions have been utilised to influence NGOs and GROs including 'sticks' (closure, deregistration, investigation and coordination) and 'carrots' (tax exempt status, access to policy makers and public funding). Farrington and Bebbington's (1993) description of state–SNGO relationships as being those of 'reluctant partners' appears to characterise the situation in many countries, but these relations are complex and vary enormously. While Bratton (1989) has argued that African states have tended to take a relatively control-oriented approach toward NGOs, Anangwe (1995) points out that in Kenya the heavy handedness of the state has focused mainly on larger NGOs, based in Nairobi and with urban programmes. Smaller NGOs working in remoter rural areas are allowed to operate with a much higher degree of autonomy as they do not threaten the state. In Asia the state appears to have been able to accept NGO independence more easily but, as Wanigaratne's and Perera's chapters in this volume illustrate, much depends on the specific regime: NGOs in Sri Lanka found themselves under attack from President Premadasa after years of governments that had been relatively relaxed about NGO activity. While this book has much to say about state–SNGO relationships it does not directly examine state–GRO linkages (relationship 5).

This shift in focus has left NNGOs with an identity crisis. As SNGOs and SNGO alliances and networks strengthen their capacities in project planning and implementation, capacity building and policy lobbying, what role is left for NNGOs? Is the NNGO–SNGO relationship becoming redundant (relationship 6) as donors finance SNGOs directly, as SNGOs assert their primacy in influencing their governments and as south-south linkages become increasingly effective in training and institutional development? Or is there still a key role for NGOs in the North in international development, albeit radically different to the role that they have played up until now? For many NNGOs, complacent and unimaginative, these remain questions for the future rather than the present. But they are central to the themes of this book and we return to them in our Conclusion.

The increasing role of NGOs in development has meant that southern states and donors now include policy toward NGOs within their 'policy dialogues' (relationship 7). In most cases this item is low on the agenda compared to items such as structural adjustment, macroeconomic policy and public sector reform. However, donors are keen to have easy access to SNGOs, to support them without having to go through cumbersome procedures and to promote domestic policy environments that facilitate NGO activity (see Blair and Clark, in this volume). The governments of developing countries have approached such dialogue with mixed feelings. On the one hand they recognise the advantages of adopting, or at least appearing to adopt, a pluralist position. Pragmatically, letting donors fund NGO activity can at times pull in additional aid funds. On the other hand, SNGOs are often regarded with suspicion because of their foreign ties, and SNGO activity often substitutes for state service provision, thus reducing state control over resources and services and strengthening the case for public sector reform (something which few governments are keen to pursue). At the extreme, countries such as Bangladesh have felt that donor conditionalities have challenged national sovereignty by insisting that the state reduce its role in overseeing and coordinating NGO activity.

The avowed *raison d'être* of development NGOs (northern or southern) and GROs is poverty reduction. This can take a variety of forms ranging from a focus on material conditions to more holistic approaches involving empowerment, sustainable development and reduced economic and social vulnerability.[7] Development NGOs have done well out of the poor. The swelling ranks of the poor (estimated to number 1.1 billion in the mid-1980s by the World Bank, 1990:29) and the belief that NGOs are more effective and efficient in helping them than other agencies has fuelled NGO growth. But have popularity and growth led to NNGOs and SNGOs losing their roots?[8] Most NNGOs now accept that their 'roots' are not at the coalface of poverty and have over the last 20 years attempted to minimise their direct management of development programmes in the South (relationship 8). But if one looks at their northern roots (within their own civil societies), how much of their time and resources are used to mobilise support for actions to help poor people in the South, and how much for public relations in order to ensure that contributions keep on flowing? Is the use of television advertising and 'tele-sales' approaches business-like, or does it show that some NNGOs are themselves businesses? As the latest round of aid cuts in northern countries shows, NNGOs have not persuaded the citizenries of western Europe and North America to take a deeper interest in the problems of developing countries or to demand that their governments provide more effective assistance. Even more significantly, NNGOs have neglected the most important tasks that might lead to real change in international relations: values of interconnectedness, humility and service; relationships of respect and equality; and lifestyles which promote sustainable development over short-term gain.

SNGOs have a choice as to whether they seek to work directly with individual households (relationship 9), or whether they work with GROs that link the poor to SNGO programmes (relationships 10 and 11) or simply provide support to GROs. As SNGOs have grown then the preferred operational mode for many has been mobilising village organisations or community-based organisations according to a standard format which the SNGO believes to be optimal. This facilitates mass outreach and helps to reduce administrative costs. However, it also raises the likelihood that pseudo-participation (Uphoff, 1986) will displace the active participation of the poor in GROs. In effect, GROs become a convenient means of aggregating poor 'customers' rather than locally based organisations that are at least partially accountable to local people. While this problem has been identified in many countries it has been highlighted especially in Bangladesh (see Wood in this volume). Hashemi (1995) argues 'only through the development of a system of accountability to the poor can NGOs truly transform themselves into organisations of the poor... NGOs have to make a choice; between the four-wheel drive vehicle that comes with government licensing and donor funding, and the much harder conditions involved in living alongside poor people'. This question – whether (by volition, cooption or coercion) SNGOs are concentrating on their linkages to states and donors to such a degree that their relationships with the poor are being eroded – is critical. We return to it throughout the book and in the Conclusion.

Finally, in this section, the reader should note that while individual chapters make reference to organisations and forces in the environment beyond the actors identified in Figure 1.1, we do not systematically examine these external factors. This is not to imply that northern states, transnational corporations, markets and the private sector in developing countries have no influence over the evolving role and nature of NGOs, but to provide a focus for the analysis of relationships that we believe to be of particular importance.

THE STRUCTURE OF THE BOOK

The first part of the book, including this chapter, seeks to establish an analytical framework and present overviews of key issues in NGO, state and
donor relationships. In Chapter 2, Harry Blair examines the ways in which
donors (and particularly USAID) have sought to strengthen civil society in
developing countries and democratise state–society interactions. Two basic
strategies are identified and analysed: improving the policy environment
for civil society organisations (including NGOs), and supporting specific
organisations directly. The chapter identifies the wide range of options
available to donors and points out that selection needs to be based upon
objectives and contexts. Blair underlines the analytical sophistication that
donors will need if they are to make appropriate choices and work effectively with NGOs to strengthen civil societies. In this respect this contribution stands in stark contrast to the simple assumption that underlies most
donor action; that working with SNGOs automatically strengthens society.
John Clark (Chapter 3) examines the opportunities for NGOs to assist the
poor and disadvantaged to participate more effectively in development
processes. He argues for NGOs to shift from a 'supply side' approach to a
'demand side' approach, while donors should pursue a policy dialogue
with southern states to foster a more enabling environment for NGOs. The
issue of whether NGOs, and particularly SNGOs, are neglecting demand-
side preferences is a point that is elaborated in the Conclusion. In Chapter
4, Mark Robinson tackles the contentious issue of whether the voluntary
sector is being surreptitiously privatised. From an extensive literature
review he concludes that there is little evidence that NGOs are becoming
significantly involved in public-sector contracting. Where contracting is
evident then it is closely associated with donor activities, usually in neo-
liberal policy environments and in areas where NGOs have achieved high
levels of technical competence. In a provocative piece, and in contradiction to the thrust of Robinson's contribution, Geof Wood (Chapter 5)
argues that state functions (particularly for welfare provision) are being
'franchised out' to NGOs. Civil society, and in particular poorer citizens,
are witnessing the erosion of citizen rights as externally-financed NGOs
with little downward accountability become increasingly important to
welfare provision. The chapter is illustrated by reference to Bangladesh
where NGOs have become so significant in service delivery. The final
chapter in Part I provides a broad review of trends in the Asia–Pacific
region with a particular focus on the empowerment of individual citizens
and the role of citizen associations. Morales and Serrano's contribution is
heavily influenced by the thinking of NGOs and GROs in the Philippines.

They also point to the duplicity of donors (such as the UK and US governments) who link aid to democracy in their policy statements but treat countries on a differential basis when it comes to practice. Indonesia may score low on democracy and human rights counts, but donors pledged it US$5 billion at the Paris Club in 1994! Like Marguerita Bosch and Mohsen Marzouk later in the book, Morales and Serrano are more interested in the broader questions of where NGOs and GROs 'fit' in the evolution of state–society relations and sustainable development than in the narrower questions (which preoccupy donors) of how inputs and outputs are related at the level of projects or individual agencies. Indeed, a criticism made by commentators from the South is that the whole debate on NGO performance, accountability, legitimacy and cost-effectiveness is framed exclusively in Western (liberal) terms. This is an important criticism which we have not answered sufficiently in this volume.

In Part II, the focus shifts to NGO and donor relationships. Tony Bebbington and Roger Riddell (Chapter 7) present a summary of the major review that they have conducted on the direct funding of SNGOs by official aid agencies. They examine the modalities that this can take and provide examples of such practices. Their conclusion counsels that donors should adopt a cautious approach to direct funding as their capacity to do this effectively may be limited and the consequences of a rapid shift to this approach could ultimately be counterproductive. Tom Dichter (Chapter 8) focuses on NNGOs, particularly those in the USA, involved in the microfinance sector. He too sounds a cautionary note and questions whether the growing numbers of NGOs in this field are not moving away from their espoused missions to fulfil a donor-led agenda. Chapter 9, by Steve Commins, reviews the experience of World Vision International (WVI) which has developed increasingly close ties with official agencies in recent years. It recognises the dangers of getting 'too close' to donors, but argues that (at least to date) closer relationships are producing positive results and that WVI has been able to 'at least partially balance the accountabilities of project work and of policy work on aid issues'. He does not counsel complacency, however, but concludes that although WVI has learned how to lobby on aid and relief policies it has not (as with other NGOs) developed strategies to challenge or critique international economic trends, transnational enterprise or patterns of consumption and lifestyle. How NGOs might tackle these deeper issues that are so central to keeping poor people poor is another issue considered in the book's Conclusion.

Jehan Perera's account (Chapter 10) of Sarvodaya Shramadana's recent experience provides a case study of an SNGO that had developed direct links with donor agencies through a donor consortium. It provides alarming insights into what can happen when such close relationships turn sour and charts the breakdown in the 'partnership' between Sarvodaya and its financiers. Sarvodaya was not blameless in this sad story, but the 'contract culture' of the northern donors certainly proved inimicable to a satisfactory resolu-tion of the problems that did arise. The donor consortium weakened Sarvodaya's negotiating position and this case suggests that large NGOs may best defend their autonomy by bargaining separately with donors.[9] Part II concludes with a study of a major NGO financier (the World Bank) in Sri Lanka. Roland Hodson (Chapter 11) analyses the way in which the World Bank sought to work with NGOs in that country through a 'social fund'. Despite the foolishness of the initial conceptualisation of the Janasaviya Trust Fund (JTF) – the 'John Cleese Poverty Project' (that is, how *not* to alleviate poverty) – he concludes that ultimately the JTF may strengthen local NGO capacities and that the Bank has an experience from which it could learn how to work more effectively with NGOs. Key questions remain, however, as to whether Bank techniques and approaches – cost–benefit analysis, hasty visits by peripatetic task managers, rigid plans and opulent lifestyles – can build long-term relationships with a domestic NGO sector. If the Bank does not learn then 'the elephant (World Bank) will trample the grass (NGOs)'. Those with a more jaundiced view of the Bank than Hodson may claim that the Bank has already learned this lesson, but turns a blind eye when it would mean that an adjustment associated social safety net would be out of sequence with adjustment measures: better to have 'implementation problems' than adjustment policies that admit that there will be social consequences that cannot be mitigated!

In Part III, we focus on NGO–state relationships through a series of country and regional case studies. The first two chapters look at two parts of the world in which relatively little is known about the activity of NGOs. Mohsen Marzouk (Chapter 12) reviews the growth of NGOs in the Arab world and argues that rapid growth has not been associated with greater impact. The relatively authoritarian nature of regimes in the region, allied to weak civil societies that harbour a capacity for violent action, has led to NGO activity which follows social change rather than promotes it. Processes of democratisation open up opportunities for a greater role for NGOs, but it remains to be seen whether these opportunities will be seized (and, indeed, whether democracy will take root). Jude Howell (Chapter 13) provides an overview of state–NGO relationships in China, where NGOs are new on the scene and are treated with suspicion. Donors have relatively little leverage over the Chinese state as compared to the situation in many African countries and Bangladesh. It seems unlikely that

NGOs in China will experience the growth and prominence that has characterised NGOs in South Asia. Ranjith Wanigaratne (Chapter 14) reviews the Sri Lankan experience from the deep historical roots of voluntary action in that country to the assault that President Premadasa launched on NGOs in the early 1990s. (Readers wishing to get a detailed understanding of the dynamics of NGO–state–donor relationships in a single country should read the chapters by Wanigaratne, Perera and Hodson as these constitute a powerful Sri Lankan trilogy.) Margarita Bosch focuses on the evolution of state–NGO relations in Brazil, where democratisation has seen NGOs modify the confrontational stance they adopted to previous military regimes. Her conclusions are strongly internationalist, arguing that the solution of many of the country's problems requires new North–South relations: thus, SNGOs must turn their energies to linkages with other SNGOs beyond their national boundaries. The last chapter in Part III reaches relatively positive conclusions about state–NGO relationships. Richard Mawer (Chapter 16) argues that in South-east Asia Save the Children Fund and local NGOs have been able to influence and improve government policies relating to disabled children. Through a series of pilot projects that feed information into formal and informal lobbying, and supported by a relatively low-profile multilateral agency (UNESCO), changes have been promoted in both 'tiger' (Thailand) and 'transitional' (Laos) economic contexts.

In Part IV, the contributions focus on the future of NGOs in relation to poverty alleviation and poor people. Jenny Pearce (Chapter 17) analyses the choices that Latin American NGOs now face, utilising the concept of associational culture. She posits that if they move closer to the state they will become 'co-opted'; but if they stick to the radical ideas that influenced their foundation they may be irrelevant in the contemporary context of a 'new world order'. A third way can be identified, however, focussing on their relations with the poor and disadvantaged and how they might help to empower them. In effect, NGOs should not seek to be advocates for the poor but must help them develop their own capacity for advocacy. This may not be Freire (1972) but it has a Freirian flavour which veteran NGO personnel may find attractive.

The Conclusion (Chapter 18) summarises the key points to emerge from all the other chapters. As the reader will appreciate, this cannot be in the form of narrow generalisations. The materials in this volume show that, even if current processes of globalisation are leading to a convergence in NGO philosophy, structure and practice, this is such a recent phenomenon that diversity still remains the hallmark of NGOs. This applies within countries as well as between countries. While some states[10] are able to dictate the nature of NGO activity (Howell and Marzouk's chapters) in others the direction of influence can be reversed and NGOs can contribute to the reshaping of public policy (Mawer). While it can be argued that NGOs are assisting policies that 'franchise out' state functions in Bangladesh (Wood) the international evidence for NGOs becoming public service contractors is limited (Robinson).

The contributions to this volume do add weight, however, to arguments about the ways in which donors continue to influence the scale and nature of NGO operations. Although Commins argues that World Vision International has been able to interact more closely with donors without being compromised and Mawer identifies positive linkages between Save the Children Fund and UNESCO, on balance it is clear that donor influence on NGOs is much greater than NGO influence on donors. Dichter, Perera, Hodson and Pearce illustrate the relative power of donors to reshape NGO activity, both by design and by accident. The tail (NGOs) is not wagging the dog (donors).

Our main conclusion is that NGOs must 'return to their roots' if they are to promote poverty reduction on a mass scale. With respect to this conclusion we posit a number of questions. Could it be that many SNGOs are so involved in service delivery that the local level associations they create empower NGO personnel and leaders but not the poor and disadvantaged? This can certainly be argued for some of the large NGOs in Bangladesh. Have NNGOs got so involved in lobbying donors directly that they have neglected their role in creating active citizenries that, through more diffuse political processes, can demand effective aid policies and other policy changes (for example, in trade, debt relief and foreign affairs) that will assist the poor in poor countries? The pressures on NGO leaders to devote their energies 'upwards' (to donors and states) and on NGO personnel to look 'upwards' (to their supervisors and senior managements) facilitates the weakening of the special relationships that NGOs claim with their supporters and beneficiaries. In the North greater efforts are needed to ensure that NGOs activate the energies of their supporters and help to create a society that finds poverty and global inequality unacceptable and demands that both they and their governments attack such problems. In the South, in Pearce's words, it means pursuing a 'third way' which avoids the cosiness of donor cooption and the irrelevance of being a radical but marginal critic. As Clark (this volume) and Montgomery (1995) argue, NGOs must be more cautious about the supply side opportunities that the last decade has unleashed: effective NGO activity is dependent on the capacity to respond to demand side pressures and, where these are weak, to help mobilise the poor and disadvantaged so that they can make their own demands – on NGOs, states and donors – more forcefully.

Notes

1. Throughout this book a distinction is made between non-governmental organisations (NGOs), which are intermediary organisations engaged in funding or offering other forms of support to communities and other organisations that seek to promote development and grassroots organisations (GROs), which are membership organisations of various kinds. Other authors make the same distinction, but use different terms. For example, Carroll (1992) distinguishes between 'grassroots support organisations' (which are NGOs) and 'membership support organisations'; GROs are also sometimes called 'community-based organisations (CBOs). The most important difference between the two groups lies in their accountability structures: GROs are formally accountable to their members, while NGOs are not. However, many other authors use the term 'NGOs' to cover all forms of non-profit organisation.

   The term northern NGOs (NNGOs) is used to refer to NGOs with their headquarters in the 'north' (that is, OECD countries) and southern NGOs (SNGOs) for NGOs with their headquarters in low-income and middle-income countries.

2. Official aid agencies are those which are funded by northern governments either directly (bilateral agencies such as the British Overseas Development Agency or Swedish SIDA) or indirectly (multilateral agencies such as the World Bank and the European Union).

3. The state refers to the entire set of governmental organisations that make and enforce rules for society. It includes the political leadership, the legislature, the executive, the judiciary, the bureaucracy, the police and the military at the national, intermediary and local levels.

4. Except for a brief period in 1994 when irregularities over Overseas Development Administration financing of the Pergau Dam in Malaysia hit the headlines. These are now forgotten and the British public's awareness of the existence of ODA has receded.

5. For the European Union alone that represented US$300 million in 1992 (Overseas Development Institute, 1995:1).

6. The figures here vary considerably, as do methods of calculating aid transfers to and through NGOs, and NGO dependency on official agencies. For example, the proportion of SIDA funds channelled through NGOs increased from 9 per cent in 1990/91 to 30 per cent in 1994: SIDA funds over 2000 NGO projects, while the British ODA is already funding over 450 Indian NGOs directly, and a similar number in Bangladesh. All five of the largest NGOs in the UK show a significantly increasing level of financial dependence on ODA, while in other countries (such as Canada, the USA, Germany, the Netherlands and Norway) dependency ratios of between 50 and 90 per cent are common. In the south, the large south Asian NGOs such as BRAC receive most of their funding from external sources, though it is difficult to specify whether more of this is coming from official agencies rather than traditional northern NGO sources. The availability of official aid under 'social compensation funds' in adjusting economies has, however, been an important source of support for NGOs in countries such as Bolivia and Uganda (Arellano-López and Petras, 1994). For details of these trends

see Smillie and Helmich (1993), Good (1994), Bebbington and Riddell (this volume), Edwards and Hulme (1994) and German and Randel (1995).

7. For an excellent discussion of the meaning of the terms poverty, vulnerability and deprivation see Chambers (1995).

8. For a discussion of this issue also see our earlier works (Edwards and Hulme, 1992 and 1995).

9. The Kenyan Rural Enterprise Programme (KREP) reports that it moved towards having a donor consortium in the early 1990s to co-ordinate activity and reduce demands on its management. However, it took a strategic decision not to have a consortium as it decided that this would potentially transfer too much power to its donors.

10. Anangwe (1995) observes that while it is common to ascribe NGO underperformance to state interference there is often an alternative explanation: that many NGOs are weak and ineffective and this is why they fail to mobilise beneficiaries and reduce the incidence of poverty.

2 Donors, Democratisation and Civil Society: Relating Theory to Practice[1]

Harry Blair

As the wave towards democratisation has grown in recent years, the international donor community has experienced a similar swell of interest in supporting democracy. The Development Assistance Committee (DAC) of the Organisation for Economic Co-operation and Development (OECD) adopted a consensus statement of donor support for democratisation in 1993 (DAC, 1995) and various members of DAC have put together their own approaches to provide material assistance to democratisation (for example, Norway, 1994). The United States Agency for International Development (USAID) has also put together a programme to support democratisation. Indeed, first the Bush administration (1989–93) and now much more so the Clinton administration (since 1993) have been pushing democratic development as a centrepiece of foreign aid strategy. In the Bush era, the 'democratic pluralism initiative' was one of USAID's four main policy agendas (see USAID, 1991), while for the Clinton White House 'sustainable democracy' has become one of the four principal themes of the foreign aid programme (USAID, 1994).

On the academic side, there has also been mushrooming interest in democratisation but this analysis has been virtually all theoretical. Very little effort thus far has been directed to connecting the realms of theory and practice by building what might be called 'applied democracy theory' that would begin to answer the donor practitioner's principal needs, which can be characterised as:

- how to go about developing a strategy to promote democracy?
- what to give the highest priority, given that there are never enough resources to do all that might be worthwhile?
- what sequences (if any) would make sense in designing and implementing a democracy support strategy over time?

There are many sectors in which donor assistance has been offered in recent years: justice systems, human rights, political parties, legislatures, decentralisation, elections and the media are but a few of them.[2] All stand in need of some applied theory that could inform donor strategies. USAID has sponsored analyses in several of these sectors with a view to assessing recent experience and distilling strategic ideas that could inform future programming.[3] Although it is perhaps a bit grandiose to label this kind of analysis 'applied democracy theory', it can at least be termed the first steps in building such theory.

The present chapter aims at developing the beginnings of an applied theory for one of these democratic components: civil society. The analysis begins by defining civil society, then showing how it can support (as well as possibly constrain) democracy. Thirdly, a model depicting the linkages between civil society is presented, and finally a number of strategies employing civil society organisations in support of democratic development are discussed.

DEFINING CIVIL SOCIETY

Civil society[4] inhabits the area between individuals (or families) and the state,[5] and is made up of associational groupings of all sorts. In its widest sense, civil society would range from political parties on the more public side of this terrain over to business corporations on the more private side, and it would include groups aiming to influence the formation and implementation of public policy as well as groups that have no concern for the public domain at all.

In constructing an operationalisable approach to civil society, however, it makes sense to narrow the definition so that it embraces primarily non-governmental organisations (NGOs) emphasising public rather than private goals, or more specifically, voluntary groups concerned *inter alia* with influencing state policy. A concentration on influencing the state need not be an NGO's principal concern for it to be of interest here, but such a focus must be at least a significant part of the group's activities. Thus we would exclude such essentially single-purpose organisations as a business enterprise or a political party; the former's main goal is to make a profit, while the latter's is to take over state power (as opposed to influencing it, as with the institutions of civil society).[6]

The characteristic institution of civil society is what we may call a 'civil society organisation' (CSO), which can be defined as an NGO that has as one of its primary purposes influencing public policy. Thus while all CSOs

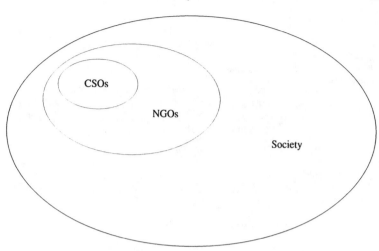

CSOs = Civil society organisations
NGOs = Non-governmental organisations

Figure 2.1 Relationship of civil society organisations to NGOs and society

are NGOs, by no means are all NGOs also CSOs. In most Third World systems, only a portion of the total society is included within the total universe of NGOs, and only a portion of all NGOs are also CSOs, as indicated in Figure 2.1. A purely service-oriented NGO (say, in the health sector) could become a CSO if it added policy advocacy to its agenda, and by the same token a CSO could become an NGO if it dropped its advocacy activities to concentrate solely on service delivery.

One useful way to think of civil society is to characterise it as having a kind of 'in-betweenness'. In its usual definition, civil society lies between the state on one side and the individual or family on the other. But civil society also sits between what is usually thought of as the public and private sectors (some writers see it as a 'third sector' in addition to these two). And there is an additional dimension as well, in that CSOs are usually not (although some may be) profit-seeking, but neither are they generally what we think of as non-profit, service-providing organisations (though at times they might be). To sum up, civil society comprises the collectivity of those social organisations that enjoy *autonomy from the state* (are not a part of the state or creatures of it) and have as one important goal among others to *influence the state* on behalf of their members.

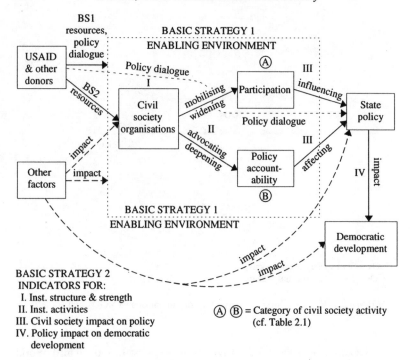

Figure 2.2 Civil society and democratic development

SUPPORTING CIVIL SOCIETY

Two Basic Strategies

In supporting civil society to strengthen democracy, donors have two basic strategies that can be pursued, as indicated in Figure 2.2: *Basic strategy 1 – system reform* (BS1), where donors can focus on the 'enabling environment' or 'rules of the game' for civil society by working to improve the conditions in which it can function effectively; *Basic strategy 2 – sectoral agendas* (BS2), where donors can work within a given civil society environment by *supporting specific CSOs*. Although BS1 logically precedes BS2 (in that the conditions propitious for civil society should be in place before it can function most effectively), USAID in the past has tended more to support BS2, even when the conditions aimed at in BS1 were not in place. That is, the Agency often supported specific CSOs as part of its project effort despite a weak civil society environment in the host country.

At least three reasons can be adduced to account for what at first glance might seem such an illogical approach. First, BS2 was to a large degree the *limit of the possible* in many situations, given Cold War strategic concerns and United States geopolitical considerations. In such circumstances, when USAID found itself supporting authoritarian regimes, pressing host country governments to open up their political systems to CSO participation was often not a feasible policy option. Accordingly, USAID for the most part could only follow BS2, which meant supporting the delivery and (to a lesser extent) self-governance purposes of civil society.

Second, geopolitics quite aside, donors including USAID have until fairly recently tended to '*think apolitically*', operating primarily within the context of a 'technology transfer' model of development, in which economic growth was the main goal and donors focused mainly on projects rather than policy. In this milieu, the donor emphasis tended to be on 'thinking technically' or 'thinking bureaucratically' rather than on 'thinking strategically' and 'thinking politically'.

Third, where USAID and other donors like the Asia Foundation have 'thought politically' in devising their aid strategies, it was reasoned that *supporting BS2 could itself be a transforming approach*, a way to improve an inauspicious enabling environment, on the basis that some civil society activity could itself lead to a better environment for civil society. This approach might be labelled a 'trickle-up strategy'. This kind of civil society effort, of course, had to be largely participatory in nature, as opposed to policy accountability-oriented, in view of the relatively unfriendly enabling environment extant at the time.

As the 1990s began, however, the Cold War ended, making the first constraint on BS1 much less powerful. In addition, donors had by that time already been thinking for some time along policy lines in the economic development sphere, for example in pushing 'structural adjustment' approaches. In a word, it had become much more feasible to engage in BS1 as well as BS2.

As a research issue, BS2 implies a *political behaviour* approach in which the central questions are: what happened? who did what? who got involved in decisions? who made policy? On the other hand, BS1 implies more a *political economy* approach, where the guiding queries become: who benefits? who loses? what classes are in control?

Sequencing the Strategies

As implied in the discussion above, the two basic strategies have been sequenced in different ways, which can be set forth as follows:

- *BS1 leads to BS2.* This is the logical sequence, in which the donor first works to improve the enabling environment for civil society and, then when the climate is suitable, begins to support individual CSOs as they pursue civil society activities. In this approach, the two strategies could overlap, if the donor feels that the climate is sufficiently receptive to BS2 to begin work along that avenue but wants to continue pushing to shore up the environment. Thus the donor could be working both to continue improving the environment (BS1) and to support civil society efforts (BS2) in the existing environment.
- *BS1 is unnecessary, BS2 proceeds.* Here the environment is already receptive to CSOs, and so the donor can simply move ahead with BS2.
- *BS2 leads to BS1.* In this 'transforming approach', the donor finds itself constrained (usually by geopolitical considerations) from pursuing BS1 but is able to give some support to BS2. The organisations supported are likely to be NGOs that are not at the same time CSOs (see Figure 2.1), but the donor hopes to turn them into CSOs in the course of supporting them. It hopes further that these incipient CSOs will have some catalytic impact in improving the civil society climate in the host country.

Basic strategy 1 can be broken down into two components, both directed to political advocacy: participation and accountability. Both are part and parcel of a functioning democracy.

Widening Participation

How do participation and accountability relate to democracy? A strong civil society directly supports democracy by widening participation in several ways:

- educating and mobilising citizens generally to exercise their right to participate (for example, through civic education programmes);
- encouraging previously marginalised groups (such as women, minorities, the poor) into the political arena to participate; and
- building a complex net of groups having members with overlapping multiple affiliations in many organisations, thereby serving to moderate the potentially destabilising effects of single memberships in exclusive groups (especially those based on ethnic, religious, territorial or economic cleavages).

Deepening Policy Accountability

A strong civil society also supports democracy by deepening policy accountability to its citizens – the distinctive hallmark of democracy – along two dimensions. In a negative sense the state must be kept from abuse and venality, which is the theme of the preceding paragraph. But accountability also has a positive aspect, in that the state must be responsive to the needs and wants of its people.[7] The citizenry, in other words, must be able to exercise a role in telling the state what policies to pursue. Both aspects embody a deepening involvement of the people in the affairs of the state, in contrast to the participatory dimension discussed above.

A strong civil society promotes this positive accountability in either a pluralist or a corporatist fashion.[8] In the *pluralist* variant, which is more familiar in the United States, the political universe is one of rough-and-tumble competition between all comers. Here civil society enhances accountability by:

● facilitating a constant flow of citizen inputs to the state, which, being continually reminded of what its citizens want, finds it difficult to wander too far from those wishes;
● fostering pluralist competition by encouraging all groups to press their agendas on the state, which accordingly discovers itself having to accommodate conflicting voices in such ways that it cannot surrender to any one voice or small coterie of voices.

In the *corporatist* version of accountability, which is more common in the continental European democracies, citizen interests are generally aggregated into apex organisations representing farmers, women, health sector workers, and so on. Here the behavioral mode is one of bargaining and negotiation between representative organisations and the state rather than the conflict and competition that characterises pluralist systems. In this milieu civil society promotes accountability through:

● representing citizen interests to the state; and
● negotiating on behalf of those interests.

Limitations of Civil Society

In addition to the constructive effects on democracy explored here, there are also indications that civil society can have more dampening repercussions, in both its pluralist and corporatist versions. In the advanced pluralist democracies in particular, concern has grown that too much interest

group influence on the state over too long a period may well lead to immo-
bilism and a hardening of the democratic arteries or 'gridlock' rather than
to a rich and vibrant democratic polity.[9] A debilitated state continuously
pummelled by conflicting special interest groups may well then become
too feeble to act in the interest of the citizenry as a whole.

In corporatist democracy, on the other hand, the representational monopoly accorded to apex groups and the relatively small number of such groups
can lead to a parasitic mutual dependency between civil society and the
state, in which rigid allocation of public benefits inhibits innovation and
growth. An associated danger here is Michels' (1915) famous 'iron law of
oligarchy', according to which organisational leadership (in this case
unconstrained by rival groups threatening to steal its membership base)
comes to substitute its own interests for those of its members.[10]

There is also the danger that with both types of civil society, any real
sense of the larger public good may be effectively suffocated in the rush of
interest groups to appropriate societal goods for themselves. If the polity
becomes consumed either with smaller, competing groups (the pluralist
system) or with larger, negotiating groups (the corporatist system), the
overarching national good may get lost in the shuffle.

Civil society, then, is not an unmitigated blessing, and it may have dele-
terious as well as beneficial effects on democracy.[11]

A MODEL FOR CIVIL SOCIETY AND DEMOCRATIC DEVELOPMENT

The two basic strategies for supporting civil society to promote democratic
development are portrayed in Figure 2.2. USAID and other donors support
civil society either by endeavouring to improve the enabling environment
(BS1) or by supporting specific organisations within civil society (BS2).
BS1 is more policy-oriented (and thus more abstract, as hinted by the
dashed lines in the figure), while BS2 is more project- or institution-
oriented (and hence more concrete, as indicated by the solid-bordered
boxes in the figure's central portion). To the extent that BS1 works (or is
unnecessary because the enabling environment is already in place) and
BS2 succeeds (that is, CSOs pursue their activities successfully), they
affect state policy, with the ultimate result of furthering sustainable
democracy within the host country's polity, as shown by the box in the
lower right-hand corner of the figure entitled 'democratic development'.

There are two levels of dynamic at work in the model, one at the level
of the individual CSO and the other at the aggregate level of all CSOs in

the political system. At the individual CSO level, different organisations each pursue their own different and self-directed paths. Several examples will illustrate. First, a middle peasant producers association may invest its efforts in mobilising its potential constituency and then supporting electoral candidates favoring its cause. The association may also lobby the state to set higher floor prices for staple foodgrains. Secondly, a chamber of commerce may focus its energies on pressing the state to further deregulate its control of the economy. And thirdly, a women's advocacy group may work on energising a wider constituency to participate in politics, follow and publicise what the state is doing (and failing to do) to benefit women and put pressure on the state to promulgate affirmative action regulations.

So far as the individual CSOs and their members are concerned, these activities will (usually in partial degree) succeed or fail, to their benefit or cost. Collectively, these activities could create some conflict in the system. With the examples just cited, farmers demanding higher foodgrain prices (that is, more regulation) could be opposed by businessmen in the chamber of commerce wanting lower foodgrain prices (that is, less regulation) so as to minimise upward pressure on urban wages. At the same time, both groups might well be against the women's agenda; the farmers could fear that a move sponsored by the women's CSO towards equal property shares between sons and daughters as inheritance would disrupt family integrity through time (as daughters marrying out of the family would take their shares with them), and the businessmen could be concerned that they would feel considerable heat over the low wages and unsafe working conditions prevalent at their 'export platform' garment factories. This kind of conflict, of course, is what feeds democratic development, either in its pluralist variant (as the various agendas become partly realised through the give and take of the political process) or its corporatist version (in which apex organisations representing agriculture, industry and women negotiate their positions with the state).

The Donor Role in Supporting Civil Society

As indicated in Figure 2.2, donors directly contribute resources (largely financial support and technical assistance) to strengthen civil society, generally in the form of foreign assistance projects. The first phase of effort (indicated by the Roman numeral I in Figure 2.2) is primarily an institution-building one, with donor support providing core overhead costs for CSOs, basic equipment, training for personnel, and the like. In the next phase (II in Figure 2.2) of CSO activity, there is often still some direct donor support as technical assistance and tactical guidance, but the recipient organisation is largely on its own here. Then in the third and fourth phases (III and IV), things are largely (though not completely – there is, after all the 'policy dialogue' mentioned above) beyond any direct donor influence. Donor work, in sum, is for the most part restricted to building and strengthening CSOs and then, with a little guidance, setting them on their own course. After their initial launching, the CSOs become, as it were, missiles that are largely internally guided, still subject to some direction from the ground (donors disbursing successive funding tranches when specified conditions are met) but mainly on their own.

Causality Issues

Needless to say, donor support is scarcely the only factor affecting state policy and democratic development. The wider society, economy, polity (conveniently labelled 'other factors' in Figure 2.2) all have an impact on state policy and on democratic development as well, collectively much more strongly than donor support working through CSOs. And even within the range of what donors do, there are many influences at work besides support for CSOs. Other foreign assistance efforts have their effects; a 'structural readjustment' programme that cuts state support to education, for instance, may have a long-term negative impact on democratic development that far outweighs whatever good foreign-assisted CSOs might do. Or the 'policy dialogue' carried on between the donor embassy and the 'host country government' (reflected in the dotted line in Figure 2.2) may have a much bigger influence on improving the human rights climate than CSO agitation against a repressive regime. Establishing precise causality in this model, in other words, may be difficult.

CIVIL SOCIETY DEVELOPMENT STRATEGIES

One good way to gauge what civil society can do, in an operational sense, to support democracy is to ask, 'What problems can civil society-based efforts address?' Table 2.1 poses nine such problems, which are first categorised in row 1 according to the two basic strategies depicted in Figure 2.2: system reform and sectoral agendas. The sectoral agenda strategies are then divided according to whether they emphasise participation or policy accountability more strongly.[12]

Each of the nine strategies (row 2 of the table) is cast first in terms of the 'development problem' to be dealt with (row 3), then the programme purpose and longer-term goal (rows 4 and 5). In the sixth row are shown the major project elements likely to be chosen. Row 7 lists some examples of the kinds of NGOs that might be enlisted to implement these project elements, while row 8 gives the most likely motivations for these groups to become involved. The ninth row indicates expected 'end-of-project' outputs for the different strategies, and the next row lists some initial ideas for measuring project success in realising those outputs. Finally, rows 11 and 12 present, first, issues and problems that might create difficulties for the various strategies, and then some tentative responses to such challenges.

An example will illustrate. 'Democratic culture' strategies (depicted in column 2 of Table 2.1) are aimed at institutionalising democratic culture and so fit into the system reform category (BS1) of activity. Such a strategy would be especially appropriate in some of the more advanced developing countries of Latin America, where the polity has only recently emerged from a period of sustained authoritarian rule. The social infrastructure in terms of education, media and associational life, is there to support democracy, but the democratic environment or culture is still somewhat feeble and artificial; it has not yet taken firm root and thus far is still in danger of a relapse into authoritarian rule (as happened in Peru in 1992). The development problem, then, as indicated in row 3, is a democratic system that is in place but may well prove unsustainable over time.

Accordingly, a democracy project addressing this challenge would have as its purpose (row 4) contributing towards a stable democratic polity; such a polity can best be sustained over the longer term (row 5) if it is supported by an enduring democratic culture, that is, a commonly held set of social values within the citizenry holding democracy to be the only acceptable way to manage the country's affairs.

A USAID project in this context (row 6) would likely be one in the civic education area, which would support efforts to inculcate and strengthen democratic values in the population. Appropriate NGOs to undertake such work (row 7) might be in-country groups similar in their functions to what the League of Women Voters does in the United States, local election monitoring groups and the like. Such associations could be expected to be motivated (row 8) largely by middle-class impulses towards good government and public rectitude. The most important tangible result of a project in this area (row 9) would be continued adherence to democratic practices (which over time would contribute to the purposes and goals shown in rows 4 and 5). One way to measure success (row 10) in strengthening democratic culture would be to use opinion surveys to assess how people feel about democratic values. A major problem to be expected over time (row 11) is that of keeping up the momentum of such a

Table 2.1 Development strategies incorporating civil society

1 Basic strategy & category (cf. Figure 2.2)	Basic strategy 1: system reform				Basic strategy 2: sectoral agendas				
					Category A: participation			Category B: policy accountability	
	1	2	3	4	5	6	7*	8	9
2 Type of strategy	Democratic transition	Democratic culture	Human rights	Democratic integrity	Democratic capitalism	Democratic pluralism	Social mobilisation	Human resources	Sustainable environment
3 The development problem	Autocratic state with minimal participation	Unsustainable democratic system	Human rights abuses	Unaccountable & corrupt government	State control of economy, 'dirigiste' rigidity	Unrepresentative government	Marginalised groups	Counter-productive state policy on PQLI NGOs	Natural resource mismanagement
4 Programme purpose	Widening political voice	Stable democratic polity	Decline in abuses	Corruption decline	More inclusive market economy	Expanded body politic	Group empowerment	PQLI improvements	Natural resource decline reversed
5 Longer-term goal	Transition to democracy	Sustainable democratic culture	Secure human rights	Integrity, predictability in government	Sustainable economic growth	Pluralist polity	Equal opportunity society	Healthy & productive society	Sustainable natural resource regime

Table 2.1 Continued

| Basic strategy & category (cf. Figure 2.2) | Basic strategy 1: system reform | | | | Basic strategy 2: sectoral agendas | | | | |
					Category A: participation			Category B: policy accountability	
6 Project elements	Support all NGOs (some will become CSOs)	Civic education	HR monitoring HR reporting HR advocacy	Investigative journalism, political reporting	Market-oriented & producer organisations	Organisation building	Adult literacy & conscientisation	Umbrella NGOs	NR monitoring NR reporting NR advocacy
7 NGO examples	All NGOs	LWV groups, election watch groups	In-country HR advocacy groups	Investigative journalism NGOs	Chambers of commerce, water user associations	Professional associations, peasant groups	Women's rights, minority rights groups	Health sector umbrella NGOs	Environmental advocacy CSOs
8 Motivation for groups	All motivations	Democratic norms	Human rights	Journalistic professionalism, whistle-blowing	Self-seeking	Representing membership	Self-assertion	Service delivery	Public goods
9 EOP outputs	Some CSO influence on the state	Adherence to democratic practices	Effective HR CSOs operating	Active media	Interest group lobbying	New groups pressuring state	Micro- & macro-level advocacy	CSOs influencing state policy	User group & environmental group advocacy

Table 2.1 Continued

1 Basic strategy & category (cf. Figure 2.2)	Basic strategy 1: system reform				Basic strategy 2: sectoral agendas				
					Category A: participation			Category B: policy accountability	
10 Performance measures	Movement away from autocracy	Acceptance of democratic values (surveys)	HR improvement	Corruption exposed	More players in system, more state responsiveness	Increased representation at all levels	Increased minority representation	Spatial & class equity in PQLI	Decreasing environmental degradation
11 Issues and problems	Government hostility	Sustaining momentum	State opposition	Rent seekers' opposition	Gridlock, 'demo-sclerosis'	Continued elite domination of polity	Ethnic tension, majority backlash	Urban bias	Collective action issue
12 Possible responses to problems	Lower CSO advocacy profile	Continual reinforcement	International publicity	Public pressure	Executive autonomy	Stronger non-elite advocacy CSOs	Consociational polity	Rural focus	User groups

Notes:

Acronyms   CSO = civil society organisation; EOP = End of project; HR = Human rights; LWV = League of Women Voters; NGO = Non-governmental organisation; NR = Natural resources; PQLI = Physical quality of life index.

* This strategy can be an element of both Category A and Category B approaches to BS2.

project; people can become fatigued at hoeing the same row again and again, for example in promoting civic studies efforts with successive cohorts of schoolchildren or monitoring successive elections. To counter such flagging enthusiasm, somehow the motivation for such efforts has to be continually reinvigorated and reinforced (row 12).

Civic-minded CSOs are scarcely the only kind of organisations to be supported through civil society strategies, however, as a second example will illustrate. Self-promoting NGOs, concerned primarily with the welfare of their members, can also become CSOs contributing to sustainable democratic development. The 'democratic capitalism' strategy depicted in column 5 of Table 2.1 is such an approach. Here, for example, agricultural water user associations might be encouraged to form an alliance to lobby the state at both local (the district water engineer) and national (the water development ministry) levels. Their agendas might be more farmer control over water allocation, more equity for 'tail-enders' in surface water irrigation systems or more systematic canal rehabilitation. In the process, the water user associations would be ameliorating state control of the economy by contributing to decision making and pressing the state to be more responsive to public demands.

There are dangers in such strategies, to be sure. Too many self-seeking groups making demands on the state and realising those demands can lead to an interest-group gridlock that effectively immobilises the polity, as pointed out earlier. One answer to gridlock would be more autonomy for the executive branch to act in a national interest, as opposed to the parochial interests of the CSOs, but then this would of course bring its own dangers.

Assessing Civil Society Strategies

How can we tell if foreign aid-assisted civil society strategies have had any impact (positive or negative) on democratic development in a given country? It was this question that formed the core inquiry of a USAID assessment conducted in 1994, involving extensive field visits to five countries: Bangladesh, Chile, El Salvador, Kenya and Thailand. The model presented here facilitated that effort by pointing out successive phases for assessment, which can be framed here as consecutive questions (which correspond to the roman numerals in Figure 2.2):

I   What institutional strengths were CSOs able to build? How well equipped were they to engage in civil society activity?

II   What did the CSOs do (both individually and collectively)?

III   Did these activities have any effect in changing state policy?

IV   Did changes in state policy have any effect on democratic development?

A fifth topic for assessment (which would be too complex to show in Figure 2.2, since it would cover most of the chart) was the impact of USAID and other donors on this whole series of processes:

V   How can we tell if what USAID did actually contributed to what happened?[13]

The USAID assessment has been reported on elsewhere, but by way of brief summary it might be stated here that CSOs pushing system reform (BS1) were found to be effective under some conditions in a country that has not yet negotiated the passage to democracy, and that during democracy's early phases such CSOs continue to be most effective. But as new basic rules of the game come to be accepted, it makes sense to support CSOs more oriented toward sectoral agendas (BS2). Nonetheless, there is at least a secondary place for sectoral CSOs in the early phases and for system reform CSOs in the later period, even after a polity could be well consolidated, for there is always a need to firm up the fundamental rules of the system, for example with respect to human rights. Also, as indicated in the analysis above, sometimes only BS2 strategies are possible when a regime is still authoritarian and has yet to become democratic. And finally, one donor approach that will be increasingly needed as foreign aid budgets continue their downward path in the coming years is to promote self-sustainability among CSOs. The days when CSOs could count on renewed foreign grants if they proved themselves effective are rapidly disappearing. Effectiveness in the future will have to be measured in part by an organisation's ability to sustain itself in the wake of donor departure.[14]

SOME FURTHER QUESTIONS

The theory constructed thus far raises a number of further questions, some of which are briefly sketched out in this section. The most pressing questions come under two headings: sustainability and success.

Sustainability, Pluralist Competition and Corporatism

How can a civil society (as opposed to individual CSOs, as discussed just above) best sustain itself and in the process sustain democratic development? Under what circumstances has civil society failed to sustain (or contributed to a failure in sustaining) democracy? The answers would appear to differ according to whether the polity is more pluralist or corporatist in orientation.

Pluralist Sustainability

Here the key factor is ensuring competition. Unless groups energetically compete with each other, the polity faces serious dangers, either (1) that a few CSOs will dominate the policy terrain and skew things in their own interest, or (2) that a larger number of CSOs will simply collude to divide benefits (especially subsidies) among themselves at public expense, resulting in a kind of 'interest group gridlock' that hobbles the political system. The crux of the problem is that excessive accountability to individual groups (or coalitions of groups) can mean a lack of accountability to the polity as a whole. Only a healthy competition can prevent such untoward outcomes. How can this competition best be achieved and maintained?

Corporatist Sustainability

With its emphasis on 'consociational' behaviour (wherein leaders of potentially hostile or competing constituencies negotiate co-existence arrangements), corporatist democracy also runs a double risk. The first danger is that group leaders will cut deals that immobilise the polity and economy by dividing up all available resources into rigidly fixed shares and thus locking public policy into place indefinitely, while the second is that a self-serving cabal of leaders will themselves benefit inordinately while depriving associational members (who have no recourse in the corporatist set-up that provides only one hierarchical structure for each societal grouping). Yet another danger is that in a society organised along corporatist lines (as with many Latin American countries) civil society as a mechanism for ensuring accountability may never really get launched, for the state will prove too strong in its desire to control social life through corporatist organisations. In the corporatist case, accountability has to come from competing political parties and an energetic media that will ferret out and publicise corrupt behaviour. How can such accountability best be maintained?

Problems with Success

Just as an anaemic or undernourished civil society is dysfunctional to democracy, so too an overactive civil society may well bring problems of its own. Two in particular deserve mention in this context.

Policy Insulation

Policy makers are generally thought to need some insulation against populist pressures if they are to undertake serious efforts at structural reform, especially in the economic sphere. In some cases, strengthening civil society may make policy reform more difficult (for example, stronger labour unions better opposed to dismantling wasteful parastatals, or an energised 'comprador' business community against trade deregulation). What are the trade-offs here? Is there a case to be made for supporting NGOs selectively rather than across the board?

Antidemocratic Civil Society

Under certain circumstances, civil society could become antithetical to democracy itself; it could in a sense lose its civility. The institutions of civil society can after all promote destructive ethnic conflict and religious intolerance just as they can foster constructive pluralism. There may also be other ways in which competition can go too far beyond pluralism in destructive directions. Are there ways to help channel civil society into more constructive paths? Could this be done without manipulation and co-optation?

BUILDING AN APPLIED THEORY

What has been offered here is essentially a starter on what I hope will become an 'applied theory of civil society in Third World democratic development.' In the present chapter, I have put together some outlines of such a theory, but much lies ahead. USAID's assessments of several democracy sectors has begun this task, but there is a great deal of work yet to be done. Donors seeking to promote democratic development through CSOs, NGOs and other means have only rudimentary theoretical frameworks for exploring what the likely consequences of their actions may be. CSOs may be a key element in promoting pluralism but, as pointed out in this chapter, they can also take an antidemocratic role.

It would be appropriate to close with an analogy to economics. One thing that virtually all economists now agree is that, *ceteris paribus*, market systems do a better job than other systems at enabling consumers to signal producers what they want and at enabling producers to signal consumers what they can offer. But what are the *'ceteris'* (other things) that must be *'paribus'* (equal) for democratic development, and what kind of policies are needed to ensure their maintenance? And what can governments and donors do to promote such policies? This is where applied economic development theory comes in. Pluralism in politics is similar in that it appears to be the best way to enable citizens to tell governments what they want and for governments to respond. But if we are to promote democratic pluralism we need to know a great deal more about what it really does for the polity, about determining just what are the *ceteris*, and about ensuring that they remain *paribus*. There is indeed a place for an applied democracy theory to help donors understand the polities in which they are intervening.

Notes

1. The chapter is based largely on work conducted while the author was on leave from his academic post, on assignment with USAID. The analysis and interpretation made in the chapter are the author's own, however, and not necessarily those of USAID, which bears no responsibility for the chapter's contents. Much of the chapter has appeared earlier in Blair (1993 and 1994).

2. A study conducted by the United States General Accounting Office (GAO) found that USAID had provided just over US$700 million in democracy assistance during the fiscal years 1991–3, of which 23 per cent went to judicial reform, 22 per cent to civil society, 11 per cent each to legislatures and elections and the remainder to a variety of other sectors (GAO, 1994: 12–13).

3. Thus far one assessment has been published, on legal system reform (Blair and Hansen, 1994), with a second on civil society scheduled to appear shortly (Hansen, 1995; for a much briefer version see Blair, 1995). A third USAID study began in 1995 on legislatures, and it is planned to begin a fourth on decentralisation in 1996.

4. The idea of 'civil society' has a long history, tracing back to Hobbes and Hegel (see Hyden, 1995 for a brief history), but in its contemporary usage it has come into the political science literature only quite recently; earlier terms with a similar meaning were 'interest groups' or 'pressure groups', but these were applied largely to the political systems of the advanced industrial countries. Today 'civil society' is the term most widely used to describe this sector in the development field.

   There is considerable debate on just what should be included under the rubric of 'civil society', and a consensus understanding on this issue is yet to emerge. For instance, some (for example, Diamond, 1992) would include the media as a part of civil society, while others would exclude it, essentially restricting the definition to voluntary organisations. See also Diamond's later attempt (1994) to pin down a definition.

5. The 'state' as used in this chapter has been in widespread usage at least since the mid-1980s – longer than 'civil society' but still relatively new in its meaning here as the whole set of governmental organisations, ranging from local to national, that make and enforce rules for the society. The state is thus not only the political leadership or the bureaucracy, and it does not exist only at the national or (as in the United States) intermediate level, but

rather it is the collectivity of office-holding political leaders and bureaucracy at all levels.

6. Some political parties may be included in civil society by this definition, if their primary goal is to act as a pressure group rather than take power; some of the European Green parties would be examples here. The number of such parties in the Third World is probably small, however, especially in the absence of the proportional representation electoral systems that tend to encourage their continuance in the western European political scene.

7. Elections serve this accountability function, of course, but they occur only at periodic intervals and by their very nature demand accountability for a programme, that is a whole package of issues. The kind of accountability civil society provides, on the contrary, can take place any time – whenever CSOs can press its case successfully with the state – and it concerns particular issues, i.e. those of interest to the CSO involved in presenting them.

8. The participation aspect of civil society discussed just above in the text applies similarly in both pluralist and corporatist democracy. It is only this policy accountability aspect that operates differently in the two variant types of democracy.

9. A recently coined term for this condition in the domestic American context is 'demosclerosis' (see Rausch, 1994; also Olson, 1993). It is also possible that, even if they do compete vigorously with each other, CSOs may simply become so numerous that they clog up and overwhelm the state's capacity for responding, as Huntingdon feared some 25 years ago (1968). For a broader critique against pluralist strategies in the LDCs, see MacDonald (1992).

10. In addition, corporatism is also a political culture that can have stifling effects on the very emergence of meaningful democracy, as has often been the case in Latin America (see Wiarda and Kline, 1993, esp. pp. 112 ff).

11. For an extensive discussion of the negative sides of civil society, see the special issue of *Politics and Society* devoted to 'Secondary Associations and Democracy' (1992), in particular the long essay by Cohen and Rogers (1992).

12. The intent in Table 2.1 is to be inclusive, but significant categories of civil society activity may have been omitted. Also it may prove possible to combine some strategies, for example, those in columns 6 and 7 of Table 2.1.

13. These evaluation questions, along with a provisional methodology for addressing them, are discussed at some length in Blair (1994).

14. For a thorough analysis and synthesis of the five country studies that concentrate largely on system reform strategies (BS1), see Hansen (1995). For a much briefer treatment that focuses on both system reform and sectoral agendas (BS1 and BS2), see Blair (1995).

3 The State, Popular Participation and the Voluntary Sector

John Clark[1]

NGOS AND PARTICIPATORY DEVELOPMENT

Could the contribution of the voluntary sector to development be more fully realised given greater current emphasis on poverty reduction, the environment and participatory development?

When a government endeavours to give greater weight to reducing poverty, to redressing gender or ethnic biases, to combatting environmental degradation, or to involving the poor and their communities in development decision making and resource allocation, it is likely to find its normal macro instruments inadequate. Economic policy, the provision of services and infrastructure, regulations and market mechanisms are rarely sharply directed towards vulnerable groups. Participatory development approaches are required.

Non-governmental organisations (NGOs[2]) may provide instruments which, whether invited or not by governments, emphasise the participation of the poor. This is by no means uniform and depends on the NGO, the government and other factors. NGOs may keep their distance from the state and run their projects parallel to those of the state; in some countries NGOs effectively play an oppositional role; while elsewhere NGOs seek to represent the voice of the weak and help them organise in their communities to achieve a more powerful voice in the making of decisions and the allocating of resources. The latter NGOs are emerging as critical ingredients of civil society. They are moving beyond a 'supply-side' approach, concentrating on the delivery of services or development projects, to a 'demand-side' emphasis, helping communities articulate their preferences and concerns so as to become active participants in the development process.

This is not an either/or situation. Some of the most effective operational NGOs (such as BRAC – the Bangladesh Rural Advancement Committee,

43

the Philippines Rural Reconstruction Movement and the Worldwide Fund for Nature) are becoming effective in challenging development orthodoxy and promoting new people-centred approaches while they are increasing the scope of their own programmes.

Many argue (OECD, 1988; Elliott, 1987; Fernandez, 1987; Garilao, 1987; Bhatnagar and Williams, 1992) that NGOs may be best placed for the tasks of fostering popular participation which include articulating the needs of the weak, working in remote areas, changing attitudes and practices of local officials, and nurturing the productive capacity of the most vulnerable groups such as the disabled or the landless. In some countries there may be a rigid divide between the voluntary, public and private sectors whereas elsewhere there is a high degree of interaction. It appears (Tandon, 1991) that where the interaction is high the climate is most favourable for poverty reduction and other social priorities, though cause and effect may be difficult to separate. Whether a strong NGO sector encourages governments to pursue such priorities, or assists them to do so, this vehicle of civil society has potential importance which has hitherto been largely neglected.

In many countries the voluntary sector concentrates on operating its own projects (Fowler, 1992, Bratton, 1989 and 1990) improving local situations but doing little to bring its experience to bear on the government's service delivery or policy making. It appears that where the voluntary sector is not only sizeable but also where it interacts with the public and private sector it is able to achieve a significant multiplier effect on its own efforts (Bratton, 1988 and 1990).

NGOs may interact closely with local government and play a strong role in local development activities even where the central government has weak links with NGOs. Studies of decentralisation and land reform programmes in a range of countries have demonstrated that the active involvement of local organisations is a key factor in influencing the degree of benefits reaching to poorer citizens (Fisher, 1993).

'Scaling-up' of NGO experience has been the subject of considerable study in recent years (see, for example, ANGOC 1988 for a report of the Manila conference, and Edwards and Hulme, 1992). In addition to increasing its size by building up its capacity as an alternative provider of services and development projects, the voluntary sector can influence mainstream development in the following ways (Clark, 1991):

1   encouraging official aid agencies and government ministries to adopt successful approaches developed within the voluntary sector;
2   educating and sensitising the public as to their rights and entitlements under state programmes;

3 attuning official programmes to public needs through acting as a conduit for public opinion and local experience;
4 operational collaboration with official bodies;
5 influencing local development policies of national and international institutions including decentralisation and municipal reforms (Ritchie-Vance, 1991); and
6 helping government and donors fashion a more effective development strategy through strengthening institutions, staff training and improving management capacity.

The moving beyond the development 'supply-side' to 'demand-side' activities requires that NGOs develop new skills, partnerships and ways of working in order to help communities articulate their concerns and preferences, to manoeuvre into a negotiating position with official bodies, and to mix technical operational skills with 'information age' communication, advocacy and networking skills. The literature which describes this evolution (Tandon, 1992; Clark, 1991; Edwards and Hulme, 1992) sees NGOs as becoming important agents of the civil society.

Governments do not necessarily resist this trend. For example, in the late 1980s the municipal reform programme of the Colombian government (responding to popular pressure) provided an important opening to the NGOs in a wide range of local development and service delivery functions. In June 1989 the Colombian Health Minister announced an innovative policy of involving community committees in the design and management of primary health care programmes. With the coming of age of Colombian NGOs they have increasingly joined regional and international networks and have fostered a 'culture of democracy' among their constituencies (Ritchie-Vance, 1991).

The donor community now widely advocates agencies that effective development requires appropriate macroeconomic policy and 'good governance' – a healthy political environment. The critical elements of the latter are transparency, accountability, freedom of speech and association, greater participation in political decision making, and due process (Lateef, 1992). But these elements, firmly installed in the capital city, do not necessarily mean changed circumstances for poorer members of society, particularly in remoter areas. The poor are normally much more concerned with, and affected by, *local* governance. It is more important to them whether local officials are passing on benefits to which they are entitled, whether their efforts to form a peasants' union are repressed, or whether they are provided information about or are granted a say in the planning of a nearby infrastructure project which may adversely affect their lives.

Participatory development is often used to mean little more than establishing user groups to ensure that beneficiaries are involved in project implementation. The 'demand-side' approach, as pioneered by an influential school of NGOs is a local-level complement to 'good governance'. Such NGOs assist citizens in finding out about activities of the government and others which might affect them; they use advocacy and political influence to hold local officials accountable for activities (or inactivity) which are damaging to the poor; they help communities mobilise and form societies to express their concerns, and help guard against reprisals; they construct fora in which officials can consult people about development plans and listen to alternatives presented by the people; and they help ensure that individuals disadvantaged by government decisions receive just compensation, negotiated wih the affected parties.

POTENTIAL CONTRIBUTION OF NGOs

NGOs have achieved importance in development assistance for various reasons: (a) their scale – Northern NGOs act as conduits for 12 per cent of total development assistance (Clark, 1991); (b) their ability to reach poor people especially in inaccessible areas; (c) their capacity for innovation and experimentation, which are difficult for official agencies (Tendler, 1982); (d) their representativeness – often having close links with poor communities; and (e) their skills of participation (Bratton, 1988 and 1990). Moreover, their resources are largely additional, and they not only 'fill in the gaps' but serve as a response to failures in the public and private sectors (Salamon and Anheier, 1991; Bratton, 1990).

These NGO attributes have become increasingly important in recent years as official donors and many governments have given greater attention to poverty reduction and environmental sustainability. 'Rolling back the state' where it has become overextended also gives greater prominence to NGOs and the private sector. Moreover, the 'good governance' debate has highlighted the need for pluralism and a prominent citizens' voice in national development planning, which NGOs can contribute to in many ways including through the promotion of participatory development (Bhatnagar and Williams, 1992).

The degree to which the NGO potential is realised depends on many factors including the tradition for voluntary activity, levels of tertiary education (indigenous NGOs are usually founded and led by those educated in universities, particularly in Northern Europe or North America), and the interests of donors and Northern NGOs in funding development activities in the country in question. A paramount factor is the nature of the relationship between the NGO sector and the state. Government policies, practices and even attitudes can have a pivotal influence on the capacity of NGOs to operate and grow.

HEALTHY STATE–NGO RELATIONSHIP

A healthy relationship is only conceivable where both parties share common objectives. Where the government's commitment to poverty reduction is weak, NGOs will find dialogue and collaboration frustrating or even counterproductive. Likewise, repressive governments will be wary of NGOs which represent the poor or victimised. In such situations, NGOs will probably prefer to chart their own course, giving all instruments of the state as wide a berth as possible.

Where the government has a positive social agenda (or even where individual ministries do) and where NGOs are effective there is the potential for a strong, collaborative relationship. As Tandon (1991) clarifies, this does not mean the sub-contracting of placid NGOs, but a 'genuine partnership between NGOs and the government to work on a problem facing the country or a region... based on mutual respect, acceptance of autonomy, independence, and pluralism of NGO opinions and positions'.

As Tandon points out, however, such relations are rare, even when the conditions are met. The mutual distrust and jealousy appears to be deeprooted. The government fears that NGOs erode their political power or even threaten national security (Fowler, 1992). And NGOs mistrust the motivation of the government and its officials.

Though controversial and risky, many of the more strategic NGOs are overcoming their inhibitions and are seeking closer collaboration with governments (Fernandez, 1987; Tandon, 1991; ANGOC, 1988; Garilao, 1987, Aga Khan Foundation, 1988). By so doing, they believe, they will be better able to contribute to participatory development as described above, and they will be able to expose the government to a grassroots perspective which might otherwise be neglected. However, there might be increased risk of corruption, reduced independence, and financial dependency.

The planning of projects and policies can be strongly influenced by inviting NGO leaders to serve on government commissions or by holding public consultations in which grassroots organisations are able to voice their concern and experience. As Michael Bratton commented (1990): 'Once the question was "how can development agencies reach the poor majority?", now it is "how can the poor majority reach the makers of public policy?'"

World Bank experience (Cernea, 1988) drawn from a survey of 25 Bank-financed projects, indicates a strong correlation between project success and the participation of grassroots organisations. More recently the Bank is deriving important insights from the public consultations included in Environmental Assessments in which NGOs often play a major role. Such consultations are effective where all parties are prepared to be objective and to learn from each other. Where NGOs use selective reportage or distortion in order to heighten criticism of the government, or where the government is not receptive to outside advice, 'consultations' are likely to be no more than confrontations.

Even where there has been a largely adversarial relationship, however, consultation can be a surprisingly productive process and even reduce tensions. The Environmental Congress – a network of NGOs in Sri Lanka – initially adopted a fairly confrontational style with respect to the government. On one issue the government proved receptive to their concerns, and dropped plans for a major project. After this, the NGOs developed a more constructive dialogue with the authorities. The government, in turn, invited five NGO representatives on to the National Environmental Council which reports to the prime minister on the environmental ramifications of all major development projects.

Conversely, dialogue with NGOs may be unproductive where the state–NGO relationship is too cozy. NGOs may then accept too readily the government's information and its role in coordinating all development activities, including those of NGOs, and be too prepared to fill in gaps as directed by the authorities. In not questioning state activities, they fail to inject the grassroots perspective. A degree of financial autonomy of the NGO sector is necessary to ensure their independence.

NGOs are often described as offering 'development alternatives' but this is misleading. The dictionary defines 'alternative' as meaning 'either of two or more possible courses; ...mutually exclusive'. The population of any country does not have a choice between the development model offered by government and that by NGOs. NGOs can play an important role in helping certain population groups, or filling in the gaps in state services, or in pressing for a change in the national development strategy, but they rarely offer realistic alternative pathways. Their innovations may test out new approaches, but these only become sustainable or of significant scale if they influence national development. If they achieve this then they may be commissioned by the government to continue providing the service (for example, with BRAC in Bangladesh), or the NGO approach may be adopted by the government as a model for replication, as with the Escuela Nueva education programme in Colombia (Ritchie-Vance, 1991) or the National Rural Support Programme in Pakistan (based on the Aga Khan Rural Support Programme). In such situations the NGO approach becomes mainstream rather than alternative.

When both parties look to complementary rather than competing contributions, collaboration becomes possible, even though they may harbour very different goals. The government may be keen to harness foreign funds and the NGOs' capacity for service delivery. The NGOs may seek to re-orient development priorities toward poverty reduction. Such unshared objectives may make for friction but not necessarily incompatibility.

By offering or withholding support, official aid agencies can clearly have a major impact on the NGO sector. Through their project and policy dialogue with governments, they are also able to influence the state–NGO relationship, perhaps enhancing the political will for constructive engagement. Some are realising, in promoting participation and 'good governance' that the growth of a healthy NGO sector is an important contribution to development. The health of the state–NGO relationship is sector-specific. Steps to improve the quality of relationship will also, therefore, be sector-specific (see, for example, discussion of NGOs in the agricultural sector in Bebbington and Farrington, 1992 and 1992/3b).

BARRIERS TO A HEALTHY NGO–STATE RELATIONSHIP

The following factors, identified by a range of commentators, are the major determinants of the health of the relationship between governments and NGOs (see especially A. Fowler, 1988 and 1992; Salamon and Anheier, 1991 and 1992; Bratton; 1988; Clark, 1991; Edwards, 1991; Tendler, 1982; Tandon, 1987 and 1992; Brown, 1988; Elliott, 1987; Brodhead and Herbert-Copley, 1988).

Policy Environment

NGOs often fall in the opposition camp while the government or ruling party may see itself as the sole legitimate voice of the people. In such highly politicised policy environment neither party would have sufficient trust in the other to be able to work together, nor would they desire to do so. NGOs would not seek to improve the delivery of public services to the people or even help make official development programmes more participatory if by so doing they would increase the government's popularity.

Conversely governments would not lend legitimacy to agencies which they view as political opponents. And they may, consequently, not want to foster a healthier NGO sector for fear of bolstering the opposition. It does not necessarily follow, however, that NGOs are crushed by governmental hostility. In some countries they have thrived on such controversy.

An NGO's dependence on foreign sources of finance might also lead to governments and nationalistic political parties. Conversely NGOs which are largely funded by their members have maximum authenticity. Where foreign-funded NGOs simply provide uncontroversial services, particularly in programmes which are co-ordinated by or under the auspices of the government, tensions need not arise. But where the NGO has activities which are in any way controversial, where it challenges government decisions, where it mobilises people against the vested interests of local elites, or where its participatory approaches leads to the empowerment of population groups which are traditionally exploited, it is likely to find its motives impugned as being 'guided by a foreign hand'.

The Bangladesh Rural Advancement Committee (BRAC), for example, has recently suffered a spate of burning of its primary schools. Islamic fundamentalists have felt threatened by the fact that these schools provide equal education to girls and boys. Since BRAC funds overwhelmingly come from abroad, the fundamentalists have whipped up a popular but unfounded fear that BRAC is a covert Christian operation, whose ulterior motive is to steal souls.

Government Factors

Where the government's commitment to poverty reduction and participatory development is weak, there will be little interest in working with NGOs or in improving their operating environment. Such governments, however, mindful of current donor interests in channelling funds through NGOs, may seek to create or foster their own 'government-oriented NGOs' (GONGOs) which then receive funds from less discriminating donors. Considerable tension often exists between such GONGOs and the more legitimate, people-oriented NGOs.

Government–NGO relations may also be strained where corruption and nepotism are rife, or where there is a shortage of competent staff especially at local level. The jealousy of civil servants toward NGOs can exacerbate policy tensions. The former often resent the access to vehicles and other resources, the opportunity to travel abroad and, perhaps, the higher wages which major indigenous and international NGOs often afford to their top executives. In countries riven by civil conflict there is often a legitimacy issue when much of the country is not under government control.

NGO Factors

NGOs often display a distinct preference for isolation. They are not only unwilling to dialogue with government but they co-ordinate poorly with one another. For some NGOs isolationism is a means for escaping attention, and therefore outside interference. By keeping a low profile, however, they may actually be making themselves more vulnerable to government control, as illustrated by the case of the Savings Development Movement (SDM) in Zimbabwe – an effective but little-known NGO whose operations were temporarily suspended and whose board was amended by the government because of alleged corruption (Bratton, 1990).

In recent years, however, there has been an increased trend for Southern NGOs to network nationally, regionally (especially in Latin America) and internationally (Fisher, 1993; Ritchie-Vance, 1991). Such networking is often weakest and most evidently donor-driven in Africa. Regional and international networks often concentrate on global issues such as environment, debt and the General Agreement on Tariffs and Trade (GATT). NGO isolationism is decreasing, though the practically oriented, operational NGOs (as opposed to NGOs concerned with research and advocacy) often remain weakly connected. Even though there is an increased tendency to share information, practical collaboration is still uncommon outside the context of multiple NGO involvement in government or donor programmes.

NGOs may represent a very narrow constituency, such as one kinship group, or the poorest farmers. In such situations, the government may consider an NGO too selective since it must consider the common good. Similarly, NGOs have the 'luxury' of picking one or two issues which dominate their attention, while governments must juggle with a multitude of concerns. NGOs may also not live up to the claims made in their literature. Their projects may not be as effective or well-directed, the stated levels of popular participation may not be realised, the professional skills of their staff may be wanting, they may have weak accountability to the grassroots, and they may have weak management and poorly developed strategic planning.

Donor Factors

The pressure on successful NGOs from major donors to receive more funds may lead to a decline in performance, if this entails institutional growth faster than the management capacity of the NGO can cope with, or a shift in direction away from the proven competence of the NGO. For example, the Voluntary Agencies Development Assistance Organisation of Kenya was deflected by donor pressure from its original institutional development function to acting as a funding intermediary. This has occurred at the expense of both its original agenda and its relationship with other NGOs. This has consequently undermined its advocacy effectiveness towards the government (Bratton, 1990).

When the NGO sector is dominated by foreign or international NGOs problems can arise between the government and the NGO, if the government feels that it is being squeezed out of development decision making. This has been documented by Edwards (1991) and Hanlon (1990) in the case of Mozambique where, in 1990, 170 foreign NGOs were running programmes in complete isolation from the state. Hanlon describes how these 'new missionaries' have divided the country into 'mini-kingdoms'. Edwards describes how his own NGO – Save the Children Fund (UK) – decided to work closely with the government, providing technical assistance at local and national levels in the fields of health and food security. This has had an important scaling-up effect; for example, SCF has helped devise mitigatory measures to protect vulnerable groups from the decontrol of prices and economic liberalization under adjustment programmes.

FOSTERING AN ENABLING ENVIRONMENT

How can governments construct a policy environment conducive to the strengthening of the NGO sector, particularly so as to foster enhanced popular participation? This will depend significantly on the initial relationship between the two sectors, as described by Tandon (1991).

The first form of relationship is where NGOs are in a dependent client position *vis-à-vis* the government, in which NGOs implement state-prepared programmes and/or receive funding through the state (a dependency of money, ideas and resources). Examples include Tanzania (especially during the 1980s) and China. The second type of relationship is adversarial in which there are no common starting points and no wish from either side to search out areas of agreement. Examples include Zaire, Kenya and Pinochet's Chile. The third and most constructive relationship emerging in certain liberal democracies is a collaborationist one in the sense of a genuine partnership to tackle mutually agreed upon problems, coupled with energetic but constructive debate on areas of disagreement. Examples include India and Brazil. These only indicate a national pattern and require a caution. As with companies in the private sector, individual NGOs differ enormously from one another and hence there is a variety of NGO–government relationships.

From an NGO perspective, the most favorable policy setting is when legal restrictions are minimised, when they have complete freedom to receive funds from whomsoever they choose, to speak out as they wish and to associate freely with whoever they select. The NGO sector is likely to grow most rapidly (in particular, the number of NGOs is likely to rise rapidly), but 'bigger' does not necessarily mean 'better'. Growth of the sector can be a mixed blessing.

Where regulations and reporting are most lax, the door is open for unhealthy and even corrupt NGO activities which may taint the sector as a whole. Where the expansion of the sector has been most rapid (as in South Asia and certain African countries) there is considerable concern about the rapid ascension of 'bogus' NGOs which serve their own interest rather than those of vulnerable groups. An assessment is needed as to which regulations merely hamper the contribution of the NGO sector and which are necessary to ensure that incentives provided are used for the intended purpose.

Even if it were possible to curb bogus and corrupt NGO activities, a non-interventionist policy environment may not make for the healthiest NGO sector. The individual NGOs may be healthy, but collectively there may be insufficient coordination, duplication of effort, and important gaps left unaddressed. All these problems are illustrated in a recent report on the NGO sector in Uganda (World Bank, 1992).

POLICY INSTRUMENTS AFFECTING THE POLICY ENVIRONMENT

Various state instruments influence, for good or ill, the health of the NGO sector (Brown, 1990). Governments' stance can be non-interventionist, active encouragement, partnership, co-option or control. A conducive policy environment can help make the whole greater than the sum of the parts, through judicious use of policy instruments, as discussed below.

'Good Governance'

Governments are able to use social and political policies to encourage a healthy civil society and public accountability of state institutions in ways which promote participatory development and foster a strong NGO sector.

Such policies would help the government become better attuned to popular concerns, and to improve its efficiency.

Of particular relevance are issues of plurality (rights of association, rights to organise interest groups) and information (public access to information about development programmes). Governments might reduce implementation problems and enhance public support for their pro- grammes by easing access to information and allowing affected communi- ties the opportunity to voice their concerns.

NGOs can play an important role as interlocutors and facilitators of public consultations, and can catalyse public debate and contribute to improving governance.

Regulations and Fiscal Legislation

Government-imposed NGO regulations and reporting requirements must strike a balance between nurturing NGO growth, and guarding against cor- ruption, management ill-discipline and other malpractice. Restrictive laws and procedures designed for the political control of NGOs clearly hamper legitimate NGOs.

Fiscal policies should be transparent and even-handed, providing incen- tives for legitimate NGO activities (conforming with State development priorities). Tax concessions may be used to encourage indigenous philan- thropy and income generating activities of NGOs. And legitimate NGOs should be able to receive foreign funds and donated goods without onerous bureaucratic delays. There should be no arbitrariness, bias or 'rent seeking' in the awarding of these privileges.

Operational Collaboration

Governments may present opportunities for NGO collaboration. Where this allows the NGOs to retain their own agenda and remain accountable to their traditional constituency, this can offer a 'win–win' situation, espe- cially in the promotion of participatory development approaches. Valuable roles which NGOs might play within government programmes include (Salmen and Eaves, 1989): articulation of beneficiaries' needs to project authorities, providing information about the scheme to communities, organising communities to take advantage of the scheme's benefits, deliv- ering services to less accessible populations, or serving as intermediaries to other NGOs.

The effectiveness of such collaboration will depend on the particular sector, on the attitude of the relevant central and local government officials to such collaboration, and on the attitude of the major NGOs to collaboration. Other important factors include: the degree of encouragement, guidance and training provided for such collaboration; the process for selecting the NGO partners; and the stage in the project cycle at which collaboration is sought.

Effective collaboration may profoundly influence the official structures, for example in encouraging greater transparency, or responsiveness to the opinion of local communities. Collaboration may also influence the NGOs, for example in instilling strategic planning, and other management disciplines, or fostering awareness of the macro-level concerns of government. But collaboration may also deflect NGOs from their traditional constituencies and purpose, or lead to a polarisation within the sector.

As governments move towards contracting out services that were previously provided by public employees, it is important to learn from experience what has worked and where pitfalls lie. NGOs may be able to deliver services in a cost-effective way, but they may not be sustainable, and they may depend on structures (such as village committees) which are parallel to and duplicating existing ones. There may also be implications for the management of the remaining public sector facilities, if both the NGO and public sectors are to avoid damage.

When NGOs become involved in development programmes to make them more participatory or responsive to the needs of vulnerable groups, they are not always well equipped to represent a broad cross section of stakeholders. For example, in development projects which entail considerable involuntary resettlement, NGOs may represent the legitimate concerns of those displaced. This may result in considerable improvements in the compensation packages awarded, but if the campaigns are waged very strongly – perhaps internationally – the legitimate interests of other groups (such as those who stand to benefit by the projects) may get lost or eclipsed.

Policy Debate and Formulation

Governments can involve NGOs in fostering public debate and in helping to formulate policy in many ways. Firstly, they can provide information to NGOs for dissemination to their constituencies. In some sectors such as AIDS prevention or environmental awareness this is relatively uncontroversial; in other sectors such as in combating gender, ethnic or caste bias or in promoting family planning it may be highly controversial.

Second, NGOs can help governments organise public consultations, ensuring that affected parties are adequately represented in planning enquiries and environmental assessments. Third, governments may invite NGO leaders to serve on official commissions and other official bodies. For example, the Indian NGO, DISHA, has been an influential member of the Central Government's Commission on bonded labour.

Coordination

The ideal is for the government to foster but not dominate coordination. Having NGO Units in the most relevant line ministries or organising NGO consultative committees enables the government to plan its programme in full knowledge of the activities of others and enables NGOs to do likewise and to plan their programmes more strategically. Sensitive co-ordination does not amount to controlling NGOs, but it encourages NGOs to avoid duplication, attend to geographic or sectoral gaps, eliminate religious or ethnic bias and avoid activities which are unrealistic or which contradict state programmes.

The government may also encourage or facilitate the training of NGO staff, for example, by ensuring that its own training institutions offer courses of relevance to NGOs. It can provide other fora for co-ordination and the sharing of experience and plans. And it can permit NGO involvement in aid processes such as regular donors' meetings and Consultative Groups.

Government Funding

Governments may provide funds, contracts and training opportunities to NGOs so as to give them special encouragement for priority activities and for operating in priority areas. Care is needed to avoid undermining NGOs' autonomy and independence. It is necessary for the government to reach broad agreement with leading NGOs and/or NGO umbrella organisations on such priorities. The funding may come from the government's own resources or from donors.

Transparent and consistent mechanisms are necessary for the channelling of official funds. Fora such as the Council for Advancement of People's Action and Rural Technology (a leading body for channelling government funds to NGOs in India) and the new Community Action Programme (a local government scheme for financing NGOs and community initiatives within the Northern Uganda Reconstruction Programme) are illustrations. To guard against any negative impact on the work, constituency and autonomy of the NGO sector, it is useful for NGO leaders to be consulted on such funding.

CONCLUSION

In all of these areas there is potential for conflict: conflict between NGOs and the government, between different NGOs (because in most countries they are far from a homogeneous group) and even within an individual NGO. Official support for NGOs involved in service delivery may be resented by others in the same organisation who are actively seeking reforms in government policies and practice.

The factors determining the NGO–state relationship and the policy instruments available to the government to influence the operating environment for NGOs are necessarily country specific. They depend on the anatomy of the NGO sector in a given country, and on a range of government and societal determinants.

The emphasis of governments and donors on poverty reduction, popular participation and the environment has led to increasing interaction with NGOs, particularly at the operational level. This necessitates detailed knowledge of the NGO sector in a given country and of the way it relates to the government, communities, the private sector and donors.

There are many reasons cited for involving NGOs in government activities. NGOs may be cost-effective, they may deliver services to difficult-to-reach population groups, they may be able to innovate and they may display other attributes. The most important factor, however, is their potential for helping to ensure that people – in particular vulnerable groups – become more involved in decisions that affect them in development planning and resource allocation. It is the pursuit of genuinely participatory development which should be the motivating force in improving state–NGO relations and in fostering a more enabling environment for NGOs.

Notes

1. This chapter reflects the author's views and not necessarily those of the World Bank or its affiliated organisations. It was presented at the Manchester Workshop in 1994 and was originally published (under the same title) in the journal *World Development* Vol 23(4), pp. 593 to 601 in April 1995. The editors wish to thank Elsevier Science Ltd. for granting permission to reprint this paper.
2. In this chapter I focus on non-governmental organisations (NGOs) which work in relief, development, environment, welfare and human or civil rights. I will also, for the present, assume definitions offered by Salamon and Anheier (1991 and 1992) restricting attention to organisations which are formally constituted, non-governmental, self-governing, non-profit (that is, not organised chiefly for business purposes), not overly partisan (in a

party political sense) and characterised by some degree of voluntary involvement. This is a broad scope including international, national and grassroots organisations; special interest organisations, networks, service providers and public service contractors; funding, operational and advocacy NGOs; professional associations, community associations, co-operatives and membership organisations of the poor, and many other categories.

NGOs may be membership or non-membership organisations. The former (including organisations which are not formal membership bodies but which de facto represent a sizeable constituency) may play an important role in participatory processes. They usually provide a service which is regarded as a priority by its members. Sectoral polarisation of the NGO community varies considerably from country to country. In some countries, for example, NGOs concentrate on income-generation activities, in others, environmental concerns, while elsewhere support for and mobilisation of the landless dominates. In some countries, international organisations play a more prominent role than national NGOs, but elsewhere the reverse is the case. In some countries, indigenous intermediary or umbrella organisations provide intellectual and operational leadership.

4 Privatising the Voluntary Sector: NGOs as Public Service Contractors?[1]

Mark Robinson

PUBLIC SERVICE CONTRACTORS AND THE VOLUNTARY SECTOR

It has become increasingly common for NGOs to be categorised as part of a discrete organisational sector with a distinctive identity and characteristic features, namely the voluntary or third sector, alongside the government and commercial sectors. In conceptual terms, Brown and Korten (1991) distinguish between the three sectors on the basis of the options available to organisations to mobilise resources. The commercial sector depends on negotiated exchange through market transactions, the government sector rests on coercion and legitimate authority exercised through hierarchical systems, and the voluntary sector derives its impetus from shared values in consensus-based systems. In this typology, voluntary organisations are principally driven by shared values rather than by the quest for economic or political power, and their constituency is the poor and disenfranchised, rather than citizens or consumers.[2] As value-driven organisations, voluntary organisations operate in a variety of ways, providing services, catalysing development initiatives, and providing support services. But there are other types of NGOs that do not strictly fit into the three-fold categorisation outlined above, which form the subject of this chapter.

The term public service contractors (PSCs) was coined by David Korten (1990) to denote those NGOs which function as market-oriented non-profit businesses serving public purposes. Such organisations, he argues, sell their services to aid donors and government agencies to implement projects and programmes. They are distinguished from voluntary organisations in that they are driven more by market considerations than by values, and thus have more in common with private businesses, even though their avowed purpose is to provide services to third parties. According to

Brown and Korten (1991:62), the conceptual difference between a voluntary organisation and a PSC is clear: 'A value-driven NGO defines its program based on its social mission, and then seeks the funding required to implement it. The market-driven PSC starts with an assessment of prospective funding sources and defines its program on that basis.' But in reality, they acknowledge the difficulty of making a cut and dry distinction between the two types of organisation since many NGOs rely heavily on government support, and many PSCs share a strong commitment to social goals and the same type of legal registration and related tax benefits that apply to NGOs. However, in practice, few NGOs think of themselves as PSCs and continue to maintain their independence from the funder's agenda and continue to stress the importance of value-driven goals. Indeed Korten acknowledges that many PSCs are in fact a hybrid type of organisation, combining a strong market orientation with a clear social commitment and high ethical standards, and that such hybrids are likely to be an important trend in the future.

According to Korten, the features that donors look for when seeking to engage NGOs as implementors of projects are technical competence, well-developed management systems and a concern with cost-efficiency. Moreover, he claims that there are pressures on voluntary organisations to become PSCs. These include: uncertain and precarious finances and the attraction of donor funding; strains induced by constantly combating established values and practices; the difficulty of maintaining value consensus and organisational commitment in the face of growth; an obligation to provide job security to paid staff; the belief that the resources made available by contracting will increase the opportunities to concentrate on priority tasks; and pressure from donors to recruit more specialists with a view to professionalisation (Korten, 1990:103). It is therefore difficult for all but the most committed of NGOs to be lured by the attraction of contracting, but in so doing they may be in danger of losing sight of their catalytic role and value-driven orientation.

Korten (1990:103) predicted that there would be 'a substantial increase in demand from donors for legitimate, qualified public service contractors to manage large-scale implementation of social projects that government has proven incapable of handling'. In the five years that have elapsed since this prediction was made there is certainly evidence of such a trend, but there is surprisingly little documentation of contractual arrangements involving NGOs. In the available literature, questions of accountability, effectiveness and performance have been addressed only very tangentially. But it will be argued that there are very compelling reasons for these issues to be given greater attention, and that experience of contracting needs to be shared more widely and subject to detailed scrutiny, to enable NGOs to consider the costs and benefits of adopting this approach, and determine their preferred terms of engagement with donors and governments.

PRESSURES TOWARDS CONTRACTING

Pressures on NGOs to enter into contractual arrangements with governments and donors do not only stem from factors associated with funding, professionalisation and organisational growth. There are also broader structural and ideological determinants at work which reflect economic realities and neo-liberal influences. The first stem from policy responses to economic decline in the 1980s in the form of stabilisation and structural adjustment. Stabilisation measures generally entailed sharp reductions in public expenditure and devaluation raised the prices of goods and services. Adjustment measures invariably focused on reducing the size and role of the state and promoting the growth of the private sector through privatisation and institutional reform. NGOs expanded their social delivery functions in response to cutbacks in spending on health, education, rural development and other public services, often with the active encouragement of aid donors. Reductions in state capacity and public services went hand in hand with an increasing volume of donor support channelled through NGOs, principally in the form of grants, but increasingly by means of contracts.[3]

Ideological factors also shaped thinking about the role of NGOs in public service provision. Government was typified as inefficient, hampered by bureaucracy and in the thrall of self-interested politicians, whereas NGOs were perceived to be low-cost, flexible, participatory, and able to reach the poor. In other words, concern focused on the role that NGOs could play in compensating for 'government failure', particularly in the provision of public services (Roth, 1987).

These perceptions derived from neo-liberal critics of the social democratic consensus around the welfare state in the West, and exerted a strong influence on development thinking. In the United States there was a profound shift under President Reagan away from an emphasis on state provision of social welfare to contracting out the financing and delivery of social welfare services to public agencies, non-profit agencies and private sector organisations to provide services of a specified quantity, quality and cost (Bernstein, 1991). This trend has also been taking place in Britain, with a move away from grants as the principle source of public funding for voluntary organisations to what has been characterised as a 'contract culture', in which charities compete for contracts from government agencies (Hawley, 1992; Kendall and Perri 6, 1994).

The third main influence on an expanded NGO role in public service provision is political in nature. Political liberalisation and democratic transition in many parts of the developing world has created a climate which is more conducive to voluntary action. As Bebbington and Thiele (1993:45–7) have shown, this is especially the case in Latin America, where most countries reintroduced competitive electoral systems under civilian regimes in the 1980s, although formal political democracy has not meant that all constraints on voluntary activity have been automatically removed. A similar trend is now underway in sub-Saharan Africa, and observers note the prospects for an expanded NGO role as a consequence of the transition to democratic rule, even if there are limits on their contribution to democratisation (Fowler, 1993). In Latin America, administrative decentralisation has taken place alongside the reinstallation of democratic regimes, which has not only increased opportunities for political participation, but has created new opportunities for NGOs to assume expanded roles in the implementation of local government programmes (Bebbington and Thiele, 1993:47–8).

ADVANTAGES AND LIMITATIONS OF CONTRACTING

The conceptual rationale for focusing attention on non-profit organisations rather than commercial private sector organisations stems from perceived disadvantages of the latter in the provision of public goods. Where it is difficult to assess the quality of the service provided, there will be a preference on the part of the consumer (purchaser) for a non-profit provider, since commercial firms have an incentive to cut quality in an effort to increase profits when monitoring is problematic (Meyer, 1992). A variant of this argument, which is especially relevant in the development context, suggests that purchasers of services tend to prefer non-profit providers when the purchaser (donor) is not in direct contact with the clients (recipients) which makes it difficult to monitor the quality of service provision. In development work donors can feel confident that public resources will be used primarily for the benefit of the intended beneficiaries since there is little scope for private appropriation of surpluses (Brown and Korten, 1991:46). The public sector can also benefit from the flexibility of non-profit providers which are able to tailor their services to the needs of individual clients and operate on a smaller scale than government agencies or commercial organisations (Salamon, 1987). As noted by Meyer (1992:1117), there are additional advantages to the public sector from competition among non-profit service providers for government contracts. Hence when government agencies award competitive tenders to PSCs they hope to combine the advantages of smallness and flexibility associated with the voluntary sector and qualities such as technical competence, effective management and cost efficiency associated with the private sector.

But there are also a number of limitations implicit in this approach, which largely derive from experience with contracting public services through the non-profit sector in the West. There is evidence from the United States that contracting results in the poorest being served least and less-needy clients receiving better services. When government funding is reduced, services to the poor are cut disproportionately because agencies serving them cannot compensate for these losses either from their own resources or from user-fees due to heavy dependence on public resources and the limited capacity of the poor to pay for services (Bernstein, 1991:4).

There are also problems of accountability and control. In the absence of national policy implemented through a basic system of services in which there is a certain clarity about roles, functions and priorities, there can be excessive influence on the policy and direction of government purchasers by service providers, which can result in turn in a segregated and inequitable distribution of services (Bernstein, 1991:4). In other words, in the absence of core service functions, government agencies can become over-dependent on the policy and programme priorities of service providers. A related problem is that of quality control, which is particularly problematic among non-profit providers because programme objectives are often diffuse, resources are limited and technologies are inexact and difficult to measure. While the difficulty of monitoring expenditure might be eased when engaging non-profit providers, this does not solve the problem of monitoring the quality of service provision. According to Bernstein (1991:4–5):

> These problems are exacerbated when contracts are involved because it is difficult to develop valid, realistic contractual requirements sufficient to achieve accountability but not so burdensome that they result in more compliance activity than service. When contracting occurs among different government levels, increased political influences and constraints complicate quality control. When contracting occurs between one or more levels of government ... and non-profit and for-profit agencies, or

a combination of the two, this complexity has staggering implications for accountability.

There are, finally, a set of operational problems that arise in the context of the provision of public services by non-profit agencies. Financial problems are among the most significant of these, including delays in reimbursement, insufficient reimbursement, and restrictions on budget modifications (Bernstein, 1991:5). Contract requirements are costly and difficult to manage, and as Hawley (1992:51–2) reports from British experience, voluntary organisations often incur additional costs by having to hire in legal and accountancy expertise to assist in the preparation of tenders and negotiation of contracts. The contracting process itself also poses problems such as short submission time for proposals, frequent turnover and inadequate training of government staff, time gaps before renewals, and award and approval delays (Bernstein, 1991:5–6; Hawley, 1992:58–60). Finally, contract compliance introduces a further layer of complexity since regulatory requirements may be too onerous, or subject to evasion and manipulation,[4] and reporting and auditing procedures can be costly in terms of staff time and effort involved in statistics and compiling documentation.

These perceived advantages and problems of voluntary sector provision may be intrinsic to the particular forms of contracting favoured in Britain and the United States, in which competition is built in to the contracting process through competitive tendering, with successful bids selected on the grounds of cost and quality. In other words, the underlying objective of the government purchaser is to secure the highest quality of service at the lowest possible price. But this element of competition may not be so prevalent in NGO contractual arrangements in developing countries, where subcontracting of service provision and project implementation is often determined by other considerations and governed by procedures which differ from those which obtain in the West. Nevertheless, they do provide some guidelines on the basis of which examples of contractualisation through PSCs in the south can be analysed. In order to do this, it is clearly important to distinguish the forms that these different contracting arrangements assume among donor agencies and developing country governments.

CONTRACTING BY AID DONORS

A range of approaches are employed by donors to contract out public services, project planning and implementation, advisory, research and extension work, and technical assistance to non-profit providers. An important distinction alluded to in the previous section, is between competitive tendering and subcontracting on a non-competitive basis. In the former, the purchaser draws up a tender specification for a development project or public service and non-profit providers submit tenders along with commercial firms. The contract is awarded on the basis of the quality of the proposal and cost considerations. This is the mechanism employed by USAID and the World Bank for many of the contracts awarded to NGOs. In general, however, contracting through NGOs is carried out on a non-competitive basis with the donor or government agency commissioning inputs from organisations selected for their track record in implementing projects and programmes.

The trend towards contracting out the provision of public services to the private sector in the United States has also influenced aid agency practice. USAID increasingly favours contracts as the principal means for project implementation, in which NGOs tender alongside private sector agencies for contracts for the procurement and delivery of food aid, the implementation of development projects and advisory services. The ODA in Britain also employs competitive tendering in awarding consultancy and research contracts, although the principal means of funding NGOs is through grants rather than contracts.[5]

The World Bank also uses contracts for involving NGOs in development projects. Out of 218 Bank projects involving NGOs in the period 1973–88, 68 (31 per cent) were through contractors. These PSCs worked as consultants to government agencies or financial institutions to strengthen institutional capacity, or as contractors designated to construct roads, schools and other public works with clearly specified implementation guidelines. Many PSCs working in this capacity behaved like private sector contractors, receiving market rates for their services, but operated on a not-for-profit basis and derived their funding from sources other than contracting. As shown in Table 4.1, almost half the Bank projects involving NGOs in infrastructure and urban development were implemented through PSCs[6]; the other significant area of PSC involvement was in agriculture. Moreover, two-thirds of the projects involving PSCs were in sub-Saharan Africa, indicating a marked regional trend (Salmen and Eaves, 1991:103–5).

There are a number of useful lessons to be learnt from the Bank's experience of contracting through NGOs. Aside from specialist skills and expertise, cost was usually the principal reason for using NGOs to implement Bank projects, since they benefit from low overheads and tax advantages. This stems from a widely held assumption that NGOs are more

Table 4.1   Frequency of NGO involvement in World Bank projects, by type as delineated by the 'public–private' continuum, and by sector, 1973–88

| Sector | Public–Private Continuum | | | | |
	Community association	Policy advocacy NGO	Service-provider/ intermediary NGO	Contractor	Co-operative
Agriculture	26	6	30	19	38
Education and training	2	0	8	10	0
Population and health	8	0	21	4	2
Industry and health	0	3	5	13	2
Infrastructure and urban development	3	2	20	22	2
Relief and compensation	3	1	4	0	1
Total[a]	42	12	88	68	45
Percentage[b]	19(16)	6(5)	40(34)	31(27)	21(18)

Notes:
[a]Since projects may involve more than one type of NGO, some may be double-counted across columns.
[b]As a percentage of total projects in universe (218). Figures in parenthesis are percentages of table total (255).
Source: Salmen and Eaves (1991:105).

cost-effective than government agencies and private firms in implementing particular types of development projects. Evidence from two CARE projects in West Africa under contract from the Bank provides mixed results: road construction in the Sierra Leone Eastern Integrated Agricultural Project was relatively expensive because CARE adhered to high quality standards, whereas the construction of primary schools in the Liberia Second Education Project was estimated to be 30 per cent less than the amount charged by private firms. In the Liberian case, CARE was selected to build 100 schools on the basis of its reputation for cost-efficient construction, in which it used voluntary community labour. This made it much more attractive than local contractors which were known to be more expensive and only moderately skilled, and the Ministry of Public Works, which judged that it could not undertake the task. The project completion report found that in undertaking the assignment on contractual terms, CARE did not capitalise on its perceived strength of working closely with local communities and as result there was not adequate participation in school use and maintenance (Salmen and Eaves, 1991:121). This example suggests that NGOs involved in project implementation on contractual terms, especially in construction projects, may face a trade-off between keeping costs low and adhering to a participatory approach, unless they can negotiate with the Bank on integrating participatory issues into the project design.

The experience of PSCs with contracting procedures operated by the Bank also offers some useful insights. The agreements drawn up with contractor NGOs are similar to those with private firms. However, private contractors tend to work on an expense-reimbursement basis, whereas non-profit PSCs are unlikely to have the capital reserves required to fund construction while awaiting reimbursement (Salmen and Eaves, 1991:121). Lack of flexibility in contracting procedures can be a cause of project delays and implementation obstacles as a local NGO in Burkina Faso found to its cost. The NGO in question was contracted to build health centres because of its expertise in stabilised-soil construction technology. The NGO tried to undertake work simultaneously on three sites, but in the process overextended its supervisory and financial capacity. Funds were disbursed on verification and certification of the work completed, but inspection was often slow and funds were not released to the NGO when required, and large sums could not be accounted for, as a result of which further advances were blocked. In other projects, NGOs have found themselves subject to rigid government procurement procedures which have caused delays in project completion. However, Salmen and Eaves (1991:122) note that the Bank can influence the flexibility of procurement procedures since loan agreements are usually dependent on the policies of the borrower government. They suggest that financial difficulties resulting from rigid contracting procedures could be lessened by setting up a special revolving fund to cover expenses whilst awaiting verification and repayment.

NGOs have also played an important role as contractors in compensation programmes designed to ameliorate the effects of structural adjustment on the poor, which are invariably implemented with World Bank support. Among the most prominent are the Bolivian Emergency Social

Fund (ESF) and the Programme for the Alleviation of Poverty and the Social Costs of Adjustment (PAPSCA) in Uganda, both of which were premised on extensive NGO involvement.

The Uganda Government chose to implement the PAPSCA programme through the Ministry of Education in collaboration with eight international and local NGOs. The intention of PAPSCA was to provide quick relief to those most at risk from the effects of structural adjustment, namely widows and orphans, although the programmes initiated under PAPSCA were intended to lay the basis for sustainable development over the longer term. World Vision and ACTIONAID both became involved in the implementation of the PAPSCA programme at the request of the Government of Uganda (GoU) towards the end of 1990. The ACTIONAID contribution to the PAPSCA programme is in the form of financing for a small scale infrastructure project in Kamuli district. The objective of the project is to enhance community capacity to identify, plan and manage small infrastructural projects which meet community needs. The projected cost of the project was $4 million over three years; 73 per cent of the cost was to be met by the World Bank, 8 per cent by the GoU and 19 per cent by ACTIONAID (Randel, 1992).

The apparent attractions to the GoU of involving ACTIONAID in project implementation as against a private contractor were threefold: a flexible contract which does not specify physical targets; reduced implementation costs since project administration is covered by ACTIONAID; the provision of a training programme to promote sustainability; and good accounting for the use of project resources. The perceived benefits to ACTIONAID were as follows: access to additional resources; the experience of working with non-ACTIONAID intermediaries and using a modified approach to community capacity-building; the possibility of expanding its coverage at relatively low cost; and the opportunity to derive lessons from close interaction with the World Bank and official donors (*ibid.*).

The main operational risk was that delays in procurement and funding resulting from the disbursement procedures employed by the World Bank and the GoU could create additional costs, since ACTIONAID's staff, office and vehicle expenses are fixed. Should such an eventuality result, the options would be to re-negotiate the credit or end the project after three years as specified in the contract. Moreover, if the GoU failed to pay its contribution the World Bank commitment would end and the contract would be terminated with four months' notice (*ibid.*).[7] Although many of these anticipated costs and benefits of ACTIONAID involvement were somewhat speculative, some insights into the experience of NGOs involved in the implementation of the PAPSCA programme can be gleaned from a mid-term evaluation of World Vision's contribution.

World Vision was asked to submit proposals for orphan care and the rehabilitation of health services in four programme areas as part of the PAPSCA package, through an approach founded on community-based development. Rather than establishing orphanages, the programme equips widows and extended foster-care families to care for orphans within the community. There is provision for extensive participation in planning, design and resource contribution (Voorhies, 1993). The mid-term evaluation found that significant results had been achieved in the 18 months since its inception, despite extremely difficult circumstances. The difficulties encountered by World Vision in project implementation derived from the contracting process that the PAPSCA programme entailed. A major problem was the delays caused by the international competitive bidding procedures employed by the World Bank, which require at least 12 months, but in practice took 18–24 months, which meant that basic supplies, including vehicles, were not available at the start of the project. Further, the original design of the programme did not allow sufficient time for mobilising community participation.[8] Further delays were caused by the GoU Central Tender Board procurement procedures, which require that all items of expenditure in excess of $1000 go out to tender. NGO employees and the staff in the government programme monitoring unit were unfamiliar with the tendering procedures which were complex and time-consuming. As a result of procurement delays, some NGOs did not begin work until halfway through the three-year time period and one major NGO even threatened to withdraw from the project (Voorhies, 1993).

Additional problems encountered by participating NGOs were that the overall co-ordination of the PAPSCA programme was not effective in assisting NGOs in programme implementation, because staff in the monitoring unit were unfamiliar with Bank procedures and operating systems, and the Unit was not adequately staffed to enable it to deal effectively with the GoU bureaucracy. Several of the implementing NGOs reported problems caused by delayed decisions, loss of documentation and poor communication, which were attributed by staff in the monitoring unit to unwieldy disbursement and procurement procedures. Additional weaknesses were that NGOs were not significantly involved in the design of PAPSCA, and a lack of clear policy within the Bank regarding NGO-government collaboration. However, implementation problems did not result exclusively from Bank and Government procedures; staff from the monitoring unit observed that several of the indigenous NGOs participating in the programme were new and lacked adequate staffing and expertise.

The second example of a compensation programme where there has been significant NGO involvement is the Bolivian Emergency Social Fund (ESF) (Arrellano-López and Petras, 1994). The ESF was the first of series of social investment funds promoted by the World Bank and other multi-lateral agencies. Unlike PAPSCA it was designed as a quick-disbursing mechanism which had clear criteria for financing small and technically simple projects on a demand basis. More than 500 organisations were involved in implementing the programme, of which 80 per cent were NGOs. NGOs accounted for one third of the projects and 25 per cent of the funds allocated to the programme. The 3000 projects funded through the ESF in the period 1985–91 contributed to substantial wage rises and the provision of social services and infrastructure for the benefit of the poor. According to Sollis (1992:170), additional benefits were improvements in NGO–government relations, and proof that municipalities and NGOs could serve as effective channels for large-scale government and donor funding. In particular, since the ESF involved both public agencies and NGOs there was more even sectoral and geographical coverage than would have resulted if only one of these channels had been utilised. At the same time, many of the projects did not reach the poorest and the unemployed, and there was duplication and inefficient investment due to limited contact with national and sectoral planning processes. Bilateral negotiation with NGOs proved time consuming, and problems arose with NGOs which were still at a formative stage of development and lacked the necessary expertise (Sollis, 1992:171).

The Bolivian model has been influential elsewhere in Latin America, but far less successful, in part because of lack of effective consultation with participating NGOs. In Guatemala, NGOs were drawn into the planning process through a consortium. Their motives for participating were to influence national development policies with a view to providing a favourable policy environment for NGO activities, to diversify and increase financial support, to promote NGO coordination and cooperation, and demonstrate the effectiveness of NGO service providers relative to other development agencies. The government's willingness to cooperate with NGOs stemmed from the World Bank's desire to involve them, as a means to access financial support for its social investment fund from foreign sources. A major problem that surfaced was the limitations placed on NGOs in having to conform to the World Bank's operating procedures, which many of them were ill-equipped to handle. Ultimately, the proposed fund failed to get off the ground for political reasons, which focuses attention on the limitations of replicating an approach that has worked in one context, but cannot simply transplanted to another where relations between the government and the NGOs are rather different (Sollis, 1992:173).

CONTRACTING BY GOVERNMENTS

Evidence on the experience of contracting out project implementation and service provision to NGOs by developing country governments is limited and fragmentary. The few documented examples that exist derive from Latin America, especially Bolivia and Chile, which have actively sought to increase private sector involvement in public service delivery over a period of years (Meyer, 1992; Arrellano-López and Petras, 1994). There were no documented examples of NGO contracting on a competitive basis by governments in Africa and Asia which were outside a donor-funded aid project despite the increasing involvement of NGOs in service provision and programme implementation in these regions, and a marked trend towards World Bank contracting through PSCs in the former.

In their discussion of state withdrawal from agricultural technology development in Latin America, Bebbington and Thiele (1993) distinguish between the privatisation of implementation, where responsibility for funding remains with the state, and privatisation of funding, in which responsibility for financing agricultural technology development is also handed over to the private sector. One example of the first type of privatisation is in the provision of technical assistance in Chile, where the bulk of technology transfer expenditure is covered by the public Institute for Agricultural Development (INDAP), but with private institutions carrying out the work. AGRARIA is a Chilean NGO that has accepted a large number of INDAP contracts as a means of influencing government policy on rural development and poverty alleviation. In the process, it has taken on many additional staff and adapted its working practices to fit in with contractual obligations to INDAP; this has created imbalances within the organisation between its older, more political, remit, and the exigencies placed on it by contracting (Bebbington and Thiele, 1993:143). But the programme also offers advantages to AGRARIA: it provides financial stability and enhances the status of the organisation, it allows AGARARIA to expand into many new areas, broadening its experience of rural conditions in the process, and it frees up funds which enable it to develop new types of activities (*ibid.*:223).

In the second case the state simply withdraws from service provision in the expectation that the NGO sector will assume responsibility for financing and delivery. An example of this is IBTA in Bolivia which was responsible for agricultural extension in the country, but has ceased to offer extension services in the *altiplano* region with such an outcome in mind. Another variant on this approach, which has been tried out in five countries in Latin America and the Caribbean with the backing of USAID, is the creation of foundations with donor funding, which contracts NGOs, private firms and public agencies to implement agricultural development programmes (*ibid.*:52).

The trend towards privatisation of agricultural development and extension services poses a number of dilemmas for NGOs involved in service provision. One is that by accepting contracts they may be perceived as wilful accomplices in the privatisation of services. Second is a concern that they will be assigned a subordinate role in implementation and not consulted in the design and planning of service provision (Bebbington and Thiele, 1993:54–5, 141). A third issue is that increasing dependence on one-off contracts could increase their financial insecurity and reduce their capacity for independent initiative.

A good example of NGO contracting is in the case of rural water and sanitation projects in Bolivia. These form part of a $20 million USAID-funded Child and Community Health (CCH) project, which included $5 million for improving rural water supplies and sanitation in the three most populous of Bolivia's nine geographical departments. The Division of Environmental Sanitation (DES) of the Ministry of Health has responsibility for rural water and sanitation but was not very effective because of staff shortages, conflicting responsibilities and bureaucratic inertia. Largely for these reasons, very little was achieved in the two years since the project commenced in 1989 and USAID was considering termination of the project. To avert this possibility, it was decided that all community-level work would be contracted out to NGOs in order to increase the efficiency and effectiveness of project implementation. Private sector firms were excluded from tendering for the contracts because it was felt that they lacked the necessary experience with the social components of the project, which included community organisation, the training of operators and water committees and health education. However, only six NGOs were deemed as having the requisite experience with rural water and sanitation programmes, and none had the ability to work in an area larger than a single department. The expectation was that these NGOs would develop piped water supplies and household latrines in 129 communities in the target areas, with approximately 70 000 beneficiaries (Karp, 1992).

The contracting process operated in the following manner. Invitation for proposals were only sent to those NGOs which had expressed interest and possessed the expertise required to undertake the work. Contracts were initially awarded for one year, to allow the CCH to assess the performance of participating NGOs before committing further funds. Each contract was limited to one department, and amounted to less than $100 000 in each case. In a departure from its usual procedures USAID approved an informal bidding process to expedite the contracting process. Detailed implementation instructions were devised which all organisations interested in participating in the project had to adhere to. An evaluation committee was set up to assess the proposals, using a weighted point system which took into account social and technical considerations, as well as cost and scheduling. Once the contracts had been awarded, workshops were held in each of the three departments to clarify the responsibilities of the various agencies involved in the project. As the first 16 communities had already been identified and promotional work undertaken by the local health authorities, it was possible for the NGOs to begin work immediately after the workshops had been held. An internal evaluation conducted six months after the new approach had been introduced found that progress was much greater as a result of contracting NGOs rather than through the DES.[9] From this experience Karp (1992:25) concludes:

> It is both possible and beneficial for a government programme to implement projects via local NGOs. Care is required in the contracting procedures, and the government may logically continue to set priorities and to select communities, as well as overseeing the work of the NGOs. Nonetheless, when working at the community level, NGOs can avoid many of the problems which inhibit the effectiveness of government-sponsored projects.

Although a large proportion of World Bank projects awarded to NGO contractors are in Africa, there was no documented evidence of African governments entering into contractual arrangements with NGOs independently of donors. There are understandable reasons for this. Effective contracting through NGOs presupposes government commitment and a capacity to resource public service provision which many African countries simply lack. Expenditure on public services and poverty reduction programmes declined markedly in the 1980s in most African countries. NGOs have expanded their service delivery functions in a gap-filling role, to provide services where the public sector is absent or failing to meet its obligations (De Coninck with Riddell, 1992; Muir with Riddell, 1992). Aid donors have also been promoting increased NGO involvement in the delivery of public services, usually through grants rather than under contract. For this reason, NGOs, especially church-based organisations, account for a significant proportion of health and education services in Africa. For example, in Malawi church-based NGOs provide 30 per cent of health care services, equivalent to 12 per cent of health sector expenditure. In Ghana, 40 per cent of the population is covered by NGO health care provision, and in Zimbabwe 40 per cent of all health contacts are through NGOs (Gilson *et al.*, 1993). In 1990, 18 per cent of health dispensaries in mainland Tanzania were operated by NGOs. It is estimated that NGOs contribute 35 per cent of health services in Kenya and 40–50 per cent of education provision (Mushi *et al.*, 1992). This high level of provision is all the more significant in view of the fact that NGOs tend to concentrate their activities in rural areas and primarily serve the poor and disadvantaged, but no evidence was found of a trend towards government contracting of service provision.

There are trends towards increased NGO involvement in public service provision in South and South-east Asia, although there is a higher level of state commitment to basic services by comparison to most African countries. In India, the government has taken steps to involve NGOs more actively in the implementation of rural development and poverty alleviation programmes. At present this is done through grants allotted to NGOs from a fixed share of Plan resources, although there are indications that District Rural Development Agencies (DRDAs) are beginning to subcontract local infrastructure projects such as minor irrigation works, rural roads, and low-cost housing to NGOs in preference to private contractors, who are more costly and less attentive to quality and maintenance. It is possible that this may become more formalised by the government requiring that NGOs tender for projects along with private contractors, but to date subcontracting NGOs has not taken place through competitive tendering. The initiative to involve NGOs in local infrastructure projects rests with the DRDAs, who identify and contract individual NGOs known for their special expertise, competence and community-based approach. Geof Wood (in this volume) suggests that this process has gone further in Bangladesh, where the state effectively franchises responsibility for large-scale, donor financed service provision (in primary health and education, adult literacy, and rural banking) to NGOs as a matter of course, which represents a variant of contracting, but again without an element of in-built competition.

CONCLUSIONS

This brief review leads to the conclusion that NGO contracting in developing countries is not a very widespread phenomenon.[10] In view of the limited experience of government contracting NGOs for service provision and project implementation, it would appear that aid donors are the driving force behind this trend. The main examples of NGO contracting are from donor projects, especially those funded by the World Bank and USAID, although in the former there is still a preference for involving NGOs in projects through non-contractual grant-based arrangements. The trend towards contracting-out public services to the voluntary sector in the United States has been a major influence in this regard, and USAID is keen on promoting increased NGO involvement in service provision in developing countries through contracting. For this reason, one can expect continued pressure on NGOs to function as PSCs, although there are obvious limits on the ability and willingness of NGOs to operate in this capacity.

Although lack of documentation prevents any detailed assessment of sectoral and geographical trends, it would appear that the trend towards contractualisation is most pronounced in Latin America, reflecting greater policy emphasis on privatisation and measures to enhance private sector participation in public service provision. It also reflects the technical competence of Latin American NGOs and the types of expertise they have gained in implementing large and complex development programmes in collaboration with government agencies in the 1980s. There is also pressure on Latin American governments from USAID and the World Bank to move in this direction, although neo-liberal ideas have received widespread acceptance in Latin America and have exerted a strong influence on policy choice. Contracting-out on a large scale is also dependent on the capacity of the government to effectively monitor and coordinate the activities of different service providers, which is lacking in many African countries.

In general, there are three categories of NGOs that are operating in the contracting mode. The first category are highly specialised non-profit consultancy firms who are experienced in advisory work and implementating donor projects: these are the 'true PSCs', but they constitute only a very small proportion of the NGO sector. They are usually, but not exclusively, based in the United States, and derive the bulk of their funding from competitive aid contracts. Evidence from World Bank projects with NGOs indicates that these organisations focus their attention on infrastructure projects, for example, in rural electrification, small-scale construction and road building. The second category are the larger international NGOs which are accustomed to implementing large-scale development projects or which possess specialised skills. These organisations, which include CARE, World Vision and ACTIONAID, are valued for their participatory approach and ability to operate on a large scale at relatively low cost, tender selectively for aid contracts in countries where they are already working and where the projects are consistent with their broader development objectives. But donor contracts are generally not their principal source of funding (the exception being NGOs which derive the bulk of their income from food aid contracts with USAID) and such organisations are primarily value rather than market driven.

The third category of contractor NGOs are indigenous voluntary organisations. A small minority, principally in Latin America, are like their US counterparts, essentially operating on market principles as non-profit service providers competing for government contracts with private sector firms. The majority are development NGOs involved in project implementation, either in compensation programmes and social investment funds, or in the delivery of public services and technical assistance. For the most part, indigenous NGOs are working with public agencies in a partnership mode with the funds being provided in the form of grants by aid donors and governments. Examples of NGOs acting as PSCs are few and far between, the major exceptions being NGOs with specialist skills who are subcontracted to implement discrete components of larger development projects.

The examples reviewed in this chapter suggest that there are advantages and limitations of NGOs working in a contractual mode. The attractions of contracting are that they can gain experience from working in a contractual arrangement with the major aid donors, they may be able to inject a more participatory focus into project design, and the prospect of additional funds which can enable them to increase their geographical coverage, and release resources which can be deployed for other activities. The disadvantages are that involvement in project implementation and service delivery through contracting can deviate NGOs from their primary objectives and compromise their autonomy. It may also lead to a change in working practices and create conflicts in NGOs between those who are motivated by values and a voluntary ethos and those who are responsible for managing contracted work and all the bureaucratic requirements that this entails. There are also problems inherent in the contracting process. World Bank projects usually entail complicated procurement procedures which can lead to delays in implementation, even though there may be scope for introducing greater flexibility. Finally, reporting and accounting requirements tend to be stringent and it may be necessary to recruit additional staff with specialist accountancy or legal skills for this purpose.

In the absence of detailed case studies or evaluations it is difficult to make any definitive statement about NGO performance when operating in a contractual mode. The evidence surveyed for this review suggests that NGOs have performed well in relation to project objectives, although this has sometimes been at the expense of community participation. It was not possible to assess the claim that the poorest may not benefit when services and development projects are contracted out to NGOs and private sector providers, as evidence from the United States appears to suggest. The assumption that NGO involvement will reduce costs is not always borne out in practice, either because a participatory approach can increase the length of the project, or because procurement problems result in delayed implementation. All these aspects of performance require further detailed research in order to arrive at a more conclusive assessment of the impact of NGO contracting.

The pressures for NGOs to function as PSCs are unlikely to abate in the current economic and ideological climate, and there will be continued emphasis on increasing private sector involvement in public service provision, largely at the insistence of aid donors. However, there has not been such a pronounced shift towards contractualisation among NGOs as Korten predicted, and NGOs have for the most part taken up contracts in a fairly cautious and piecemeal fashion.

Notes

1. I am grateful to Jake Ross and Peter Ferguson who played an invaluable role in identifying and collecting background materials for this study.
2. For a dissenting view see Uphoff (1995) in which he argues that most NGOs belong to the private sector, and that the third sector is more properly the domain of people's associations and membership organisations.
3. As Bebbington and Riddell argue (in this volume), donors are seeking to increase direct funding of southern NGOs and contracting may offer an attractive approach to this end, although it has to be seen in the light of Randel and German's observation that official funding for NGOs is unlikely to increase significantly over the coming years.
4. Bernstein (1991:7) lists a number of ways in which service statistics are vulnerable to manipulation: over-reporting of services rendered; reporting existing services as new; reporting services provided under one source of funding when funded from another source; reporting of clients eligible for services who do not fit the eligibility criteria; and creative reporting to fulfil contract conditions even though activities do not conform to the requirements of the funding agency.
5. ODA has involved NGOs in contracting arrangements for project implementation, for the most part southern NGOs which can access ODA funds for discrete elements of a bilateral aid project, but these are not awarded on a competitive tendering basis.
6. It should be noted that one specialist contractor with expertise in developing and managing transportation systems, the World Organisation for

Rehabilitation and Training (ORT), accounted for a large proportion of these. Although those NGOs designated as contractors maintained a not-for-profit status and manage independent development projects, they operate in the same way as private consultancy firms (Salmen and Eaves, 1991).

7. Voorhies (1993:11) reports that the GoU was only able to provide 15 per cent of its PAPSCA counterpart funding which resulted in cuts to travel and salaries, but not in the termination of the programme as feared by ACTION-AID.

8. Ironically, in World Vision's case, procurement delays actually facilitated this process, premised on a revised implementation schedule.

9. The DES was abolished around this time as part of a public sector reform process, with its functions being divided between other ministries and government agencies.

10. The qualification is that there are probably unpublished case studies or evaluations of NGOs operating as contractors in the project documentation in the possession of NGOs and aid donors, but clearly further substantive research is required to identify possible sources of relevant documentation.

5 States without Citizens: The Problem of the Franchise State
Geof Wood

GOOD GOVERNANCE AND THE FRANCHISE STATE

In international development discourse, it is now clear that we have entered the era of 'good governance'. There is much hypocrisy embodied in the Western preoccupation with this theme, and much room for debate about concepts and meanings. In the West there is a presumption of a successfully working democratic process with strong accountability between state and people, removing the prospect of dictatorial oppressive governments and underpinning, therefore, the protection of fundamental human rights. It is often difficult, however, to recognise this description of ourselves and our political systems. I can be accused of arguing out of perspective; that by comparison with many societies in Asia, Africa and Latin America, the democratic political systems and strong civil societies of the West do deliver accountability and human rights. While I can concede some of this comparison, I maintain that our systems are fragile in many respects and when tested quickly resort to the curtailment of people's rights and the suppression of truth. I would, however, go further and argue that via processes of labelling and ideological manipulation unwary citizens in the West are managed more subtly but no less completely. Furthermore, it is noticeable under recent conditions of higher unemployment how quiescent European citizens are. In short, I am suggesting that 'good governance' represents a revival of ethnocentric, modernising ideology, attempting to make the myths of one society reality in another.

Part of the claim for 'good governance' is *participation*, a wider involvement of citizenry in managing their own affairs, taking responsibility for them and so on. For many in the UK, such a theme verges on a sick joke. The idea that hospital trusts or locally managed schools empower consumers with choice is laughable as budgets are constrained and increasingly earmarked. Local government in the UK has been systematically undermined since 1979 by the very forces which are now placing 'good governance' on the agenda of other societies with much weaker traditions of local government in their political culture. If a highly literate, IT-saturated society cannot manage successful voice, how ethical is it to expect, indeed insist, on better performance elsewhere? However, I often fantasise about group mobilisation among the poor and dispossessed in the UK – perhaps good governance is more possible elsewhere than in those countries which purport to be the keepers of the discourse!

In the context of Bangladesh, a specific aspect of the 'good governance' issue concerns the franchising of state responsibilities to NGOs and more generally the relationship between government and NGOs, mediated to a considerable extent by the ideological prescriptions of donors. Within the community of donors and their immediate clients, it is easy to overestimate the significance of NGO development and service activity. The debate, therefore, about the state franchising its responsibilities to NGOs is about a trend which needs to be examined carefully before it takes further root in the society. There are now several large NGOs in Bangladesh in effect tendering with government and donors for the franchise to take over major services: primary education; adult literacy; primary health; rural banking. Since these and other NGOs are also involved in other sectors (agriculture, pisciculture, forestry, horticulture, rural works, veterinary, crop storage and sericulture) through institution building, training, extension and credit as well as monitoring and performance evaluation, there is no reason to suppose that this 'tendering' will not continue with the support of donors who are increasingly turning their back on the inefficiency and corruption of government. NGOs look like a better bet for spending the revenues of hard-pressed Western taxpayers.

Many questions can be raised about whether NGOs enjoy a relative advantage over government in the provision of services (especially rural ones), and whether these advantages continue as NGOs expand the scale of their operations. Such questions would be central if NGOs were to attempt universal, nation-wide coverage in any of these sectors. Some of these questions arise from the implications of organisational size, and the extent to which procedures have to become increasingly bureaucratised to cope with the maintenance of universal standards and services, and whether in this process the relative advantage of flexibility and adaptability (associated with small organisational size) is lost. There are further points, also, about organisational culture. Small, ideologically and ethically motivated organisations in the early years of their formation may be able to insulate themselves from the prevailing patron-client norms of the surrounding hierarchical and authoritarian culture with a strong deference to status and leadership. Such organisations are, almost by definition, insignificant in the sense of not challenging the norms of the society in their objectives for it. However as they become larger, both more significant in the realm of ideas and policy as well as in actual implementation and the allocation of scarce resources and as employers of the educated middle classes, so that insulation is harder to preserve.

However, despite the importance of these issues, they are not the main ones addressed in this chapter which focusses upon the problem of governance and the state in the context of the NGO franchise option: hence my coining of the term 'The Franchise State'. To what extent do citizens lose basic political rights if the delivery of universal services and entitlements is entrusted to non-state bodies which would at best only be accountable to the state rather than directly to those with service entitlements? Can the state devolve responsibility for implementation without losing control over policy (since practice is policy) and therefore losing responsibility for upholding the rights of its citizens? If the answer to the first question is 'yes' and to the second 'no', then we have states without citizens. The irony, of course, is that the international advocates of the process of democratisation are the same ones who wish to privatise the functions of the state, thus rendering the purpose of democracy toothless and meaningless.

STATES WITHOUT CITIZENS

The argument about good government is both a conventional preoccupation with political scientists and theorists or apologists of democracy as well as a sign of the times. Although we may understand the recent history of ideas about state and society relatively easily in the context of Western societies, the picture is not so clear for other societies. It is complicated by differential histories of insertion into international economic structures, by particular post-colonial legacies, and by indigenous organisational culture set in wider frameworks of status systems, property relations and deference. A key element of this complexity is the problem of the nation-state and legitimation for any kind of national level, universal institutions whether in the state or the society. The market itself has limits to its universality in the absence of generalised morality about economic transactions and exchange (Granovetter, 1985). But the state has even greater problems of legitimacy as essentially a foreign institution, regarded with suspicion and hostility, dealt with instrumentally and reluctantly when in monopoly control of certain sets of resources but best avoided whenever possible. It is in this sense that we observe states without citizens.

Some of the concern with good government rings hollow under these conditions, especially when translated into conditionality. It is not so much that conditionality around some notion of a human rights agenda is intrinsically unethical, but that the setting of impossible and unrealistic conditions is unethical. This is why careful analysis is so important: ethics are contingent on realpolitik.

THE PROBLEM OF ACCOUNTABILITY

The problem for states without citizens is accountability – the culture and structures for it are missing. It is impossible to address the issue of 'good government' without tackling the issue of relativism both in the sense of cultural expectations about performance as well as in the sense of distributional outcomes (arranged by class, ethnicity, gender, age, household composition and so on): good for whom in whose eyes? Probably, therefore, the question of what is 'good' cannot and should not be resolved in a universal sense, out of context: such an exercise is too normative and likely anyway to be strongly ethnocentric since the relativism applies also to any author on the subject. What can be addressed is: how 'good in context' can be obtained. This is a question of the *process* of good government where the problem of accountability returns us inevitably to Hirschman's (1970) propositions concerning exit, voice and loyalty. The conclusion from that discussion seems to be that the process of accountability is contingent upon several factors: the monopoly character of the service or provision and the opportunities for non-degraded exit; the significance to the agency of the voice being exercised (the voice of some can be more easily ignored than that of others); the capacity of different groups in the society to exercise voice effectively, and over what aspects of agency performance (since governments have many products and many discrete sets of clients); the degree of exposure or responsiveness of governments to criticism in terms of legitimation (especially when it is explicitly reliant upon popular support); and the extent to which the creation of specialist client constituencies has ensured loyalty and dependency. As in committees, are we supposed to take silence for assent, indicative of satisfied customers? Apathy has long been regarded as an ingredient of democracy. Are good governments identified by the extent of voiced opposition and criticism, or by the absence of such voice? Is loyalty just co-option?

THE PARADOX OF NEO-LIBERAL VIEWS ON GOOD GOVERNANCE

There are some paradoxes in the notion of good government, where the thrust of policy is to undermine the monopoly of the state in service provision and the allocation of resources, thereby creating more opportunity for exit choices and thus reducing the necessity for governments to be good. More exit means less voice and loyalty. The preoccupations with privatisation and markets on the one hand and good governance on the other do not easily sit side by side. Furthermore adherence to neo-liberal views about the efficacy and responsiveness of the market as an allocator of public goods crucially slides over the issue of responsibility. If the theme of good government means anything it has to concern rights. In the market one has exchange entitlements but not rights.

Rights and responsibility go together. The state as guarantor and regulator implies a different view of responsibility to the state as implementer. When my local government subcontracts the allocation of tennis courts to a private company to whom do I complain about the principles of allocation and to whom do I complain about the operation of those principles? One is never consulted about these principles in the first place, let alone the principle of subcontracting which disperses both responsibility and the process of accountability.

Along with accountability, responsibility and rights, we must reflect upon 'participation'. There are further ironies here since those concerned now with 'good government' have not been so interested in the more established theme of participation. Participation has attracted different supporters, having a bottom-up career by contrast to the top-down 'good government' agenda. To a considerable extent participation started with grassroots radicals preoccupied with class and gender struggles, dealing directly with the unsophisticated consciousness of poor, isolated, alienated people well aware of their own conditions but with limited empathy for others and a consequent inability to translate immediate senses of grievance into sustained political and armed action. Such radicals were informed by classic revolutionary theory which had brought them to an understanding that cadre leaders eventually betray their followers (Moore, 1966). For activists with a longer vision and a conscience, this problem had to be overcome: hence conscientisation leading eventually to participation (Freire, 1972).

So far so good: a decent career despite the contested nature of the concept, especially when the moment of truth arrives and activists are expected to relinquish their leadership roles in favour of the mobilised and animated. But then the trouble starts as mobilisation takes the form of projects. Participation enters the project lexicon and becomes rapidly subverted by tokenism, routinisation and overuse. At this point there is a fundamental assumption to be examined: does participation ensure improved project performance? Is participation a precondition for good development; or is reference to it merely a sign of quality, a hallmark? As the concept moved from means to ends status in the lexicon, so it finally merged into the contemporary concerns with human rights and good government, and in the process was made technical and stripped of its erstwhile radical implications.

FRAGMENTING RESPONSIBILITY FOR DELIVERY

The concern with 'good government' would seem then to be less a concern with improving the capacity of the state and more with restructuring it with a sharper distinction between the functions of defining, guaranteeing and regulating entitlements on the one hand, and delivery on the other. While the government remains responsible for the former as part of the maintenance of political and human rights, it is seen in most societies (especially poor ones) to reach quickly the limits of its own competence when it comes to the delivery of such entitlements.

This conclusion has led to a widening of the organisational landscape to legitimate the public activity of alternatives to government: the private sector, parastatals, NGOs, QUANGOs, management companies, consultants, education and other service institutions. Such agencies are similar to each other in sharing contracts with the state, but they may differ in other important respects. Their degree of dependence upon 'government' work or the composition of their public/private portfolio; profit-taking philosophy; their relations to clients; assets held or owned; tax liabilities; internal management styles; the existence of consumer bodies specific to the service.

This fragmentation of the delivery function entails a corresponding fragmentation of voice, with political parties and unions sidelined in the process, their respective voices denied primacy and legitimacy in the specific, sectoral contexts of service provision. In this way accountability is diluted at both ends: source and destination. The function of resource allocation and public expenditure is performed by disaggregated non-public, non-transparent agencies, insulated from a universal system of accountability. The state has discarded responsibility along with implementation by extending and diluting the definition of what constitutes the state.

The theme of 'good government' therefore risks self-contradiction by diluting these dimensions of responsibility and accountability through the creation of the franchise state as a solution to delivery incompetence. It is as if the basis of citizenship has been systematically removed: the right to attribute performance to the state alongside the existence of formal mechanisms to bring that bureaucratic performance to account.

This suggests that the 'good government' formula is a trick that cannot work since it is based upon convincing us that this distinction between defining entitlements and implementing them is tenable, and that the former function is accountable through the disaggregated, quasi-state directed monitoring of the latter. This separation enables responsibility for policy to be side-stepped by focussing accountability upon 'implementation'. In this way, the meaning of participation is restricted to the management of outcomes. Citizens become consumers though often without meaningful access to a choice of suppliers. The loss of rights in the state is not adequately compensated for by acquiring them in the market.

The proposition, therefore, that 'good' can be achieved either through improving accountability, or through less government, or through greater reliance upon consumer rather than citizen models looks rather fragile when examined. Certainly these variants of the proposition amount to a substitution of the corporate state model by a franchise state model.

FRANCHISE MODEL: ALTERNATIVE TO STATE AND MARKET

In the West, while we continue to deal with the consequences of such policy (especially in health and education, but also in key public utilities such as transport), the philosophy itself is under attack. The market is increasingly revealed as an inefficient allocator of resources in the real world, as opposed to the theoretical models of economists. The experience of East Asian NICs has prompted this re-assessment along with the evidence of crisis in the North Atlantic economies.

The problem for poor country economies, dependent on key international agencies such as the IMF and the network of development banks, is that while this re-assessment is under way in the North Atlantic economies they remain trapped within a monetarist perspective in terms of advice received and conditions set for financial aid. But can the critique of monetarism applied in the North Atlantic economies be transferred to a poor country context? Perhaps the big distinction here is that the poor country state has been palpably more incompetent and indeed corrupt (for structural rather than pathological reasons: Wood, 1994) so that, even though the market may be shown as an inefficient and unfair allocator of resources, because of its interlocked and non-transparent character, a return to direct state provision of services remains unacceptable for both theorists and the populace alike. Under such conditions, the franchise model has much going for it. But what concrete institutional forms could it take?

We have to consider the significance of political process in producing institutional forms which might be adapted to, indeed captured by, the theory. Bangladesh has been a good example of this process. This is best illustrated by the career of the NGO phenomenon: relief, political repression of political parties and unions, military regimes, advocacy, conscientisation, small-scale income generation, credit, pilot, innovation, experimentation, foreign sponsorship moving increasingly from the voluntary to the official sector, domestic government control over flows of funds and monitoring of objectives, organisational expansion, routinisation of programmes, contracts with government (sometimes as part of aid projects) both for training and project implementation in particular localities or among particular target-groups. Alongside this career has been the use of conditionality to break state monopolies in both service and goods delivery and to remove regulations and licensing to allow the market to breathe. But since the market cannot breathe normally (as demanded by theory), then NGOs in all their shapes and forms have been available to fill the institutional space arising from the critiques.

NGOs, PARASTATALS AND COOPERATIVES

At this point it is important to examine the claims of candidates other than NGOs to occupy this institutional space: such as parastatals and co-operatives. Both sets of institutions involve the notion of distance from the state, though to varying degrees. The claim of parastatals can be dismissed easily. Despite the principle of management autonomy, they have always operated within a framework of open-ended government support. The impossibility of bankruptcy and absence of personal managerial liability underpinned incompetence, inefficiency and non-accountability. In short, both in theory and practice they have been indistinguishable, in the eyes of critics, from the state. The pretence of separation from the state merely enabled responsibility to be avoided. Poor countries in the Indian sub-continent and Sub-Saharan Africa have this record in common (Lawson and Kaluwa, 1992).

Cooperative institutions, however, represent a more complicated story. Although the farmers' cooperatives (KSS) and assetless cooperatives (BSS) system in Bangladesh has been discredited among observers concerned with the long term interests of the rural poor, it raises important issues: a process of descent from the high ground of quasi-socialist principles, through a brief ideological spell as banking groups towards the low ground of incorporation into the local patronage networks run by alliances of officials and patrons. The cooperative career has moved, as it were, from the quasi-state to the quasi-market. This has happened partly because the quasi-socialist principles could not be reconciled with the inability to insulate the institutions from the prevailing organisational culture of hierarchy, command, authority and patronage (and much more). Will this history for co-operatives be repeated among the NGOs?

NGOs AND INDIGENOUS ORGANISATIONAL CULTURE

With such a strong role envisaged for NGOs, especially by the donors, in this 'franchise state' model, let us consider to what extent NGOs might conform to negative rather than positive features of the model. Although assumed to have comparative advantages over large-scale government organisations in social development, NGOs cannot easily insulate themselves from the prevailing organisational culture. This is especially the case as they become larger, more significant, receive more funds and have to account for those funds through complex review and reporting procedures. Many countries in the poor world contain strong hierarchical and authoritarian social forms, often stemming from the authority structures within peasant households and wider structures. These are reproduced throughout the political economy in all forms of social interaction (employment, credit, exchange of services), sustained through poverty and pervasive inequality, and reinforced by deeply rooted religious philosophy and associated social practices (for example, caste and gender differentiation). Within this hierarchical and authoritarian structure, relationships of dependence and deference are widespread. In the villages, these are often referred to as patron–client relations in which strong families dominate weaker ones through multi-stranded, paternalistic ties rather than single-stranded ties more associated with the idea of contracts and market transactions. These patron–client relations are transferred into official organisations, despite any appearance of rational, bureaucratic and objective practices.

Most NGOs in Asia (and Bangladesh is certainly no exception) are started by one or a few individuals who retain charismatic control over the organisation as it grows. Contacts with other large organisations (that is, government and donors) are monopolised by a narrow NGO leadership. Indeed, donors (whether official or voluntary) often reinforce the position of central leaders at the expense of other staff by insisting upon dealing with the 'executive director' only.

But these pressures are secondary explanations, compared to the expectations which both staff and family will have of their leader. He/she (though mainly 'he') will have widespread obligations to staff which will spread beyond the workplace into their personal lives. Staff will be recruited using a leader's personal networks, sometimes including immediate and extended family, but certainly including friends as favours for friends. This is not just nepotism, since the principle of loyalty among new staff has to be ensured especially if the NGO operates in a hostile institutional environment. Promotions and advancement within the organisation will follow the same pattern, other things being equal. Many trivial decisions will be pushed up to the top for resolution, through fear of giving offence. These centralising tendencies can only be overcome by establishing more standardised and less arbitrary patterns of decision making, thus encouraging a re-assertion of bureaucratic practices which nevertheless remain hierarchical for the resolution of non-routine issues (Schaffer, 1969). Participatory decision making within such structures is virtually impossible, yet the same organisation may be promoting participatory styles of collective development activity among its target group clients. There is a contradiction here, where the means are not consistent with the ends, with social development objectives undermined as a result.

Perhaps one of the most obvious areas of contradiction concerns the work of large-scale NGOs operating in a variety of regional contexts, with different ecologies, resource endowments, educational levels, social structures, cultural practices and political situations. The agency should promote location-specific analysis and problem solving between local staff and target groups. This requires local staff with considerable autonomy from the centre to commit resources and innovate as appropriate to local conditions. However, the increasing preoccupation among donors and governments for accountability among NGOs for their use of funds, the management and control functions of a large organisation overcome the participatory ones. Reporting, for example, becomes a reaffirmation of hierarchy rather than a sharing of information and experience. Staff cease to be generalists as sections and divisions are created to cope with the increasing specialisms and complexity of the programme. Vertical lines of communication replace horizontal ones with only central leaders having a sense of the whole picture.

While this kind of analysis is salutary, it arises from a critique of the proposition that NGOs can successfully broker state–society relationships. It notes the reversion of NGOs into powerful, outsider organisations – partly bureaucratic in form, but partly a reflection of indigenous authoritative culture expressed through formal organisations as well as within the societal institutions of kin and patron-clientage. NGOs may have prompted this kind of analysis simply because their own claims to a superior morality in working with the poor inevitably invites examination of their practice.

THE TRIANGLE OF STATE, MARKET AND COMMUNITY

In various ways, the arguments above have been wrestling with the institutional triangle of state, market and community. Community in this context refers not only to people's own spontaneous efforts based upon a range of social solidarities, but also what has become known as the 'NGO sector'. We have to live with the proposition that none of the three elements of the triangle can deliver on their own, but that all perform imperfectly in conjunction. We have to look for satisficing solutions, in the knowledge that those with power in any of these three arenas will not totally relinquish it and that no-one else in the society is sufficiently strong to take it all from them. This leads to the following working principles as a guide through the maze of poverty alleviation in Bangladesh.

CONCLUSION: WORKING WITH THE TRIANGLE

The significance of the market has to be acknowledged. The Marxian analysis of the market under general capitalist relations in which sellers of labour operate in buyers' markets has long dominated the discourse about how poverty is reproduced. At the same time, we have witnessed in many parts of the world, experiments to suppress the workings of the market, and to create an alternative institutional culture of transactions and exchange instead, managed by sets of officials. It has not worked. The social relations of production and service provision entail exchange which cannot be policed at every moment of transaction. The market, however imperfect and for whatever reason, is the arena of people's daily behaviour. That is to say, it is part of culture, not just a series of technical interactions, adjusting supply to demand via fluctuating prices. The mistake of anti-market dogma, based on the valid assumption that poor people cannot meet their needs in the marketplace, was the belief that people could be separated from this culture and operate in an officially managed substitute culture. Thus given the proven inability of the state to operate this substitute culture on behalf of the poor, we must search for what the market can do for the poor.

Other strategies are then only justified to the extent that the market does not adequately reflect and deliver poor people's needs, and that under some conditions effective demand has to be created or assisted, especially when the character of the market is interlocked against the interests of the poor (through being poor in social networks). Households need to be understood in terms of their capacity to perform in the different arenas of state, market and community. Rather than simply selecting people on the basis of material and human capital needs alone (which prompts asset and wage generation responses often through narrowly defined projects), a broader consideration of social networks and cultural locations can lead to more integrated thinking, perhaps prompting programmatic responses which address wider issues of longer-term capacity building for households while not necessarily yielding immediate material outcomes. Thus functional literacy, education, primary health care and education, provision for extending legal rights and so on may actually be more developmental than employment and income generation projects.

These other strategies add the dimension of rights to that of exchange entitlements, and establish that 'rights' are fundamentally a political phenomenon to be legitimated and guaranteed at the level of the nation-state, not handed over to the voluntarism of agencies which are not charged with this ultimate responsibility.

These other strategies present the dilemma of choosing between the state or non-state as implementors of policy in two senses: how are rights to be guaranteed and performance held to account; and does the choice of a non-state 'franchise' option entail the self-fulfilling prophecy of state incompetence through the state being by-passed? With this second question, we have to recognise that the key actual and potential political actors in Bangladesh are constrained in the degree of choice they can exercise over these issues. If we assume a desire on their part to be more democratic and accountable to a socially wider class of constituents. Nevertheless, they cannot easily translate this into performance if 'structural adjustment' and 'good governance' conditionality is urging them to divest themselves of responsibility through a 'franchise' strategy.

There are further issues about the franchise model. Can we envisage the non-state, 'franchise model' as a universal strategy, covering more than a minority fraction of the population? Without some kind of co-ordinated universality, the model cannot be a substitute for citizenship as a route to the removal of poverty. In this context does the 'franchise model' actually harm the majority of the poor in the long run development sense by concentrating achievement in the minority, non-state sector; or does it contribute to the improvement of parallel state performance by offering both experiment and competition? If the latter, then we are back to the triangle, with the state learning from the experience of its innovative contractors and replicating best practice on a wider scale as in the case of the Local Government Engineering Board (LGEB) through the SIDA-funded infrastructure project.

To what extent can we expect that the new political conditions of 'democracy' in Bangladesh will ensure that learning takes place and that citizenship becomes sufficiently effective to demand widespread service (whether direct or franchise) *as of right* rather than through the voluntaristic chance of being selected as a target by an NGO or a technical assistance-dominated project? Anxiety about a successful process of learning transfer has prompted the creation of an Institute for Development Policy Analysis and Advocacy in Proshika. It has also prompted the creation of a development management centre within BRAC, and ideas from GSS about a centre for advocacy. These NGOs have essentially lost faith in the conventional academic institutions and private consultancy agencies to perform this task of influencing national policy. These conventional institutions have tended to become incorporated into government and major donor agendas, and have lost their critical edge. Furthermore they have little grassroots experience where the real innovation is occurring whether in social development, institutional sustainability or environmental management.

However, there are dangers for NGOs in this process. Can they bear the burden of expectation placed upon them by donors (and the reluctant state) within a franchise model without becoming absorbed into the prevailing organisational culture from which they sought initially to escape? Some observers are attributing the possibility of NGOs, as delivery and mobilisation agencies, losing relative advantage over government as they 'scale-up'. My view is that NGOs have never been able to separate themselves easily from the prevailing culture, and that rhetoric has always belied practice to some extent. This is not to be judgemental. I do not think any less of NGOs for operating within their own culture, I just want us to be realistic about their room for manoeuvre and to have reasonable expectations. If the culture is dysfunctional to achieving social objectives, then NGOs as well as governments will have to continue to search for ways to reconcile practice with objectives.

In this sense, can best practice in development be assisted within state and non-state through support for a more deliberate and sustained challenge to the negative features of organisational culture, achieved not via training but through guided and supervised programmes of personal action-research in which hierarchical inversions are tested, underpinned by programmes of support for basic research within Bangladesh on these issues? Are such challenges, which amount to an agenda of administrative reform requiring much dialogue with sympathetic allies within government and NGOs, as well as co-ordination with other donors, best achieved by using experience from enclave, experimental projects like the Primary Education Programme (PEP), through demonstration and learning, or through strategic programme support to government and NGO associations? Increasingly I favour the latter.

6 Finding Common Ground in Asia–Pacific Development

Horacio Morales and Isagani Serrano

Compared to other regions of the developing world, the Asia–Pacific region has a greater share of the positive factors that should make for a stable civil society going into the new millennium (Serrano, 1994). It has the most dynamic and fastest-growing economies underpinned by natural resource systems that could support continued growth, at least up to a point. Trans-border conflicts, civil wars and revolutions are relics of a bygone era. Governments and political structures are firmly in place. Two decades from the end of the Vietnam war, citizens' movements are thriving, addressing a wide range of rights, development and environmental issues. By any conventional measures, Asia–Pacific development should emerge on the positive side of the balance sheet; indeed, many view the region's performance as the 'silver lining' on the cloudy picture of world development. It is democracy, not development, that should be topping the Asia–Pacific agenda. What is most needed is to spread the benefits of development more widely and deepen the process of decision-making in order to reduce the disparities which exist within and between nations and societies in the region.

SLIPPERY COMMON GROUND

'Democratising development' is a worthy slogan, but will remain, at best, an elusive common ground. In theory, it can and should be a sound basis on which to build a broad Asia–Pacific consensus among states, markets and civic sectors. No government in the region (even the most autocratic) would openly oppose it. The official aid community would be four-square behind it. Private business would probably see it as implying 'more market' and 'less government'. The voluntary sector would see more opportunities for citizen participation. However, agreement in principle may be as far as this consensus can go, for divisions will appear the moment these principles are spelled out in concrete terms. To move from one to the other will be a painful process.

A first problem is one of definition. Democratic development can mean different things to different actors. Other user-friendly themes, such as 'sustainable development' and 'human security', have acquired as many meanings as there are users. Secondly, the consensus often descends to the lowest common denominator that means little in practical and programme terms. Thirdly, it should be noted that 'people can go to war', as it were, precisely on the values they supposedly hold in common.

THE CHALLENGE OF DEMOCRACY

Democracy is at the core of the issues surrounding Asia–Pacific development. It is also the most sensitive, often becoming a source of conflict and tension between Asia–Pacific states and their citizens, and between countries in this region and countries belonging to the industrialized world. The issue encompasses nearly everything that has to do with governance and the prosecution of development. The challenge of democracy confronts every country in the Asia–Pacific region, though very few governments have risen to this challenge thus far. Considering that some of the largest economies in the world are located in the region yet have still to make the transition to democracy, one can conclude that democracy is indeed a much bigger challenge than development. As a whole, the region has to contend with a long legacy of state repression and authoritarian development. Nearly all countries have been under some kind of dictatorial rule at some point since 1945. The most economically successful among them happened also to be the most autocratic and have kept basically to the same political course throughout the last 50 years. In the name of development, many Asia–Pacific governments have been repressing and violating human rights, although the countries they represent have been signatories to the Universal Declaration of Human Rights and other relevant covenants of the United Nations. Some of them go so far as to challenge the universality and indivisibility of human rights on the grounds of national sovereignty and cultural relativism. Much of the Asia–Pacific region urgently needs social levelling. The divide between rich and poor is very marked, except in countries which have undergone revolutionary transformations. Efforts to improve access to justice run up against political structures which are insensitive and resistant to reform.

AID TO DEMOCRACY

Increasingly, donor countries (led by the United States) are holding up democracy as a central issue. Before 1989, the democracy theme was directed mainly at communist countries. Since the end of the Cold War, the USA and other donor countries have refocused on developing countries, most of whom have been or continue to be under some form of authoritarian rule which the USA and its allies supported in the first place. Democracy continues to be a hotly debated issue in official development circles. Almost every discussion about policy and funding inside bilateral and multilateral institutions is linked to the issue of democracy in some way. Over the past few years there have been some significant changes in patterns of aid. Military assistance is definitely on the decline overall, though the lobby to maintain it remains strong and, on occasions, successful. Poverty alleviation continues to command substantial resources although there is a growing doubt as to the effectiveness and impact of efforts at the grassroots level. Aid for environmental conservation and population is increasing. So is aid to democracy projects. These changes reflect the dominant thinking among donors, and new global realities.

Until recently, nearly all external assistance flowed through governments. However, there is now a perceptible increase in official aid going through non-state channels. This trend will continue as criticisms of the state's absorptive and delivery capacity increase. Recent changes in the profile and modalities of aid have in part been a response to strong criticisms by citizens' groups of the value and impact of official development assistance itself. The old issue of tied aid is still current. Aid to democracy is intended to strengthen democratic processes and institutions. On the face of it, this should pave the way for an improvement in governance, reflected in reforms in policy, legal systems, electoral processes, institutions and resource allocation. But in practice there is reason to believe that aid for democracy may be utilised to strengthen unaccountable governments in the Asia–Pacific region. Confusing signals from the donor community provide opportunities for authoritarian governments to undermine democratisation. Indonesia is a good example. At a meeting in Paris in July 1994, the Consultative Group on Indonesia (an international aid consortium under World Bank auspices) pledged over US$5 billion for the next financial year. That same month Merrill Lynch declared Indonesia as the region's best site for foreign investment, citing as evidence progress made in deregulation, and political stability. Japanese aid is also flowing in huge amounts, accounting for about 40 per cent of total aid inflows to Indonesia. With such assurances of continued support, Indonesian

President Suharto can afford to ignore Dutch Minister Jan Pronk who had been advocating for a clear linkage between aid and democracy (van Tuijl, 1994). Other donor countries tend to 'look the other way' for as long as Indonesia's oil and forest products continue to be accessible and the country remains an attractive market and site for foreign investment.

SUBSIDISING BAD GOVERNANCE

For too long, taxpayers' money has been subsidising bad governance. Additional inflows in the form of aid for democracy may end up doing the same – another case of poor people in rich countries giving to rich people in poor countries! In the Asia–Pacific region, graft and corruption run deep in the state system, regardless of whether the regime is democratic, though it thrives particularly well under authoritarianism where there is least transparency and accountability. Nobody knows for sure how much public funding is wasted this way, but the assumption is that the amounts are very large. Post-war development in the Asia–Pacific region has been basically state-directed. Notwithstanding two decades of structural adjustment programs and pressures for liberalization, the heavy hand of the state is likely to extend into the twenty-first century-Asia–Pacific order. Building a large bureaucracy has been a natural predisposition of governments. Over the last five decades, the size of bureaucracies in this region has grown tremendously. This holds true for both the civilian and military establishments and is evident from even a cursory look at the size of national budgets and the profile of resource allocation.

Centralisation has been a constant feature of this bureaucracy building. Resources and decision-making power have been concentrated heavily at the national level. Capacity at the subnational level is generally weak and local authorities are rarely able to undertake local economic development on their own. The result is usually further alienation of government from local communities. Governments also love to build monuments. As in other regions, spending public money on physical infrastructure has been a prominent feature of Asia–Pacific development, almost as though highways, dams and other mega-projects are all there is to development. This pattern of public spending has cornered the lion's share of national budgets at the expense of education, shelter, health care and other social priorities. UNDP's proposed '20:20 compact' (20 per cent of aid money matched by 20 per cent of the recipient's national budget dedicated to social spending) suggests that currently a very small proportion of public money goes to this kind of expenditure. This pattern is likely to continue in the 1990s and through to the twenty-first century. High economic growth targets have increased the demand for more physical infrastructure. In the last Annual Meeting of the Asian Development Bank, infrastructure deficits were estimated to run to about $1 trillion dollars for the region as a whole. Imagine twenty-first century Asia–Pacific glittering with all the new artifacts built in the name of development!

SHIFT TO THE MARKET

Governments in the Asia–Pacific region, like their counterparts elsewhere in the world, have long been under sustained pressure to liberalise their economies. Donor countries, and the international institutions they control, want to open up the economies of the region and reduce government control. Responses vary from country to country, but the pattern so far seems to be a combination of compliance and calculated resistance. The largest countries in the region, like China, India and Indonesia, are all recipients of huge foreign loans, investments and aid, but claim to be making the transition in their own particular ways. China trumpets 'market socialism'; India has declared that it is going full swing to the market, a 180-degree turn from a previous nationalistic and state–socialist development paths; and Indonesia claims to be making an 'orderly transition'.

China makes for a particularly interesting case study. Its market socialism is a very deliberate, well-phased transition; unlike Eastern Europe and the former Soviet Union, it is not plunging headlong into full liberalisation. Government remains in tight control and does not hesitate to suppress democratic movements. China makes no bones about its own interpretation of democracy and human rights and has come out openly to challenge the Western world on these grounds. According to some reports, China is currently undertaking a study on the subject of democracy and human rights as conceived and practised in the West, concentrating on the USA in particular. The debate between China and the USA around these issues is intensifying and becoming more complex. The battle lines have been drawn, so to speak, and the battle rages in every arena where the two countries come face to face. In the 1993 UN Conference on Human Rights in Vienna, China was forthright in challenging the universality and indivisibility of human rights. At the 27th annual meeting of the Asian Development Bank, China led the opposition to US-proposed policy conditionalities that link lending to democracy and governance issues. The debate is certain to have far-reaching and profound implications on the democratisation process in the Asia–Pacific region.

Shifting from a state-led to a market-led model of development will be very difficult in the Asia–Pacific region. Notwithstanding external pressures, countries will follow their own chosen way. The state will certainly be more prominent in this transition, given historical realities in the region. Performance is the biggest single reason. The failure generally ascribed to state-led models of development does not square with Asia–Pacific realities. China cannot be considered a failure, still less South Korea, Singapore, Taiwan and Hong Kong, which are now being heralded worldwide as resounding success stories. More recently newly industrializing countries (NICs) such as Thailand, Malaysia and Indonesia are moving in this direction. In all these cases, the state has been a dominant factor in determining the processes and outcomes of development. Market forces played a subordinate role and proved successful to the extent that they were pursuing the line of collaboration defined by the state.

RECONCEPTUALISING GOVERNANCE

In 1987, Marc Nerfin wrote 'Neither Prince Nor Merchant: Citizen' in the IFDA Dossier. The 'prince' stands for the government sector, the 'merchant' for the business sector and the 'citizen' for the private, non-profit sector. It may be added that citizen can also be citizen–prince, citizen–merchant or just plain citizen. In terms of resource mobilisation, the first sector uses command and coercion, the second trade and exchange and the third shared values and commitment (Nerfin, 1987). 'Neither prince nor merchant, but citizen': in a nutshell these words capture an emerging global phenomenon, the coming together of men and women, individuals and groups, to increase civic control over the events and processes which affect the lives of others in order, in the long term, to make this world a better place in which to live. This is the core message of citizen participation that is gaining forceful resonance the world over.

Over the past few decades, citizens of all classes, beliefs, and cultural and ethnic backgrounds have been organising themselves to fight for greater access to justice, rights and entitlements; to defend democracy and human rights; to promote a different ethos and path of development; and to respond to basic issues of human welfare. Defying the temptation of civic inertia and apathy, these citizens have been occupying public spaces on an increasing scale in order to defend and advance the common good. The Asia–Pacific region has seen some of the most potent citizens' movements this century, particularly in the Philippines, Thailand, India and Nepal. Others may not be as popular or as well-publicised. But citizens' movements of one sort or another, whether in young or mature form, small or large, quiet or otherwise, exist in all parts of the region.

The stimulus and inspiration for such movements varies from place to place, depending on social, economic, political, cultural and ecological conditions. The common threads are a determination to organise and speak out in defence of common humanity, and the willingness to take action, expressed in a wide range of responses from humanitarian aid to rebellion. The impact of these actions on people's lives, on state and corporate behaviour, and on the governance of civil society, likewise varies widely from one situation to another. In parts of the region where ethnicity and indigenous traditions are still firmly rooted, local action remains strong. Where the nation-state is the hegemonic organising and governing framework, the right to 'good government' comes out as the overriding theme, focusing on local autonomy and decentralisation.

Conventional wisdom has it that governance is the sole domain of states. Such is the wisdom that has brought about large state bureaucracies and state control of social life. Increasingly this view is coming under serious challenge, one expression being demands for more market leadership in running the economy. But the shift from state to corporate hegemony is itself under question, and for good reason: giving up one form of centralisation for another cannot be a solution to the problems causing social polarisation and disintegration in the Asia–Pacific region. State and market forces cannot ignore the resurgence of citizens' movements, especially after they have demonstrated a capacity to bring down authoritarian and unaccountable governments, as in the Philippines, South Korea, Thailand, Bangladesh and Nepal.

Increasingly, citizens are demanding a new kind of governance. Self-organisation is its most elementary form. Citizens want more space for their own organisation and are demanding that governments create and resource the right 'enabling' policy, legislative and institutional environment. Having been engaged in building an invisible social economy, citizens also want a greater share in the economic arena and will not leave this terrain solely to the will of market forces. This is the emerging shape of a new constructive engagement. Seizure of state power is not the objective of citizens' movements. A responsive and accountable state is. That is why they also want their own representatives in power and vote leaders they don't like out of office. But what is more important, these movements can become more powerful without having to capture state power or becoming mere appendages of the state system, as in past revolutionary transformations. Rather, people want to reacquire the power to do things for themselves and to be able to engage both state and market in a constructive way.

In the Philippines, citizen action has helped to shift government rhetoric toward a model which explicitly rejects the authoritarian path taken by South Korea and other South-east Asian economies. As importantly, the government has also committed itself to a concrete social reform agenda, though as yet not matched by the necesary resources or institutional framework. The recent Local Government Code does, however, represent a landmark piece of legislation earned through years of NGO campaigning for decentralisation, and has opened the door for greater public access to almost half the national budget, in addition to greater particpation in local-level decision-making (Serrano, 1994). There has been less success in efforts to scale up NGO initiatives via operational expansion, since what little improvement there has been in productivity and incomes among the poor has been offset by adverse macro economic trends. This has led to more attention being given by NGOs to macro-policy advocacy and stronger links between micro- and macro-level action. Simultaneously, NGOs (worried by the possible withdrawal of external funding, as in Thailand) are exploring ways of increasing their financial independence, something which is crucial for their future.

Amid all these changes, one thing stands out: the citizen. The citizen whose dignity and welfare suffer because of bad government and profit-seeking interests. The citizen whose sense of personal worth and capacity for caring and giving have been diminished because of exclusion, poverty, inequality, violence and oppression. At root, reconceptualising governance means putting the citizen at the centre so that he or she can attain greater security at home, in the workplace, in the neighbourhood, and in the larger community. The empowerment of individual citizens must be at the centre of governance. Putting the citizen at the centre of the agenda of the state, the corporate sector and civil society is the bottom line against which the impact of NGOs and peoples' organisations should be measured. Questions of legitimacy and accountability have little meaning outside of this context.

THREATS FROM FUNDAMENTALISM AND ETHNIC VIOLENCE

Threats to social cohesion do not only come from bad governance and the rapacious operations of the market. A major emerging threat is fundamentalism, now present in many parts of the Asia–Pacific region. This problem is not new. It has been there in less explosive form, waiting for opportunities for open expression. Long-suppressed by other types of fundamentalism, especially of a political or ideological variety, this new phenomenon is of religious or ethnic origin. It is by no means confined to one religion or ethnic group. Each of the major religions in this region bears its share of the problem. Like any other variety of fundamentalism, religious fundamentalism is rooted and thrives in bigotry. But more positively, it is a form of resistance to real or imagined oppression of a political, ideological or spiritual nature. It may also be fuelled by an unfulfilled search for spiritual fulfilment in a materialistic world. Nevertheless, the common thread is intolerance toward the beliefs and practices of others, and a totalising self-righteousness. Islamic fundamentalism is present most notably in Bangladesh and Pakistan and, to a lesser extent, in Malaysia and Indonesia. It is beginning to surface in southern parts of the Philippines. Christian fundamentalism affects both Catholics and the different Protestant denominations and expresses itself in evangelical movements that claim, like their opponents, to 'have all the answers'.

Ethnic violence is more of a political problem. Its origins go back to the beginnings of nation-state building which created tensions between majorities and minorities. The process of integrating groups of various cultural backgrounds into one nation has led to much oppression of ethnic minorities. State policies and mainstream development activities have led to further marginalisation of these groups. Spirituality and ethnicity are emerging themes in the new development paradigm. These are the missing dimensions in past development discourses, policies and practices. Bringing them into the current development debate may help in understanding these phenomena, so that ultimately situations can be found to the problems of fundamentalism and ethnic violence.

THE CHALLENGE OF DEVELOPMENT

The Asia–Pacific region has a great share of both 'goods' and 'bads'. The 'goods' are the region's wealth: more than half of humanity, rich biodiversity, great religions, diverse and enduring indigenous cultures and communitarian traditions. But it also has the greatest share of the world's poorest people : two-thirds, or 800 million, of a total of 1.2 billion. It also has the largest number of excluded, invisible, non-participating, discriminated human beings, the majority of whom are women. The region confronts a spectre of deepening deprivation, increasing civil and ethnic conflict, involuntary mass migration, prostitution, drug addiction, crime and violence, graft and corruption in government, overconsumption, and the monopoly of resources and decision-making power by the few, all contributing to the increasing disintegration of social values and social cohesion. These trends constitute a glaring counterpoint to the region's comparative advantage in economic terms over other regions of the world.

But 'look to Asia, that's where the solution to the world's problems can be found'. Such is the now-common message passed around in development circles – in the World Bank and IMF, and throughout the United Nations system. When such institutions talk of Asia they mean the economic 'miracles', the NICs of South Korea, Singapore and Taiwan and the others soon to follow in their wake. The message is being passed around as though it were the new orthodoxy that tolerates no deviation. Nobody would contest the impressive economic successes of the East Asian 'tigers'. And in a world that continues to be bedeviled by economic recession and stagnation, it would seem foolhardy to oppose the idea of economic growth 'the Asian way'. But what about this Asian miracle? The performance of the East Asian tigers is indeed remarkable. These countries have done in 30 years what Western industrial democracies took more than two centuries to achieve. It is a classic example of enlarging the economic pie, lifting entire societies out of poverty but with hardly any change in social structures. The experience of the NICs also deviates from the Western model by adhering to political authoritarianism. It is a vindication of the trickle-down model, with a big difference. This has not been *democratic* development.

As in all things, success has not been without its costs. And in the case of the Asian miracle, these costs are great. They have been borne by society and the environment. The mass of the population traded off their freedoms for bread. Not only that, they ended with a vastly degraded environment whose health cannot be easily restored without a heavy bill, if it at all. These countries chose to grow at any price and will pay the costs later. The Asia–Pacific region is transforming itself at a much faster rate than any other developing region. Its agricultural base is fast giving way to rapid industrialisation. By early in the next century, it will be home to more than half of the projected 21 mega cities of the world, each having a population of 10 million or more. Soon the region will be choked by pollution and will be confronting great losses in its biodiversity, and the marginalisation of countless inhabitants.

China is well on the way to becoming a regional and world economic powerhouse which may outrank all other East Asian economic miracles taken together. Many others in the region are following closely behind, including India, Malaysia, Thailand and Indonesia. But if China, India and Indonesia alone (three of the world's largest countries in population and land area) were to grow like their predecessor NICs, the world would bid farewell to sustainable development. In this sense, it may be said that Asia can make or break the dream of the 1992 Earth Summit in Rio de Janeiro. The growth-at-any price consensus among governments of the region, backed by bilateral and multilateral agencies and the corporate world, looms large like a juggernaut. Only the institutions of civil society and the different paradigm of development they promote remain standing in its way. Tensions and conflicts are certain to flare up. Now the question: what possible common ground is there that is forceful enough to prevent the polarisation we predict? Is it democratic development? Can states and markets be drawn into rethinking the path they are taking in order to forge a new and profoundly different kind of consensus? One can only start crossing fingers, exert the best efforts in constructive engagement and hope for the best possible results.

Part II

NGO–Donor Relationships: When Your Hand is in Another Person's Pocket?

7 Heavy Hands, Hidden Hands, Holding Hands? Donors, Intermediary NGOs and Civil Society Organisations

Anthony Bebbington and Roger Riddell

INTRODUCTION

The tendency of official donors to channel an increasing amount of funds directly to southern NGOs (SNGOs) raises a range of questions: why is this occurring; how is it being done; what are the impacts on SNGOs; what sorts of SNGOs are being supported; what does this imply for institutional and power relationships within southern civil societies; what does this mean for the relationship between state and civil society in the south and what does this imply for northern NGOs (NNGOs)? For several reasons, these are apposite and timely questions. In the north, the ever-growing interest of bilateral donors in southern NGOs raises concerns among northern NGOs that bring to the surface the longer-standing problem of how far northern and southern NGOs are really partners in a reciprocally accountable relationship. At the same time, northern NGOs are challenged to think what it is they can contribute that their increasingly strong southern 'partners' cannot, and whether their increased receipt of government funds to implement projects is distracting them from a more searching self-analysis of their 'distinctive competence' and their own identity. In the south, the discovery of southern NGOs by larger donors is bringing to the surface similar longer standing problems in the relationship between southern grassroots support organisations GSOs and popular organisations where the same questions arise as in the north: has this really been a partnership of reciprocal accountability between GSOs and popular organisations? Some, particularly those linked to popular organisations, think not, and are increasingly vocal about this, and the contribution and legitimacy of professional, non-membership NGOs (or grassroots support organisations – GSOs)[1] is being subjected to increased scrutiny.

These observations suggest that it would be wise for official donors to be cautious in moving rapidly into direct funding, because they may not have the knowledge and capacity to engage in direct funding effectively. More importantly, increased direct funding will influence both the relationships between northern and southern NGOs, and those between southern GSOs and popular organisations – relationships that are sometimes (perhaps often) fragile. This chapter is an attempt to open up some of the questions surrounding these issues (see also Riddell, Bebbington and Davis, 1994). It does so by concentrating on three questions. Firstly it looks at issues around the reasons why bilateral donors chose to support southern NGOs directly. The main message of this first section is that donors need to be clear first on what development objective they seek through supporting southern NGOs, and only then determine the most appropriate means of achieving this goal (often this may not be by direct funding). The second section looks at several donor experiences with channelling funds to southern NGOs. We close with some reflections on what seems to be happening in donor–NGO relations, and compare this with what we feel ought to be happening.

WHY SUPPORT SOUTHERN NGOs?

In large measure, the themes of performance and accountability are at the centre of why bilateral donors are interested in direct funding of southern NGOs. On the one hand, southern NGOs are supported as a means of strengthening civil society and fostering good government. On the other hand they are supported because they are deemed to perform better than government in delivering certain forms of aid to beneficiaries. Southern NGOs are assumed to be more accountable, better performers, and more effective in strengthening civil society than are northern NGOs. This section of the chapter looks closely at the reasoning behind each of these assertions, and suggests that the situation is less cut and dried than the assertions imply.

SNGOs and Strengthening Civil Society

'Civil society' is a notoriously slippery concept. It has entered donor terminology without careful definition. In many respects, the term is used as a code for a set of ideas related to participation, good government, human rights, privatisation and public sector reform. It is used in different ways by different people and those uses are not always consistent. The following definition of civil society used by the UNDP (1993), however, is a useful one:

> civil society is, together with state and market, one of the three 'spheres' that interface in the making of democratic societies. Civil society is the sphere in which social movements become organised. The organisations of civil society, which represent many diverse and sometimes contradictory social interests are shaped to fit their social base, constituency, thematic orientations (e.g. environment, gender, human rights) and types of activity. They include church related groups, trade unions, cooperatives, service organisations, community groups and youth organisations, as well as academic institutions and others.

This definition draws attention to the idea that civil society is composed of a wide range of organisations which we can call the southern NGO sector – SNGOs.[2] What unites all of these organisations is that they aim to represent or talk on behalf of the interests of particular sections of society. Southern non-governmental development organisations and intermediary service delivery organisations are not formally representatives of the social groups with whom they work, but they do work to try and convey and defend their interests. In contrast, it is membership organisations (MOs), such as unions, women's organisations and so on, which are potentially formal representatives of a sectional interest. Many of these organisations combine representation with some form of development, service delivery, charitable or self help activity. Their functions are, thus, both representational and operational. The balance between the two 'functions' varies greatly depending on the organisation.

The implication of pinpointing these distinctions is that to strengthen civil society is – in part at least – to strengthen these organisations, but in specific ways. As they have both representative and operational functions, and as their capacity and legitimacy to represent depends on their success in operating, then to strengthen them implies enhancing their capacity to perform effectively (according to their own criteria of effectiveness), their accountability to their social base, *and* their capacity to represent their members' concerns.

Strengthening civil society thus has two broad dimensions, one internal to the SNGO, the other pertaining to the way the SNGO interacts with its environment. As a result, the term 'strengthening the capacity of SNGOs' implies efforts to enhance their capacity: (1) to identify their members' (or social base's) main concerns; identify strategies to meet these concerns; and then manage their own development strategies to meet these concerns; and (2) to interact more effectively with the market and the state in order to defend and enhance the interests of their constituency.

Strengthening civil society, however, goes well beyond mere strengthening of these organisations. There are two reasons for this. First, the effectiveness of SNGOs depends on the political and economic environment within which they operate. Their effectiveness will be enhanced by a relatively strong state with the capacity (and disposition) to provide services and to defend rights, and by markets which function in a manner which does not hinder or exclude the possible economic activities and market entry of SNGOs and poor people more generally. Secondly, civil society is composed of different types of MO with different interests. A chamber of commerce, or confederation of industrialists is as much a MO as is a rural women's organisation and workers' union. This has several implications for donors. First, it is insufficient when trying to draw up specific policies to talk 'in general terms' about strengthening civil society. Donors have to identify those parts of civil society whose objectives and needs are consistent with their objectives. This is often no easy matter as certain objectives (for instance, strengthening the private commercial sector) might justify enhancing the capacity of chambers of commerce to lobby government, while other objectives (such as poverty alleviation and gender) would justify enhancing the capacity of women's sectors in trade unions to pressure government for equal wage legislation. Secondly, as the UNDP definition suggests, there are real conflicts between groups within civil society. The more that an effort to strengthen one group is successful, the more likely it is that it will begin to upset existing power relationships, and elicit defensive or aggressive responses from other groups. Thus, a strategy of strengthening civil society should also involve facilitating dialogue between different types of MO with differing interests, and involve support to mechanisms that help resolve conflicts.

What Role for GSOs in Strengthening Civil Society?

After initial enthusiasm about their role in empowering popular organisations, there has been growing concern that GSOs are not necessarily as accountable to the sectors for whom they work, nor as representative of them as has been claimed in the past (Edwards and Hulme, 1995; Pearce, 1993). Indeed, some argue that the concentration of donor support among development NGOs in the South has sometimes led to a weakened civil society and has resulted in or contributed to a disempowering of popular organisations. This is said to have occurred because disproportionate support to development service NGOs has created imbalances across civil society, as Wood (1995) discusses for Bangladesh. This has made popular organisations dependent on intermediaries for access to resources, and has cast intermediaries in the role of representing popular organisations in policy discussions. Equally, other evidence suggests that direct funding has encouraged the emergence of opportunistic organisations that call themselves NGOs but have no popular base at all. Many have been created as survival strategies for a professional middle class, and are more akin to private businesses rather than NGOs (except that they do not pay taxes!). The growth of these organisations clearly does not contribute to a stronger civil society (Bebbington and Thiele, 1993).

Linked to this emerging scepticism about GSOs, however, is a parallel recognition that membership organisations are not necessarily any more accountable to their social bases than are non-membership ones. In an evaluative survey of membership support organisations (MSOs) and non-membership support organisations, Carroll (1992) concluded that in practice non-membership organisations were just as accountable and responsive to their clients as were the membership organisations – indeed they were more successful in strengthening grassroots capacity. Carroll also found evidence to suggest that when non-membership organisations worked with MSOs this increased the accountability of MSOs to their members. Work in Mexico (Fox, 1992) and Thailand (Garforth, 1993) also shows that rural people's organisations can often be taken over by a minority and relatively elite section of rural society. These studies suggest that one needs to be extremely wary of concluding that representative MOs are any more accountable or representative than are GSOs. The implication is that unless problems of accountability are addressed first, to concentrate resources in any organisation, be it membership or non-membership, could further concentrate power, widen gaps between the leaders of an organisation and its social base, and thus weaken and not strengthen civil society.

Intermediaries and Straw Persons: GSOs, MOs and Northern NGOs

Part of the thinking behind the direct funding issue is the notion that southern organisations would sooner receive support directly rather than through/from a NNGO, and that this would turn out cheaper for the donor. But are GSO intermediaries any closer to, or any more likely to encourage, the self-development of popular organisations and the grassroots than are

NNGOs? Much evidence would suggest that this is not necessarily the case (Bebbington *et al.*, 1991; Bebbington and Kopp, 1995; Bebbington and Thiele, 1993). Similarly, calls for direct funding are often based on the claim that GSOs are more representative of, and closer to, the target population than are NNGOs. While at one level this is true, it is equally important to note that GSOs and MOs can be internally differentiated, can be controlled by small groups, need not be especially democratic nor equitable in their distribution of benefits, and therefore are not necessarily representative of the assumed target groups.

The implication is that ideal democratic, representative and policy influencing intermediary SNGOs are not queuing up to be directly funded. If badly handled, direct funding programmes run the risk of shifting the intermediary even further from the ideal. Generalisations that claim GSOs and MOs are necessarily more effective intermediaries between donor and beneficiary than are NNGOs need to be made with great caution. The more important policy questions to ask, then, are these: what type of relationship between different institutions (SNGOs, MOs, local groups, NNGOs and so on) will increase the client-orientation and accountability of each; what configuration is most likely to increase the effectiveness of what they do by linking actions and policy change; and how can a bilateral donor best operate in this sphere?

SNGOs and Aid Delivery

A second main donor reason for considering more direct work with GSOs and MOs is to use them to deliver aid within the context of the bilateral aid programme. How effectively have GSOs and MOs performed as aid delivery channels? Once again, it is difficult, and dangerous, to make sweeping generalisations. Impact depends on the type of activity, the type of NGO, and the policy context. To the extent that generalisations can be made, there is some consensus that GSOs and MOs are more effective in delivering services than they are in achieving a sustainable alleviation of poverty or in supporting the development of self-sustaining market-based activities (though there are of course exceptions) (UNDP, 1993; Riddell, Bebbington and Peck, 1995; Riddell and Robinson, 1995). Thus SNGOs have been particularly strong in provision of health care and education, and agricultural services. In the cases of the very large GSOs, a phenomenon particularly associated with South Asia,[3] NGOs deliver services on a scale analogous with ministries. Successes in marketing and small industrial and business development are far less frequent.

Are different types of MO and GSO more effective at delivering aid than others? Carroll (1992) concluded that non-membership GSOs perform slightly better in service delivery and reaching the poorest than do membership NGOs. Furthermore, given that these were membership organisations operating with a development objective (for example, co-operatives providing services to members) it is reasonable to assume that many other MOs would perform less well still in delivering services. This though does not obviate the fact that there are cases of voluntary mobilisation in civil society organisations which have been impressively successful. The popular kitchens (*comedores populares*) and Glass of Milk programme organised initially through women's organisations in Peru showed how widely a MO programme could have an impact (Friedmann, 1992).

A related issue concerns the extent to which the quality of SNGO work suffers when they increase the scale of their activities. As donors use SNGOs to deliver aid this inevitably implies an increase in the size and activities of the NGO. Some reviews, such as that of BRAC, suggest that growth can occur without compromising quality (Howes and Sattar, 1992). In other cases, growth has had an adverse impact on quality. In Sri Lanka, the growth of Sarvodaya has begun to compromise some of the participatory processes inside the organisation and in its work, and has also weakened the common mission that had previously united the staff of the organisation (Zadek and Szabo, 1994). Recent overviews suggest that whilst there is no conclusive evidence that scaling up necessarily compromises quality, this is a real risk (Edwards and Hulme, 1992). There is much evidence to suggest that rapid expansion can undermine effectiveness and institutional coherence, and that expansion has to be managed carefully and strategically, so that it remains consistent with, and contributes to, the mission of the organisation. Of particular concern is how far client participation in NGO programmes suffers when these are scaled up. The balance of evidence and evaluations suggests that NGOs *tend to be* better at fostering popular participation than government. However, this is often related to the smaller size and participatory orientation and objectives of such programmes.

NGOs and Governments: Comparisons and Interactions

Two particular questions pertaining to the issue of NGOs and government need to be addressed. First, do NGOs perform better or worse than government? Second, how far do the relationships between SNGOs and governments impede or enhance SNGO effectiveness. Once again, answers to these questions depend largely on which NGO and which government department are being considered. Yet there are some generalisations emerging in the research literature. One is that SNGOs may not reach the poorest of the poor, though they do tend to reach poorer sectors than most government programmes (Carroll, 1992; Bebbington and Thiele, 1993; Farrington and Bebbington, 1993; Riddell and Robinson, 1995).

How far GSO and MO service provision is more cost effective and cost efficient than services provided through government is more difficult to answer. Edwards and Hulme (1994) suggest that evidence is emerging that NGOs are more cost effective, and an overview of agricultural service provision in NGOs moved cautiously towards similar conclusions (Farrington and Bebbington, 1993). However, these are tentative conclusions in the face of poor data. More importantly they are conclusions about cost effectiveness, not cheapness. Indeed, there is less evidence to suggest that NGOs are a *cheap* alternative; rather their mode of working, which can be costly, generates benefits that justify the cost.

A deeper and more far-reaching concern is that continued moves by donors to support NGOs rather than government merely weakens government further. The argument that NGOs are a better alternative then becomes little more than a self-fulfilling prophecy. As funds move into NGOs, with their higher and more regular salaries, their easier working environment and more flexible management of resources, this creates an incentive to professionals to move out of government into NGOs. To weaken government in this way may in fact do a disservice to NGO effectiveness. Most evidence of NGO capacity (and in particular MO capacity) consistently points to the professional and technical constraints on NGOs. Primary health care NGOs do need the support of medical and hospital services, agricultural NGOs need access to research results, educational NGOs need an extant school and educational system etc. NGO performance is thus more likely to be effective where the state is relatively effective in social and development service provision, and where the quality of relationships between NGOs and government is cordial and constructive. The policy conclusion to draw is this: donors would provide more effective support to SNGOs if they combined funding support to these NGOs with continued efforts to strengthen (though not necessarily increase the size of) the state system at the same time, and if they worked to foster more constructive relationships between NGOs and the state.

SOME DONOR EXPERIENCES IN MORE DIRECT INTERACTIONS WITH SNGOS

The preceding discussion suggests that direct funding of southern NGOs may not always be the most appropriate way of strengthening civil society and increasing the effectiveness of aid delivery. To achieve such goals will require both a refined knowledge of the local NGO world, and complementary policies in the state sector. Indeed, when their local presence is weak, bilateral agencies may not be best equipped to engage in direct funding of any other than the largest GSOs, and even that has complications. Furthermore there may be other ways not necessarily involving funding through which bilaterals can interact with SNGOs in pursuit of these two overall objectives. Indeed donors have supported SNGOs in various ways: by fostering an environment that is more supportive (or 'enabling') for the work of NGOs; by building bridges between GSOs, MOs and wider political structures (mainly the state and international donors); as well as supporting NGOs directly and materially in order that they deliver development services and do capacity building work among their constituency.

Creating Enabling Environments for SNGO Operations

Donors can do much to strengthen SNGOs' contributions to both civil society and aid delivery without providing any direct funding support. For instance, donors can aim to influence the political, legislative and economic environment in which NGOs work in order that it be more supportive to their activities. There are a range of ways in which donors can work with governments to create this enabling environment, though the extent to which they are feasible will depend on the quality of NGO–state relationships. The main ways in which the policy environment can encourage local NGO activities in civil society and in aid delivery would include the following (Clark, 1993):

- the right to associate must be clearly respected in, and protected by, the law;
- public interest voluntary associations are given tax advantages;
- government does not discourage individuals and corporations from making contributions to the voluntary sector;
- government-voluntary sector partnerships are encouraged;

- freedom of expression and advocacy are respected and defended by law; and
- a code of conduct for the voluntary sector exists and is enforced a-politically to guard against abuses in the sector.

While the ability to influence many of these factors will often be beyond the capacity of individual bilateral donors acting on their own, larger agencies, such as the World Bank and regional development banks, have a greater ability to do so. If, however, bilateral agencies in a country were to adopt a joint approach to creating a more favourable policy environment then the potential for substantive influence would increase significantly.

One particular means of fostering more favourable environments for civil society organisations is for the donor to help create local structures and institutions for funding NGOs in a country. The donor would subsequently channel funds into these institutions, and the institutions would then make funding decisions and would compose their own portfolio of projects around principles laid down in the statutes creating the institution. The most obvious form that such institutions would take is a local endowed foundation. This would thus create a local funding mechanism which is independent of the local state. So far, there is still relatively limited experience of bilateral and other agencies helping in the establishment of such foundations, although there is increased talk of the idea. The Ford Foundation has assisted in the creation of several such organisations, for example the West Africa Rural Foundation.

Building Bridges between NGOs, MOs and Wider Political Structures

A number of donors have sought to use their position to help create and strengthen links and dialogue between SNGOs, government agencies and the donor community. One, especially interesting, mechanism for this type of work has been the Ford Foundation strategy of providing grants to NGOs and government bureaucracies in Asia, to encourage them to collaborate with each other for the purpose of making forestry agencies more responsive to the needs of local communities. One specific result has been the drawing up of concrete collaborative agreements. Sometimes these have been direct – that is between the farmer/user group and the state; at other times they are indirect – that is, an NGO signs an agreement with the state on behalf of local people. These initiatives have sometimes been complemented by activities of working groups established and sponsored by Ford which bring together different 'stakeholders' in local resource management, including NGOs. In Bolivia, the Swiss Development Cooperation hosted an informal working group at the same time as World Bank/Government of Bolivia discussions were underway for the reorganisation of national agricultural research and extension services. This allowed NGO, government and donor staff to discuss policy options in an informal setting, and facilitated NGO input into the process.

Some donors have involved NGOs in the design, planning, and monitoring of bilateral activities. Such interactions are perhaps the most effective way for donors to interact with NGOs. In effect they create a means through which civil society can influence southern and northern governments and their development programmes. For instance, German bilateral programmes have involved local NGOs in the preparation and discussion of country strategy papers, in the execution of bilateral programmes, and in decision making and evaluation of the bilateral programme. Initiatives along these lines have also occurred in several World Bank operations. In addition to increasing the potential effectiveness of the project, by involving GSOs and other MOs in design and monitoring, such a process can promote greater transparency, accountability and civic participation in the process of decision making. However, such initiatives are not without their difficulties. For instance, World Bank–NGO interaction in the design of social compensation funds in Guatemala, Ecuador, and north-east Brazil, and in different sectoral operations, have encountered problems. These have revolved around divisions within the NGO sector and the tendency of some governments to oppose and resist NGO involvement in programme design.

The scope to involve NGOs in design and monitoring is thus constrained by the overall context of government–NGO relations, and government willingness to be more transparent. In some cases, attempts to involve NGOs directly in these sorts of activities might, ironically, achieve less than if the donor were simply to exert pressure itself on the government to provide a more conducive environment for NGO participation in policy debate. For donors to facilitate this sort of interaction effectively, they must have a permanent presence in the country, and the staff responsible for organising working groups (say) must have a well developed understanding of, and sets of contacts within the NGO and government sectors. Some donors have this, others do not, often reflecting the strength of their local office and the type of staff they appoint.

A further option is to support SNGOs in synthesising and systematising their experiences, and using this as a basis to formulate proposals for programmes and policies that can be taken up by the state and the donor agency itself. Traditional northern NGO financing agencies tend not to support this type of learning work, and so it is one area that lends itself to bilateral support. There are as yet limited experiences of this. One recent attempt has involved SIDA supporting three networks of Bolivian GSOs in such a process to generate regional and national proposals for policies in a range of sectors. The principal underlying the programme is that integral to a healthy democracy is the capacity within civil society to elaborate alternative proposals to those emanating from government. The weakness is that the programme tends to assume that the GSOs are the same as civil society.

Direct (or More Direct) Forms of Funding

Funding from Home

One of the perennial problems facing donors who have attempted to initiate more direct funding relationships with SNGOs on a significant scale is how to identify which NGOs to support.[4] Without detailed knowledge and accumulated experience, to send funds directly from the North can be very risky. Conversely, to control for these problems, there will be a tendency to fund the largest NGOs, institutions that are often more akin to ministries themselves, than to NGOs, and which can become yet more akin to ministries as a result of such funding.[5]

Of course, direct bilateral contact with very large SNGOs can allow traditional NNGO donors to free up money for other smaller initiatives. Yet it is still a question as to how far and how effectively civil society is strengthened when these large organisations grow even larger and stronger. The continuing growth of these large organisations may well crowd out smaller NGOs – and even instrumentalising these large SNGOs and encouraging their further growth can lead them to lose touch with their initial motivating vision (see Zadek and Szabo, 1994, for a discussion of Sarvodaya).

To address these problems, but still fund directly, one option would be for government to establish a separate special agency for funding smaller SNGOs. There are very few examples in practice, given the expense implied. One case is the Inter-American Foundation (IAF) in the USA, which has staff responsible for interacting with NGOs in most of the countries of Latin America and the Caribbean. Even the IAF, however, has felt the need to move towards a more decentralised structure over the years in order to increase its local knowledge of the NGO world in each country. Now a significant part of its identification of local NGOs is done by an in-country organisation (called the In-Country Service) working with the IAF to this end. This increases the already high administrative costs of the IAF structure: costs in Washington are around 20 per cent of the total budget, and in-country administrative costs are about 10 per cent of total in-country project expenditure.

Notwithstanding these administrative costs, the IAF's Andean programme is now experimenting with going a step further in this process of decentralisation. The first step is to link its In-Country Services, its GSO and MO partners and other institutions in the five Andean countries in a learning exercise arranged around several themes. This learning – based on lessons deriving from the NGO sector – is then intended to generate criteria which would become a basis for defining future IAF funding priorities. The final step would be to pass management of the funding portfolio to that consortium of Andean organisations. At present (June 1995), the consortium has been created as a legal entity, with the IAF, the in-country services and strategic partners on its board. The next step is to operationalise the consortium and decentralise fund administration from the IAF into the consortium.

Funding in the Field

Another alternative is for the bilateral agency to build an in-country presence which focuses explicitly on NGOs. This gives donors the opportunity to get to know the local NGO community. Knowledge of this sort is crucial before beginning support, and deciding who to support and why. The principal difficulty with this approach is its cost. IDRC and CIDA each decentralised their staffing to the field, in part to improve local relationships with, and understanding of, their chosen partners, but this decentralisation proved too costly. IDRC staff estimate that it costs about three times as much to maintain a person in the field as in Ottawa, and the argument is that although the quality of work is better when you are in the field, it is not three times as good as the work of a staff person in Ottawa.

The period of time that the mission's 'NGO co-ordinators' stay in country is also very important. The complexity of the NGO world requires time to establish trust with NGOs, what their strategies are, what their strengths and weaknesses are etc. As the SNGO world does not have strong structures through which it can represent its concerns to donors, and because it is often too diverse to accept that one or a few structures should represent it, there is no substitute for time in building this knowledge. The career structure of many bilateral and multilateral agencies often militates against spending sufficiently long periods in country to build up this knowledge. This is not always the case though, as is illustrated by SIDA's experience in Bangladesh (Lewis, Sobhan and Jonsson, 1994).

Linking NNGOs and SNGOs

The implication of the above is that even if donors want to increase the flow of funds to southern NGOs, they will often not have the in-house capacity to do this well. High among other options is therefore to work in conjunction with knowledgeable NNGOs, building on and benefitting from their existing knowledge of the local NGO world. One mechanism for such an approach would be to decentralise both geographically and institutionally the design and management of bilateral SNGO support programmes by asking NNGOs to work in consortium with SNGOs and take the lead in defining how funding should be made more direct than at present. The attraction of this approach is that it sets out the broad guidelines for a civil society/SNGO strengthening programme, but allows the Terms of Reference for the specific activities to come out of the NGO sector itself. And it supports NNGOs in their own process of redefining the terms of their partnership with SNGOs. In many respects, this sort of approach is the most consistent and participatory way of drawing up a country strategy: it would allow the very organisations involved (NNGOs and SNGOs together) to participate in a design process that itself will outline to the donor how best to support SNGOs and NNGOs within the overall goal of supporting civil society.

Some of the partnership programmes sponsored by CIDA move in this direction, even though this has sometimes been as much a result of efforts to 'put work out' and reduce administrative costs in CIDA as due to concerns to strengthen civil society. CIDA has created mechanisms for supporting development via NGOs on a country and regional basis, spawning a number of partnerships and consortia; there are now consortia for NGO support to, for example, South Asia, Africa, Philippines (two), Thailand, Indonesia, Mozambique, and Angola (Rousseau and Sissons, 1992). While there are differences among these consortia, they share general objectives of: creating a mechanism to disburse CIDA aid through the NGO sector; involving both Canadian NGOs and SNGOs in programming and implementation; and moving the locus of decision making to a lesser or greater extent towards the SNGO world. While CIDA has influenced the broad objectives of the programmes, more specific objectives are set by the NGOs. These collaborations between NNGOs and SNGOs need not only be in the area of operations. They can also embrace collaborations in which the NGOs work together on specific policy questions, combining research, synthesis and policy dialogue. The UK's ODA, for instance, is supporting of a regional partnership of Latin American NGOs involved in rural development, partnered by 2 UK non-governmental research organisations. The partnership is working primarily on policy issues related to the changing relationship between NGOs and the state in Latin America.[6]

The Enduring Problem of Donor Consistency

Notwithstanding some of these innovative donor initiatives it is important to end this section on a cautionary note. For all their efforts to support NGOs, and strengthen civil society, donors sometimes sustain parallel policies that seem to contradict these objectives. We have already referred indirectly to some of the ways in which this may be so: that is when, by using NGOs as channels to implement programmes and channel aid, donors can in fact weaken these organisations as representative and accountable institutions within civil society. But there are other ways in which donors can pursue apparently contradictory lines of action.

One sense in which this is so relates to donor approaches to the state. One of the reasons for strengthening civil society and its organisations is in order that these organisations can make more claims on the state to increase poor peoples' ability to draw on public resources and services. A related objective is to increase peoples' capacity to claim rights and insist that the state defend those rights. Striving to achieve these objectives only makes sense when the donor is at the very least not weakening the capacity of the state to deliver those services and defend those rights. Yet, in practice, it is not uncommon for donors to talk of strengthening civil society at the same time as they contribute to, or endorse, programmes which reduce state capacity to respond to the demands of civil society. For instance, donor supported programmes which introduce cost recovery in health, education and agricultural services, could well have the effect of making state service provision less accessible to the poor (this will depend on the particular mechanisms of cost recovery and privatisation used).

Equally, to the extent that donor support is successful in strengthening GSOs' and MOs' capacity to organise and mobilise, and in contributing to greater awareness of citizenship rights among the poor, then a policy that simultaneously weakens the state's capacity to respond to MOs' claims can contribute to increased social protest. For instance in Ecuador in 1990, federations of Indian peoples that had long received international support, a significant part of which came from the US government via the Inter-American Foundation, took to the streets to protest against cutbacks in services (and a range of other grievances). Large parts of the highlands came to a standstill, and the tensions unleashed led to state militarisation of the countryside.

Such observations make clear the need for consistency between donor policy towards SNGOs and their policy towards public sector reform. They show that the question is not strong state *or* strong NGO sector: it is rather of the need for *strength in both*. The second observation in the same vein has far more to do with the internal policies of donor agencies. Engaging in programmes oriented towards the strengthening of NGOs as institutions within civil society is a time-consuming process, yet donors often do not invest the time needed. It often involves supporting the emergence of particular types of relationships between NGOs and government, and between GSOs and MOs, and among all these organisations, yet donors all too often introduce subcontracting arrangements for GSO implementation of public programmes that can in fact weaken rather than strengthen relations of accountability between these different actors. And it ought to involve developing new means and criteria for monitoring programmes which establish progress in capacity building, institutional development and so on, yet in practice donors tend to stick to more quantitative and time bound monitoring and evaluation criteria (or 'milestones').

Why? Trying to unpackage the complex answer to this question leads one into the areas of incentives and performance assessment within donor agencies, recognised within the World Bank following the Wapenhans Report (Wapenhans, 1992). One of the observations of the Wapenhans Report was that because the performance of task managers in the World Bank is based on product delivery – on getting projects approved – higher quality product development can be played down and undervalued. Developing better projects takes time; developing better projects in conjunction with SNGOs, and on the basis of participatory procedures, takes yet more time. There seems to be insufficient professional incentive within the Bank to encourage a process-type approach, even if this leads to more effective projects in the longer run. Current efforts to 'mainstream' participation in the Bank are also likely to encounter this problem of insufficient incentives and resources. Across bilateral agencies, too, personnel assessment criteria are often biased in favour of achieving concrete results. If NGO involvement and participation, and more general process and civil society work are to be given more genuine attention in donor agencies, then it will be necessary to reward innovation and risk more than occurs at present, and to reward quality of work more than quantitative output.

DIRECT FUNDING AND THE NORTHERN NGO: THREAT OR OPPORTUNITY?

To argue that a more appropriate donor response to the issue of direct funding is to work with a half way house such as joint NNGO–SNGO programming is not to say that business should continue as usual in the northern NGOs, nor that they should be a gatekeeper between bilateral donors and southern NGOs.

Indeed, one of the reasons why northern NGOs have often had a defensive response to the question of direct funding is that they recognise that it raises issues that are genuine and profound problems within the northern NGO world, and that need to be addressed. In short, many recognise that there is validity in those arguments which say that:

- NNGOs are not sufficiently accountable to their partners in the South;
- as SNGOs become stronger there is no clear reason why northern government funds should be channelled through NNGOs – it is not clear what 'value' the NNGOs 'add';
- NNGOs do not always have the skills to which their partners want access;
- NNGOs are not necessarily very good at strengthening civil society in the South;
- not all NNGOs in fact have very well conceived programme.

Furthermore, some may comment that the fact that they have such defensive responses itself suggests that they may have lost their way a little: that they may have worried a bit too much about growth and not quite enough about what their distinctive competence really is. They may also comment that this defensiveness also reveals a desire to retain power and influence over how their partners use funds, as appears to have been the case in the relations between Sarvodaya and some of its NNGO financiers. They would then go on to say that the nature of their relationship with SNGOs might improve – both in quality and effectiveness – if the NNGO could further develop a special role in development cooperation beyond raising and posting money.[7]

This is not to say that NNGOs are only fund raisers and senders – we all know that they are more than this. However, it is to say that the direct funding discussion is a harbinger of inevitable trends: that the traditional role of NNGOs will be increasingly questioned, and that there will be an increasing challenge to find a role that is consistent with their vision of development. Likely as not, some NNGOs will not respond to these questions, and will become increasingly like organisations who are in effect subcontracted to implement particular parts of the bilateral programme. The final comments of this section do not relate to these NGOs, they refer to those who feel the need to redefine a role that is specifically non-governmental and alternative, as opposed to simply private sector.

The critique of Northern NGOs has gathered momentum over recent years, some of that critique coming from within the NNGO movement itself. The 'scaling up' conference was one example of that self-critique; this current conference is another.[8] Together, these different critiques have pointed to several issues, including:

- the limited impact of NGO projects, and the constraints set by national, northern and global policy and political environments;
- the risks inherent in getting larger – particularly when this is done on the basis of government funding;
- the problem of accountability between NNGOs and SNGOs;
- the problem of the identity of the Northern NGO.

In many respects these problems boil down to a central challenge: to define a role for northern NGOs that can help enhance the impact of the work of their southern partners, and to define this role together with these partners.

Some have argued that policy advocacy is one such role linked to mobilisation, synthesis and dissemination of information that can be used for advocacy by both northern NGOs and their partners.[9] Another such role is the development of fair trade markets in the North.[10] Another role is to help SNGOs in gaining access to expertise and relevant experiences of social development in the North that could be helpful to their work in the South (for example, AIDS programmes, community enterprise programmes, self managed informal credit programmes and so on).

Yet another role is for the NNGO to begin development work in the North, as part of a group of northern and southern NGOs working on similar development issues in their respective countries. Indeed, at the time of writing Oxfam (UK) is considering opening a programme in the UK. Furthermore it was interesting that in the Oxfam Assembly that discussed this issue, some of the most fervent support for the idea of a UK programme came from Oxfam partners in the South.

The point is not that any one of these roles is better than the others. It is that there is a need to define that role and to do so with southern partners, as part of a move toward making the northern NGOs as accountable to their partners as their partners are to them. (Zadek and Gatward 1995).

CONCLUSIONS

This chapter has staked out two related themes. The first theme was something of a review of trends in, and problems with, current donor thinking about direct funding to SNGOs. We have argued that there are risks with increased direct funding, and that it has the potential to be a means through which donors increase their instrumentalisation of southern NGOs. Furthermore, in doing so it runs the risk of weakening the role of these organisations as agents of a strengthened civil society in the South. Indeed, the chapter has drawn attention to a number of tensions and contradictions in the ways in which donors link their support to SNGOs with their talk about strengthening civil society. The evidence would seem to suggest that this far, donors have been mainly interested in working with NGOs in order to use them to deliver aid – and not so much in order to strengthen them as representative and vibrant civic organisations. Further consequences of this *may* be to increase the prominence of large SNGOs, crowding out smaller SNGOs, and to distort the mandates of SNGOs so that they increasingly reflect donor concerns rather than the NGOs' initial mission. These consequences are not inevitable, and whether they occur or not will depend greatly on the strength of the SNGO to avoid them – but they are real risks.

Secondly, this chapter has argued that these difficulties should not mean that we simply reject all discussion of direct bilateral funding of southern NGOs. Rather this discussion is a fertile ground for looking critically at the role of both donors and northern NGOs in enhancing the effectiveness of southern NGOs in strengthening civil society and in doing development. The chapter has suggested that nobody is particularly a hero in this regard. We make our argument that donors must be cautious before launching into overzealous direct funding of SNGOs not made in order to defend NNGOs, and far less in order to claim that NNGOs are more effective than SNGOs. Rather the point is to question such moves as a means of creating a space within which to think about more appropriate relationships between all the actors involved (donors, NNGOs, GSOs and MOs), and to raise the issue of how best donors might support a process that will strengthen these more appropriate relationships.

In essence we have argued that donors have important roles in this, but that some of the most effective roles may not involve direct funding. Often a more effective role would be to work on improving the environment in which SNGOs operate, on facilitating interactions between SNGOs, the state and other actors, and in bringing SNGOs into the elaboration of the donors' country programmes. The challenge embraces helping to nurture and create an enabling environment in which rights of association, civil liberties and rights of access to minimal-quality services (most notably for those without current access) are achieved and protected: an environment in which training, financial and political support is given, and in which the state and markets operate in ways that do not weaken civil society.

Among the many difficulties faced by bilaterals in engaging in direct funding is to develop a sufficiently nuanced knowledge of the local NGO world in a particular country. In some cases, some local NGOs may be no more representative, accountable or responsive to beneficiaries than are northern NGOs, but the bilateral may not have the time to garner the knowledge to be able to discern this.

Thus the view that NNGOs are an obstacle to effective support to SNGOs and civil society because they are distant intermediaries is only half true. To the extent that this argument is used to suggest that there are more responsive intermediaries 'out there' it may well be fallacious. To the extent that it is used to justify instrumentalist direct funding it is intellectually dishonest. The debate about a 'more direct funding' initiative needs to avoid sweeping generalisations about 'who is better – the state, SNGOs, popular organisations or NNGOs?'

Thus if donors are to move towards increased funding of southern NGOs, there will be an important role for northern NGOs (at least those who have more knowledge and experience of the local NGO world) in helping to work out how, and with whom, this could be organised. However, even if there are many reasons to doubt whether in many contexts direct funding is a viable or sensible path for bilateral donors to pursue, the issues that it raises cannot be escaped by Northern NGOs. As we noted, part of the case for direct funding is based on the argument that if NNGOs do not add much value to delivered aid, and if they are not very accountable to their partners, then why should a bilateral programme aiming to deliver aid more effectively and to strengthen civil society work through them.

Direct funding may not be the best way to address these problems. But they are problems. The challenge to northern NGOs of the direct funding debate ought not be how to resist it, and maintain a share of bilateral funds. Rather the challenge is to respond to the issues it raises: to identify appropriate roles for northern NGOs, and appropriate relationships between them and southern NGOs in this new world order.

Notes

1. The term is Tom Carroll's in *Intermediary NGOs: the supporting link in grassroots development*, West Hartford: Kumarian, 1992.
2. When we use the term SNGOs we refer to the whole NGO sector in the South, comprising membership and non-membership, professional and popular organisations; we use the term GSO to refer specifically to southern professional intermediary organisations engaged in service delivery, advocacy, policy research and so on; the term MO refers to membership organisations in general, some of which will be base organisations, others service delivery organisations; and the term NNGOs refers to the whole NGO sector in the North.
3. Examples include BRAC, Proshika, Sarvodaya and AKRSP.
4. Several donors have small discretionary funds for in-country NGO initiatives that might include NGO projects. These are only small scale activities, and rarely have strategic objectives.
5. In practice, donors seemed to work more with these large organisations.
6. The UK institutions are IIED and ODI.
7. See the chapter by Jehan Perera in this volume.
8. Edwards and Hulme (1992; 1994).
9. For example, see Clark (1991) and Edwards (1994a).
10. See the work done by Traidcraft and the New Economics Foundation.

8 Appeasing the Gods of Sustainability: The Future of International NGOs in Microfinance

Thomas W. Dichter

INTRODUCTION

Over the last decade most international NGOs have become involved in microfinance initiatives to promote small enterprise development and alleviate poverty. A lot has been asked of these NGOs of late. They are being called upon by financial analysts to do a much better job at 'keeping score' – to talk in numbers rather than intentions or social effects. They are being asked to lower their costs. Increasingly the experience of BancoSol, KREP and a few others (Hulme and Mosley 1996) are held up to the rest of the NGO microfinance community as the ultimate goal : convert yourselves to real banking institutions. Above all be tighter, much more efficient, and focused exclusively on credit delivery.

More than ever NGOs in general are the great hope in poverty alleviation. If those who have entered the world of microfinance will take on these tough standards and deliver credit sustainably, some donors are now saying, we may, for the first time, have a shot at real progress in combatting poverty.

It is time to get some things straight about NGOs; to ask whether these exhortations are appropriately directed. Perspective is needed. Are NGOs, as a category, the right vehicle for credit delivery in the first place? Is there evidence that NGOs in microfinance have had real impact on poverty thus far? Is something being missed or forgotten in the present predilection for sustainability?

Of all the institutional categories in the development industry, NGOs have been the growth area in the last decade, exploding both in terms of numbers and in terms of the ways in which we understand and delineate this group. For example, we now recognise that the term 'NGO' designates what is basically a residual category, and in disaggregating it we find a wide spectrum, including those organisations which are contractors of the bilaterals; quasi-NGOs – part private part government-funded or gov-ernment-appointed ('QUANGOs'); donor organised NGOs ('DONGOs'), and INGOs (international NGOs). INGOs are the group most development professionals are already quite familiar with. They do business multi-nationally, tend to be based in the OECD countries, and are working for the benefit of others, as opposed to grassroots organisations (GROs), the largest category of development-oriented NGOs in the world today (and the fastest growing), which work for the benefit of their own members. There are also GSOs (grassroots support organisations) essentially large southern NGOs which are like INGOs except that they rarely operate internationally. INGOs and GSOs, not GROs, are the subject of this chapter.

INGOs remain, for the present, northern organisations, and draw their monies directly from the mass publics of the industrialised nations, or indirectly via grants and contracts with private donors, or bilateral donor agencies. There are some 4000 northern NGOs devoted to one or another aspect of what we call development (broadly defined to include relief and welfare activities). Most are quite small, but the giants are well known even outside the world of development; these include CARE, Save the Children Fund and OXFAM.

HISTORY

The decade of the 1980s was the expansion period for NGOs both North and South. Northern NGOs more than doubled during that period, and the multiplier for the South cannot even be determined, but it is high. Depending on definitions, the number of southern NGOs is somewhere between 20 000 and one million (Fisher, 1993).

Until roughly the end of the 1970s, grosso modo, most large INGOs and GSOs were content to work in a fairly well-seasoned, self-satisfied way. They were there to be of help to less fortunate others in the Third World and the public and their legislatures were generally behind this effort. But partly in response to market forces within the development industry, many NGOs began to change. At the forefront of the NGO world a new idea was quickly being embraced, that of helping others to help themselves. For example, instead of simply giving away food and cloth-ing, food for work was conceived. Instead of curing diseases, NGOs began trying to prevent them. Instead of bringing in technologies from outside,

NGOs began playing a role in developing technologies locally. And as these new ways of working became more prevalent, the recognition of the inherent complexity of development work grew. Seeing the continued persistence of poverty, many NGOs began to understand that more participatory approaches were needed, longer time frames, deeper commitments.

But complexity and competition in the donor market-place do not mix well. The tension grew between the complex reality of development at the grassroots and the demand for projects with measurable results that could use donor money at a rate appropriate for the donors. Meanwhile many NGOs themselves were having difficulty translating these new emphases into something other than welfare with a new name. When projects ended, when the funds stopped flowing, when the advisors went home – say two, three or five years later – little remained, or at least little remained that was measurable.

In response to the nagging persistence of the underlying structure of welfare, the word 'sustainability' began rearing its head. This has become the development challenge of the 1990s, and the general posture and stance of the INGOs to this challenge has become a defensive one. Self-conscious and anxious, many INGOs face the future nervously. The question being asked in this chapter is whether this state of affairs need be so.

It is important to remember that most INGOs were born out of compassion. Their founders saw needs abroad in the modern world that they felt could not be responsibly ignored given the vast resources of the well-off nations. To give to others in need, to save lives, to relieve pain – these were noble projects. And as the new agencies of what was then a nascent development industry shifted full focus from the reconstruction of Europe to the Third World as of the late 1950s, the INGOs, unlike their bilateral and multilateral colleagues, could well claim to have relatively pure motives, untainted by politics or the conditionalities of the Cold War. INGOs were not only by definition non governmental; they represented what eventually came to be called the independent or the third sector, associated *neither* with government, *nor* with the profit-oriented private sector.

But the fact is, development has always been a dynamic enterprise. It has never stood still, mostly because its subjects have not (politics, populations, disease patterns, food supply problems are in constant flux), and to some extent because priorities from donors and constituencies changed from time to time. Research and evaluation also continued to inject new doubts about what worked to accomplish what and how.

Many INGOs changed too. The larger and older ones began trying to do everything. Some, like CARE, developed a multi-purpose approach, a long corridor full of departments and divisions covering everything from food delivery to health, to education, to integrated community development and eventually microfinance and business development. And while experimentation in many development sectors continued, by the mid-1980s one area of work emerged as more startlingly new than the others. This was enterprise development, and the part of it that has now totally outstripped all others, is microfinance.

In the 1970s poverty alleviation had become a central agenda for the development industry. The call for self-help grew along with this. The role of the NGO as an effective actor at the grassroots where poverty existed in its most egregious forms became more widely acknowledged. Giving things away began to be seen as a dead end. But the idea arose that people, especially women, could be helped to generate income; with this income they could then begin to alleviate their own poverty. But the approach was fraught with problems. Women in villages would be taught to sew, and the development workers would help them to sell what they made. Undertaken by NGOs whose past experience had been in health, nutrition or community organising, these small efforts at income generation often failed because they were not seen as businesses; because markets were not thought about, because ultimately NGOs were playing at business rather than helping people meet the demands of a real market-place.

Some NGOs began lending money, but at very low rates of interest, in part because the compassionate underpinning of the welfare approach resulted in the feeling that high interest rates would be punitive. It took several years for the news of Mohamed Yunus's Grameen Bank to spread. By the late 1980s the idea that the poor could pay regular rates of interest and could be trusted to pay back their loans, became accepted. Though hardly a wholesale conversion, NGOs of many types began shifting all or part of their emphasis to what has become known as minimalist credit (ie credit with no other or very few other services).

Something radically new was afoot. Not only was money now a direct development commodity, it was to be made available to the poor as a way for them to build equity, thus actually reducing poverty (not merely alleviating it) and it was to be paid back to the lender, to be used again, or even, as we entered the 1990s, to produce a profit for the lender. Even those in development who had long since scoffed at the idea of a magic bullet, were tempted to see this new approach as a remarkable solution, one which met the heretofore unattainable goal of poverty reduction, but which passed the test of sustainability. A virtual perpetual motion machine, in a field where many were beginning to despair of ever accomplishing anything lasting, much less at no or little recurrent subsidy.

A linear continuum could describe the history briefly outlined above. The rhetoric of NGOs, if not the practice, has gone from pure welfare, to social welfare, to poverty alleviation, to poverty reduction, and has come to rest on the edge of the precipice of economic development; we dare not talk yet about poverty elimination.

In the enterprise sphere, where once only 20 years ago those who dabbled in enterprise at all were doing technical assistance purely, now the field has been turned on its head. The majority of NGOs in enterprise development are credit operators, with a few attempting to integrate minimalist credit with at least one other agenda. But only a tiny minority now engages purely in technical assistance – that is to say non-financial assistance to the poor entrepreneur – despite the fact that credit alone will not change structural factors such as demand for the labour or the products of the poor.

What we are seeing is in part a major concession by INGOs to the donor demand for sustainability. This has begun to dominate everything; self-sustainability and 'political correctness' are now one. And INGOs, for whom sustainability was never before a value (charity and compassion were after all never meant to be subject to bottom-line business values) are now often afraid to admit openly that they would still like to accomplish some things that cannot by definition pay for themselves. They are on the defensive. Some now seem compelled to de-emphasise their original or core agendas, saying that they have taken on microfinance only because it works; because it is sustainable. But, reading their annual reports, one finds that they are still quite interested in other things. Almost parenthetically, they add that they are going to do nutrition education, or population control, or community empowerment, but now, as if to appease the gods of sustainability, they feel compelled to point out that these additional activities are supplements to the credit work, indeed are supported by credit operations. But often the truth is the other way round; the micro enterprise lending may well have been put in place as a way to say: 'We are keeping up with the trends, we are sustainable (or are trying to be), and now we are free to pursue what we were founded to pursue.'

These comments are not made as an indictment of sustainability per se. Rather, they are intended to suggest the strong tendencies in INGO 'culture' to cave in unthinkingly to sustainability even when it is either inappropriate or simply unachievable.

THE PRESENT STATE OF AFFAIRS OF NGOs IN MICROFINANCE

There are today perhaps 125 microfinance projects three years old or older around the world which are run, instigated or fostered by INGOs, and which each reach more than 1000 borrowers. Recent research by this author required calling a large number of these organisations. Those which did not have well-established micro-lending programmes said, without a single exception, that they were thinking about it. There is a real band-wagon effect here. The good thing about it is that there is a recognition that microfinance is not something that one can simply just try out or jump into. The word has got out, this is a new kind of endeavour demanding new skills and new kinds of human resources. Focus and competence are the key words. Businesslike approaches are accepted, at least rhetorically. Where once the word business and the language of business were used with considerable discomfort by INGO staffers, now, short of embracing the words and the concepts, including that of profit, there is at least a familiarity and comfort level that did not exist even five years ago.

Nonetheless, the same tension between the imagery of capitalism and the imagery of compassion – the dual culture problem that one could observe five and ten years ago – persists, and the reasons for this are even more complex. INGOs, pushed to become sustainable, and pushed by their southern counterparts to let go of direct involvement, have become less sure of who and what they are. With few exceptions, usually those small INGOs who are content to remain small and who take no bilateral grants at all, INGOs (and now large southern NGOs too) are almost all in a con-stant state of transition, facing all manner of organisational problems from succession to survival, and pressures from within (boards and staff) as well as from without. Because they are now more sophisticated, more clued-in, more aware of what others are doing and have learned, they often know what to do to become more effective, but they do not want to act on what they know. This may be especially true for those who have recently entered microfinance where the problems of organisational change are added to by the newness of the fact of money as a commodity, as a tool for development. When money is involved the underlying cultural conflicts and tensions become more pronounced.

Take a large and prominent NGO in Asia (which will be discussed under the pseudonym XYZNGO). The XYZNGO focuses on building local level 'people's institutions' to manage and control resources and to take an active role in defining and achieving their own development goals. Although XYZNGO also works with individual families, its main empha-sis is on identifying, strengthening, and sometimes helping to organise various types of functional groups from informal neighbourhood credit and savings groups to larger community resource management groups, women's and youth groups, producer co-operatives and even local NGOs to which it provides training and networking support. XYZNGO's programmes range across sectors and include agriculture and animal husbandry, watershed management and forestry, resettlement and microfinance. Currently, it operates 15 major projects. Several of these involve the development of basic financial service systems for low-income men and women in rural areas. Through its successful strategy of first building up local credit groups and then linking these institutions into the formal financial sector, XYZNGO has become one of the leading Asian NGOs in the field of microfinance.

But its success is its model. That is to say that it is successful in the abstract. In reality, it is beginning to show problems which are a function both of its organisational structure and culture. It is an instructive case because it replicates some of the problems we see in many large INGOs. First it is a multipurpose organisation with different parts of its work having come on line at different times in its roughly quarter-century of history. As such it has also attracted different donors, some of which are INGOs themselves. The complexity of its activities and the different donor agendas often conflict in the same target area and as a result lines of authority and accountability are unclear. While outreach is high in micro-lending, efficiency has begun to suffer. Where the initial repayment rates were admirable, recently loan losses have been growing.

But perhaps more important is the strength of the organisation's under-lying culture. With strong initial leadership, XYZNGO had inculcated a fierce culture of participation. Translated into microfinance, this has meant that there was an unwillingness to transplant ready-made models of credit management from elsewhere, and a reluctance to standardise a credit man-agement system, especially one dictated or even suggested by the centre. With local self-control and participation as the arch gods of the organisa-tion's culture, standardised dictates from the top were anathema. The stated values are anti dominance, the group shall not be dominated by any one contingent, much less one person. Thus group representatives did not see themselves as leaders, and village animators – the working-end staff of the organisation – imbued with the spirit that they should not lead, not surprisingly became leaders by default. Role confusion and disorganisa-tion were obvious results. But since now we are dealing with money, lack of credit discipline and loan losses – results which are blatantly measur-able – also followed. And yet financial rigour, and the means to achieve it were very well understood in the organisation. In a way, XYZNGO knows what to do but does not feel good about doing it.

The sensitivities and symbols in this somewhat classic case are poignant. Larger southern NGOs of the GSO type as well as many NGOs in microfinance now live and work in a forest of symbols that cast shadows on their conscience: neo-colonialism, repression and paternalism, freedom, participation and non-directiveness, love and compassion, toughness and rigour, quantity and quality. The NGO role and that of the large southern GSO are thus further constrained. At a time when they are ironically most counted on by their big brothers in development to be of help they are often not in a position to do so.

IS THERE A FUTURE FOR NGOs IN MICROFINANCE?

What then is the future for NGOs in microfinance? Ought they to be the instruments? What is their appropriate role? Let us put this part of the industry into the larger perspective of poverty lending in general. The first thing to ask is, what is the potential market for microfinance? We can get at this by looking at Richard Rosenberg's (1994) paper from the Brookings Conference. Rosenberg talks of the impossibility of saturating the microfinance market unless leveraging is employed. He uses the example of Bolivia, a country of 7.5 million, with an estimated potential borrower population of one million. To saturate the Bolivia microfinance market at the rate of $300 per poor borrower, he surmises, US$300 000 000 would be needed. Rosenberg argues that only by using leverage (up to the international standard of 11 times) can this amount of money be brought to bear on the problem.

Now let us look at the microfinance market worldwide using similar ratios. IFAD's 1992 State of World Rural Poverty study, for example, says that in 114 developing countries there are 1 billion people below the poverty line and of these about 80 per cent are rural, 57 per cent are women. If we are to think about market saturation (which is itself an obviously debatable construct) in round numbers we need to be thinking about roughly US$300 000 000 000 in loan capital.

In relation to the world's private sector, and general consumption patterns, this is a surprisingly small amount of money. Current global advertising expenditures for example are approximately this figure of US$300 billion; in the USA alone last year, consumer instalment debt was close to three times this amount, at (US$880 billion). But in terms of current official development assistance spending on development, US$300 billion is huge. US$300 billion is around five times the entire official aid budget of the OECD countries (bilateral non-military aid).

And when we look at the actual portfolio of microfinance projects going on today, the US$300 billion figure to reach one billion poor is truly humbling. At best when we take all microfinance projects (excluding credit unions) including those which are run, instigated by, or operated by

INGOs, and those which are operated by NGO-like organisations such as the Grameen Bank, those few which have become banks, and those like BRI which are state run, we are looking at a current outreach worldwide of between 5.5 and 6 million borrowers.

Now let us look at the numbers only on the INGO side of the house. Take some of the more interesting programmes around: those of smaller organizations like Freedom from Hunger (seven programmes), Katalysis (four projects), or World Relief (five projects). In such INGO microfinance programmes, we are looking at 1994 outreach numbers of the following: 8940, 2000 and 11 772, respectively. Or take FINCA, a fast growing organisation whose 'village banking' model is now one of the industry standards. Its borrower cohort is today about 50 000. Adding up numbers like these does not get us to one million very fast at all, much less one billion, although it is interesting to note that such INGOs are aware that their success with small numbers is not good enough and so they routinely include in their reports statistical projections which show geometric increases in outreach within short periods like three to five years. Yet operationally they (and we) perhaps already know these projections are unlikely.

Now let us put the global numbers discussed thus far against the perspective of the donor world. Here again good numbers are hard to come by, and one has to be satisfied with gross orders of magnitude. In the 1990 report of the Committee of Donor Agencies for Small Enterprise Development 92 projects out of 285 listed were self-reported as somehow involving micro enterprise. As this designation was rarely alone but always alongside some other function, it is impossible to say what level of funding was devoted solely to lending. But, for the sake of argument, let us simply add up the funding for the 92 projects designated as micro in some way or another. The reported total funding for these 92 projects was $431 million. Now 1990 is the dark ages compared to 1995. Now microfinance has become a hot topic, and more money is going to it. In short, even with these gross figures and wild guesses, the following point can be reasonably made: the official donor agencies are still not coming up with the kind of money we need to be talking about if saturation is the goal, and even if leveraging is taken on board as the key to overcoming the capital obstacle, if indeed that is the obstacle.

Now recall that INGOs, however important, represent only one set of players in this potential market. And while it seems that many INGOs are in microfinance, the shift to this sort of development work is only beginning. There are a number of prominent INGOs 'out there' who have not yet come on board. Childreach (ex-Foster Parents Plan) is one example. It is a $400 million per year child sponsorship organisation which at the moment does not have any idea which of its programmes are involved in microfinance, or more important how they are doing. It is now beginning an exercise aimed at finding out, so that a future strategy with a strong microfinance component can be considered. Christian Children's Fund, World Vision, and others are at similar sorts of crossroads – on the cusp of getting involved in microfinance in more professional ways. The changes within these large INGOs are afoot and will in due time (say two to five years) make them major players in microfinance among the INGO set. Of the 4000 plus Northern NGOs (as per the OECD Development Centre directory of 1992) it is impossible to say now how many more will get on the microfinance bandwagon. Is this a wise course of action? Do we want to see 4000, 2000 or 1000, or even several hundred NGOs converting their operations to banks?

What sorts of changes or consequences are we likely to see coming out of this movement, if it does indeed continue? First it is unlikely that the tension between the two cultures living within many INGOs will abate. The compassionate founding stance of the INGO will remain at its heart, as will the sense of mission. These were originally the distinguishing features of the INGO, not its non-profit, not its non-profit status. Competition for the donor dollar is stronger than ever, and is not likely to lessen. Therefore, the need to appear different and especially to appear effective drives INGOs, as does the sense that nowadays in order to survive, one has to grow, to 'scale up' (Edwards and Hulme, 1992). And this in turn will tend to reinforce the tendency not to pause and reflect. Outreach and sustainability are great goals for micro-lending – indeed these have to be the sine qua non of micro-lending – but are outreach and sustainability great goals for INGOs? Few are likely to have the courage to ask that question.

Second, in this competitive atmosphere where the appearance of difference is important, we are ironically likely to see quite a bit of copycat behaviour in future as we have in the past. INGOs will not venture too far out in front of one another or want to be perceived as lagging too much behind trends. This too is unfortunate, but convergence seems to be the nature of things in a competitive world.

Third, since the watchword in INGO microfinance is likely to remain sustainability for some time to come, INGOs will continue to try to refine and test their microfinance techniques in the crucible of self-sustainability. In so doing, it is quite possible they will get farther and farther away from what they may do best, social intermediation at the grassroots. Montgomery (1995) has written of the ways in which pressures to maintain repayment rates is leading the field staff of big NGOs in Bangladesh to focus on 'discipling' the poor, not helping them to develop.

There are other dangers in all of this. One likelihood is that a concern for scale, outreach and financial sustainability will become so great that the original goal – development, and the growing understanding of its myriad complexities – may again be forgotten. Not only INGOs, but the whole development industry, for all its sophistication, still is subject to the temptation of easy answers; a temptation constantly reinforced by home country constituencies who are increasingly strapped for public funds, and where private funders have ever more choices of where to put their money.

One can hope that the INGOs will eventually gain enough courage to come to terms yet again with the issue of development itself. For this is the territory where the gradual honing of their original and natural advantages could lead them. The muddy swamplands of development complexity is where the real challenges lie. Self-sustainability; covering the cost of lending money to the poor may seem difficult, but it really is not. To do it means building a well-oiled lending organisation, with refined techniques and procedures, managed by a disciplined staff. In the end though, is this not something best left to those institutions whose mandate it is to do that – real banks and other financial institutions. It is funny that we often talk about 'non-bank financial institutions' in the microfinance realm. Such a term seems like a linguistic cover up, a way of allowing NGOs to 'play at' being banks. This may not be the way to go.

The role of the INGO as a direct lender may therefore be best thought of as temporary. The NGO contribution has been, as it should be, to take a chance, to innovate and experiment and to show the way to others. In microfinance, that has now been done. At least some INGOs ought to have the courage to move back as it were to the swamplands where the really difficult challenges have always lurked. The frontiers of development today are institutional development and social intermediation. Indeed, if there is a new swampland on the horizon, it is institutional development. Everywhere institutions, large and small, new and old, are struggling internally with questions of capacity, questions of efficiency and with conflicts in internal culture and mission. They are under strong pressures from competitors, donors or governance bodies externally, and from staffs and personnel internally who are less docile and more demanding than ever. But institutional transformation is only one area of need in institutional development. The other, especially in the enterprise sphere, is the creation of new institutions, the filling in the gaps in the institutional infrastructure in a region where entrepreneurial energy may be high but has come to a dead end because the local and regional economy remains unarticulated, its parts poorly connected with each other. Here new institutions need to be created or existing institutions need to develop new products or services to help articulate those parts.

Sadly, few INGOs want to venture into these areas. 'It's complicated,' they may say, or be wary of doing so since it is so difficult to measure the results. 'Who will donate money to us to do this?' they will ask. Above all they will be afraid to admit that what they may do best is unsustainable without subsidy. It is possible, however, that unless INGOs tackle such challenges, they may find themselves outstripped in the development arena altogether as more and more initiative for development is taken on by the private sector. That is already happening.

9 World Vision International and Donors: Too Close for Comfort?

Steven Commins

INTRODUCTION

'Total insanity is expecting to achieve new results by doing the same old thing.' In the few years since the end of the Cold War, the political and economic arrangements that had characterised the world have been changing at what feels to many as a dizzying pace. For those organisations concerned about issues of economic development and poverty alleviation, these shifts have generated questions outside of their previous operational frameworks. The linkages of capital markets, the emergence of derivatives, the impact of information technologies, the changing structures of employment and unemployment all serve to create a context not easily understood. It is in the midst of these and other changes that NGOs face the challenge of reviewing their work and reconceptualising their priorities. A central part of this task is appreciating the linkage between external trends and internal priorities, especially in regards to the policies of governments and international institutions.

NGOs face a serious challenge in terms of their ability to influence the major policies and priorities of donor agencies. Over the past few years, the world in which NGOs are operating is being reshaped in a manner that is altering established political, economic and social relations. The familiar landscapes that have defined the context for international development and the nature of NGOs are falling away or being changed at a pace that makes the predictability of future issues and activities especially difficult. One author has compared the events of the past few years to a great earthquake. The cracks and ruptures are being manifested in political and economic uncertainty, as well as the tragic spread of wars and civil strife in Africa, Eastern Europe and Central Asia.

NGOs are working in an increasingly globalised web of economic systems, a complex web of knowledge and information systems, along with a weakening of nation states and the resurgence of ethnic and nationalist sentiments. Technological and economic forces are shifting relationships of wealth, poverty and power, placing greater demands on NGOs at international, national and local levels. NGOs are faced with the demand to have a greater impact on macroeconomic policies and donor strategies at a time when economic trends are increasingly difficult to grasp. They are recognising that as marginalized populations are excluded from the 'new world order', there are strategic choices to be made about prioritising services to these communities or giving more attention to the wider factors that are marginalising particular regions or countries.

As NGOs consider the impact of global trends, they are also faced with the emergence of the New Policy Agenda (NPA). The New Policy Agenda is a reflection of the triumphalism associated with the belief that the end of the Cold War has vindicated a market-centred approach to social organisation and economic development. The donor-driven NPA emphasises the central importance of free markets, efficient use of limited government resources, a reduced role for the state and the need for good governance in low income countries. While the NPA has some progressive aspects, particularly its attention to environmental preservation, the empowerment of women and the role of civil society, these features are often secondary in practice to the primary goals of NPA programmes.

As NGOs consider the impact of global trends and their linkages with the New Policy Agenda, a serious complication is the growing incorporation of NGOs into the policy agendas of donor agencies. The shift away from state directed development to market driven development has been accompanied by larger amounts of bilateral and multilateral donor funds being channelled through NGOs. One challenge for NGOs is to determine whether their receipt and utilisation of public sector funds will enable them to have greater impact in their operational work and to better influence donor policies, or whether they will become domesticated by their dependence on public sector monies. In many cases, NGOs are in effect being asked to substitute for work that has been carried out by state agencies and to act more as public service contractors rather than independent agencies. The New Policy Agenda appears to call for NGOs to substitute for state programmes and to serve as implementors of public sector donor priorities. As this trend continues, a key question will be whether NGOs can utilise their experiences with the New Policy Agenda to develop alternative policy approaches, or whether they will fall in line with the main tenets of the New Policy Agenda.

The increasing flow of official funding through NGOs has raised questions about the impact of donor preferences on both public policy work and programme priorities. Do NGOs listen and learn from their partners in the South, or are they increasingly caught up with donor policies and priorities (Chapter 1)? The nature of the relationship between NGOs and donor agencies is changing, not just because of resource flows, but because NGOs are being invited to participate in aid meetings at a level beyond their previous activities. Can NGOs present an alternative set of views, or will they mostly operate at the margins of policy debates?

This chapter addresses these questions with a focus on the case of one international NGO, World Vision International (WVI). It asks:

- Can NGOs receive significant quantities of bilateral and multilateral resources and yet be able to serve as effective advocates for aid and other policy reforms?
- If an NGO is committed to tackling policy issues, what are the factors that may limit the scope and extent of this work?

As northern NGOs use public funds in their work with partner NGOs or grassroots organizations, they engage in a multiple set of relationships requiring multiple accountabilities. Accountability can be defined in a variety of ways. It includes relationships with donors, governments in developing countries, local communities, partner NGOs, and the private donor constituency of the NGO in Northern countries. There are a number of different aspects of accountability that can impact NGO decision making: legal, financial, institutional, contractual, partnership, relational. These take on various dynamics depending upon the particular NGO, the donor(s), the project partners and the ways in which the NGO approaches its accountabilities in practice. It is important to also ask whether accountability is based upon an equality and mutuality of interests, or whether there are imbalances in power that mean they are hierarchical, that is accounting to some constituencies is more important than to others. Can relational or partnership accountability with southern partners carry as much weight as the legal and financial requirements of donors?

WORLD VISION INTERNATIONAL

World Vision International is an NGO that has received and utilised public sector funds extensively in recent years. It is an international partnership of national offices operating with a focus on development and relief work. It was founded in 1950 as a US NGO with a strong base in small, private donations from individual sponsors and churches. In 1978, World Vision

International was established as the basis for an international partnership, with an international board drawn from seventeen countries, a strong emphasis on national leadership for each office, and a growing involvement in public policy and advocacy issues. WVI now has 17 national offices that raise money for programmes outside their own country, and over 50 national offices that implement a wide range of development and relief programmes. The role of World Vision International is to provide for co-ordination of programmes and budgets, to represent the World Vision partnership with international organisations (for example, United Nations agencies and the World Bank) and to co-ordinate advocacy and public policy work.

A number of offices in the World Vision partnership utilise government funds in their support for programmes and projects in developing countries. During the past decade, there has been significant growth in both bilateral and multilateral resource acquisition. The primary recipients of government funding among World Vision national offices are World Vision Australia (WV Australia), World Vision Canada (WV Canada), World Vision United Kingdom (WVUK) and World Vision United States (WVUS). In order to strengthen their capacity to work with government agencies and to take part in public policy issues, WV Australia has established an office in Canberra and WVUS has established an office in Washington, DC. The four fund-acquiring offices have also set up separate units or departments that are focused specifically on accessing government resources. The questions that this chapter will explore are whether relationships with government agencies or the World Bank become too close to allow World Vision to work for reforms in aid policies or to participate in public policy debates, and whether the scope of public policy work is limited by a tendency to focus on official aid policy priorities.

The evidence from several World Vision offices will be examined, looking at the way the lessons of programme experience and direct inputs from field operations have been linked to policy debates. With some clear caveats, the chapter will argue that it is possible to be operationally accountable to governments in terms of the use of funds and yet remain accountable to the low income communities where the NGO is carrying out programmes. Given the pressures of a changing global economy and the New Policy Agenda, however, questions remain. A further section looks at two issues that are not resolved by considering whether World Vision is willing to engage donors in wider policy dialogues. These are the pressures on the use and prioritisation of staff time and resources, and the links between World Vision's public policy work and the nature of the global trends and the New Policy Agenda. The chapter concludes with questions for further exploration and the identification of issues that World Vision and other NGOs must confront in the near future.

ACCOUNTABILITY, PUBLIC POLICIES AND DONOR GOVERNMENTS

The utilisation of public sector funding and intentional programmatic work on public policy issues are both relatively new aspects of World Vision's operations. The decision to seek out and utilise government funds was part of a continuous redefinition of the organisation's scope of work, the scale of its operations and the type of relationships it was willing to develop. The first use of government funds came in the 1960s, but this was modest in size. The major change in the composition of World Vision's funding did not occur until the 1980s, partly linked to a period of rapid expansion around the Ethiopian famine of 1984–5.

There has always been some concern within World Vision regarding whether the use of government funds would compromise the organisation's integrity. The offices that have been the primary recipients of bilateral resources have had to work with their national boards as well as with other World Vision offices in addressing the implications of official funding in terms of organisational integrity and independence. Because World Vision has had a large private donor base, the impact and implications of public sector funds has usually been reviewed in terms of programme quality, the integration of private and public resources, rather than the question of accountabilities.

Much of the initial impetus for public policy and advocacy work came from field staff who challenged the organisation to give serious attention to issues of inequity and injustice that they could not tackle. An international process to establish a paper on justice was initiated in the mid-1980s, which led to the adoption of a policy on justice and a policy on advocacy. In order to build collaboration and consensus in the organization, a Public Policy Network among World Vision offices was established in 1991 to allow for effective sharing of information and for the determination of policy and advocacy priorities. Further, an informal network of WV public policy staff focusing on major donors was established to allow for greater co-ordination on aid and humanitarian policy issues.

The identification of public policy contacts in each national office has allowed for the opportunity to attempt to scale up on both specific issues (complex emergencies, human rights) and wider policy matters (participation in UN conferences, work on aid reform and World Bank policies). For example, World Vision has utilised its network in preparing for its involvement in the UN Conference on Environment and Development, the World Conference on Human Rights and the International Conference on Population and Development. In each case, policy papers were developed primarily based upon input from the field.

While the public policy work has expanded notably in the past four years, relatively little attention has been given to the relationship between public sector funding and public policy work in terms of the potential constraints on questioning donor policies. It has generally been an implicit assumption within World Vision that it is feasible to maintain a critical distance while receiving public sector funds. How has this operated in different countries?

Australia

World Vision Australia began to receive funds from the Australian International Development Assistance Bureau (AusAID) in the mid-1970s, but at that point it was less than A$100 000, accounting for under 1 per cent of total income. By 1993 the amount was over A$20 million, accounting for about 20 per cent of income. Each year since 1977, WV Australia has participated in an annual consultation held between AusAID and NGOs receiving government grants. The range of issues has increased and now includes the impact of development assistance on women, human rights, good governance and the environment.

WV Australia and other NGOs have been critical of Australian aid priorities, which have not had a strong enough emphasis on poverty alleviation. Generally the focus of the criticism has been that aid programmes are too often for the benefit of Australian business interests, rather than low-income communities. A recent critique of Australian aid included Greg Thompson from World Vision as one of its authors (ACFOA, 1992). World Vision Australia has sought to inform its private donors about the problems with aid priorities and programmes. For example, in late 1993 it informed its Action Network that Australia's aid programme was out of line with the outlook of most Australians. The report noted that in 1991 only 23 per cent of Australia's aid went to the poorest countries, which compared unfavourably with a number of European donors. In addition, it reported that Australia had dropped from fifth to tenth on the OECD list of bilateral donors ranked by aid as a percentage of GNP.

The experience of World Vision in Australia is that aid has not been denied to NGOs that have been critical of Australian aid programmes or government policies. There are direct and sometimes quite strong exchanges between the government and NGOs on various matters. In order to keep an open relationship with the government, World Vision advises AusAID of any issues prior to the production of public statements. Even more significantly, WV Australia has developed linkages with like-minded staff within AusAID. It can provide public comments which strengthen the negotiating position of those within AusAID who are supportive of specific reforms.

Canada

World Vision Canada has been supported by the Canadian International Development Agency (CIDA) for over a decade. Government funding has increased from C$2 million in fiscal year 1984 (in a total budget of C$26 million) to C$14 million (in a total budget of C$96 million) in fiscal year 1994 (that is from 7.7 per cent to 14.5 per cent of total income). The relief/emergency nature of the 1994 funding level is apparent when contrasted to government income of C$7 million in 1991, C$11 million in 1992 and C$5 million in 1993. WV Canada anticipates little growth in development related funding in coming years as the Canadian government seeks to reduce its budget deficits. The only likely area of growth in government funding for the near future will be in relief-related resources.

WV Canada has taken an active role in policy discussions with other NGOs in relation to Canadian government policies. It has also sought to have an impact on the policies of the Canadian government in international peacekeeping operations. WV Canada initiated a process of consultation with other WV offices in order to determine what had been learned from World Vision's work in conflict situations. The comments from World Vision staff were brought together in the testimony presented to a Special Joint Committee Reviewing Canada's Foreign Policy. WV Canada joined with other NGOs in requesting a more comprehensive approach to global and national security issues, and their relationship to defence policies. It was argued that foreign and defence policies need to be better integrated, given that international peace and stability are intricately connected with environmental, economic, social and political measures. In particular, WV Canada noted the important role that Canada can play in international peacekeeping operations. It argued in its testimony that a priority for Canada should be a transformed peacekeeping policy internationally. This approach would be integrated into a broader peacebuilding approach that would address such issues as conflict prevention and work with local organisations.

The input on peacekeeping issues reflected a wider concern within the World Vision partnership about the endemic nature of complex emergencies. Over the past few years, increasing public policy and advocacy attention has been given by various World Vision offices to complex emergencies and mechanisms for reducing conflict. This has not meant a loss of concern about development issues, as WV Canada has also taken part in a number of CIDA related review processes. Rather, it represents a broadened understanding of the responsibilities of a large NGO in terms of emerging policy questions.

United Kingdom

World Vision United Kingdom is a new and relatively small office in the World Vision partnership (compared to Australia, Canada and the United States), but it has quickly established itself as a vital participant in public policy discussions both within the World Vision partnership and in the UK. In terms of bilateral funds, WVUK has developed three approaches to the UK's Overseas Development Administration (ODA). These include the special NGO budget; the Joint Funding Scheme; relief funds from the ODA Emergency Department; and regional desks within ODA. Because the level of aid has declined in real terms over the last 15 years and ODA's desire to work directly with southern NGOs (see Bebbington and Riddell, this volume), UK NGOs have had difficulty in increasing their bilateral income. At the same time, NGO policy work in the UK has reportedly taken on a more low-key approach since the Charity Commission's critical report on Oxfam's advocacy work on South Africa. This has led to greater co-operation among NGOs even though competition for government funds places demands on NGO staff to 'stand out from the crowd'.

WVUK recently communicated its concern about declining development assistance to the government, with a particular emphasis on the needs of countries in Africa. They argued that lack of resources for the development needs of Africa had held back progress that might have emerged from new policies related to democratisation and structural adjustment. WVUK staff noted that the lack of improved socioeconomic indicators undermined reforms. Africa is still locked into a negative resource flow due to debt repayments, as well as a lack of capital investment in most countries. The staff argued that the decline of UK assistance for over a decade undermined the ability of ODA to support positive reforms in Africa. Rather than continuing cuts in assistance flows, there was an opportunity to provide new resources in support of the reforms being undertaken by African governments. The WVUK communication also pointed out that given present aid trends, there was a significant danger that African countries would fall further behind other regions in terms of development indicators and capital resources. WVUK is committed to continuing to point out the desperate needs of Africa through both research and advocacy.

United States

World Vision US is the largest funding office in the World Vision partnership and has a particularly high level of demand on its public policy work owing to the international importance of US government action. In testimony before the House Subcommittee on Foreign Operations in April 1994, World Vision criticised cuts in assistance for 'human development' programmes, especially those related to child morbidity and mortality, and to the improvement of educational opportunities. The reductions in expenditures did not result from problems with the programmes funded, instead these programmes had suffered owing to a lack of domestic political support. Another point in the testimony was the need to reallocate US assistance from middle-income countries to the lower income countries.

WVUS has also sought to influence legislation in the area of complex humanitarian emergencies. This has included funding for relief efforts, conflict management and the provision of resources for political development. WVUS argued that what most complex emergencies require is a process for restoring the legitimacy and authority of local and national institutions and it noted that some of the most important initiatives in the area of conflict resolution had been severely weakened by bureaucratic infighting and turf wars in the US Administration. The presentation clearly identified problems within USAID and the State Department that prevented more effective mechanisms being created for these efforts.

WVUS is an active member of InterAction, the US consortium of NGOs which is now over ten years old. InterAction has been relatively successful in pulling together a diverse group of NGOs into an effective voice for policy concerns in Washington. When InterAction was founded in the mid-1980s, there was concern that the impact of increased US government funding through NGOs would reduce public policy work by InterAction members. A review of the past decade shows that this has not been the case. From this author's experience, InterAction has grown in effectiveness and commitment to advocacy work, even as government funding through NGOs has increased.

InterAction has made a significant contribution to building and enhancing North–South NGO linkages and has expanded its work on the overall reform of aid. World Vision US has similarly extended its advocacy and public policy work over the past decade. One prime area of concern has been the contining debate over the quality and quantity of US foreign assistance. After the Congressional elections in November 1994, WVUS staff took immediate action to brief new committee staff in both the House and the Senate on the importance of humanitarian aid programmes and the need to protect key accounts from drastic budget cuts. Although the direct results of such activity are difficult to judge, US aid policy and funding levels are likely to be a major focus for WVUS for the coming years.

MULTIPLE ACCOUNTABILITY AND THE WORLD BANK

The World Bank is the largest official development finance agency, and it is increasingly important in terms of shaping the aid policies of other donors. NGOs have given greater attention to the Bank's role in development policy making, due to its impact on donor priorities, controversy over structural adjustment programmes, and questions about the quality of Bank funded projects. The relationships between NGOs and the World Bank are complex and sometimes highly controversial. Whereas there was a time when NGOs appeared to be grateful to be allowed a place at the table with the Bank, the nature of NGO–Bank work has become more critical. NGOs have become better informed about the World Bank's work and more engaged in addressing specific and well documented issues. The establishment of an NGO–Bank Committee and a parallel NGO Working Group on the World Bank has highlighted the focus of NGOs on the work of the Bank. Relations remain complex, sometimes co-operative and sometimes contentious. The tenor of the contact varies widely and distrust remains on both sides, depending on the organisations, sectors and individuals.

World Vision first began to consider formal relations with the World Bank in the late 1980s. A paper was produced in 1987 by a WVI Vice President (Irvine, 1987) which sought to outline the opportunities and challenges for World Vision in terms of working with the World Bank. It looked at the way each organisation could learn from the other, and it noted that there were obstacles in terms of models and understanding of development, and operating style that could work against any effective relationship. The author also noted that in regard to structural adjustment lending, World Vision could contribute through enhancing the level of participation by low-income groups, encouraging advocacy for the interests of poor communities and addressing some of the social impacts of Bank policies. What was sought was a combination of direct operational cooperation balanced by critical inputs from NGO field experiences.

The progress on building a relationship with the Bank became internally contentious within World Vision for several reasons, but primarily due to concern about World Vision's participation in the World Bank funded Programme for the Alleviation of Poverty and the Social Costs of Adjustment (PAPSCA) in Uganda. Owing to the enormous needs that existed following the end of Uganda's civil war, World Vision Uganda had sought to expand its work into the areas of Rakai, Masaka, Masindi and Gulu in 1987. After a period of negotiations, in 1990 World Vision Uganda initiated several projects with World Bank funds coming through the Government of Uganda. There were a number of difficulties in the operation of this multiregional project which later became points for policy reform discussion between World Vision and Bank staff. Early in the project cycle, World Vision Uganda encountered a number of serious problems, including slow disbursement of funds and the complexities of the competitive bidding system required by the Bank. Meanwhile, there were other issues emerging as well (see Robinson, this volume).

A number of senior directors in different World Vision offices raised questions about the use of any World Bank funds, as a result of objections to the World Bank's model of development, the nature of structural adjustment programmes and the question of adding to Uganda's already crushing debt burden. From meetings in 1990 which looked at the wider scope of World Vision's relations with the World Bank, it was apparent that there was the need to develop a wider dialogue within World Vision about relations with the World Bank. In order to look at more than just the Uganda situation, a long-term process was established to create a policy framework for future relations with the World Bank.

This process included consultation with both Bank staff and noted critics of the Bank. The result of this process was the development of a policy paper outlining World Vision International's framework for its relationships with the World Bank. The policy paper was distributed in October 1992 following two earlier drafts. The priorities outlined in the paper serve as the framework for the approach to working with the Bank. The paper placed a priority on policy dialogue over funding of WV programmes and identified poverty alleviation, debt, environment and structural adjustment as the primary policy concerns. It also limited project involvement by listing a series of management and goal criteria that needed to be met in any national office prior to accepting World Bank funding. Since the adoption of the paper, WV staff have been involved in a wide range of Bank-related activities, including the 1993 Hunger Conference, work on project and procurement reform, and development indicators related to the Wapenhans Report. World Vision has sought to maintain transparency in its relations with the Bank, regularly taking part in meetings with Bank critics and sharing its own Bank related experiences with other NGOs. The World Vision staff paper (Voorhies, 1993) on the Uganda experience has been shared with a large number of NGOs as well as with a number of Bank colleagues (see also Robinson, this volume). World Vision national offices have also been part of NGO coalitions that have sought to change their own government policies in relation to the World Bank, both from the donor perspective and from countries involved in structural adjustment programmes.

Despite some concern by WV staff who were particularly critical of the Bank, the policy framework paper did not open the floodgates for greater Bank funding. On the contrary, the insistence on learning from the Uganda experience led to the rejection of several possible Bank funded projects in Africa and Asia. There was a significant amount of internal disagreement over the decision not to pursue possible Bank funding in these countries, but the long-term outcome was to strengthen the credibility of WVI policy on relations with the Bank.

The result has been a willingness to criticise Bank policies and procedures and insisting on key operational changes before implementing any Bank funded projects. World Vision staff have become more knowledgeable about Bank procedures, and are recognised by both Bank and NGO colleagues as playing an informed and critically engaged role in Bank–NGO policy discussions. World Vision has agreed to disagree with both Bank staff and NGO colleagues on various matters. In relation to NGOs that are more visibly critical of the Bank, World Vision continues to share ideas and experiences with them.

NGOs, ACCOUNTABILITY AND THE NEW POLICY AGENDA

The review of the relationship between World Vision offices and donor agencies indicates that the ability to attempt to influence and criticise donor policies is not automatically hampered by the receipt of donor funds. There are, however, some issues that remain significant for World Vision and other operational NGOs, in terms of balancing their multiple accountabilities. These include the demands upon staff to raise funds, which has to be balanced against providing analysis about the nature of aid policies, and the relative importance of the issues being addressed through public policy efforts in relation to overall trends in the global economy. This section will look at both of these issues as questions not only for World Vision but for other NGOs as well.

The establishment of separate units in WV offices dedicated to the acquisition of government funds has created a cadre of staff who are more informed about large scale development issues and the nature of government funding operations. This staff is able to provide important input into policy discussions because they are deeply immersed in the details of funding issues and have familiarity with the internal debates within funding agencies. Indeed, a key aspect of the capacity of World Vision (or any other NGO) seeking to change donor policies is the establishment of informal networks of relations that provide information beyond the public statements of the donor agency. Both the bilaterals and the World Bank have significant internal differences over policy priorities and funding strategies. Close relationships between NGO staff and donor personnel can provide the basis for understanding the best approaches to influencing policy.

The problem facing World Vision offices is that the primary measurement for most staff and departmental performance is resource acquisition. There is also growing pressure on all NGOs to reduce their administrative costs. This is a reality that cannot be avoided in assessing the effectiveness of World Vision's work on public policy issues. The World Vision offices described in this chapter all have staff who are in positions that are focused on public policy issues. They are relatively few in number, and they depend upon working closely with their colleagues who are involved in the resource acquisition work. This is generally a positive relationship, as it allows for a much deeper understanding of the policy processes within bilateral agencies and the World Bank. There are times, however, when the different roles and perspectives within World Vision offices have created serious tensions or disagreements about priorities and organisational autonomy (see Robinson in this volume).

An additional and difficult dilemma is the allocation of time for work on policy issues. This is a matter that has not been clearly discussed or analysed within World Vision. Other tensions also surface over the balance between acquisition of resources and reform work. There are donors, especially individuals, who demand excessively low operational overheads, and there are questions from partner agencies and low income communities about the expenses of large international NGOs. These are issues that will remain difficult to resolve for NGOs seeking to engage in policy work.

World Vision has opted to maintain a tenor of constructive criticism in its policy work. While it has major criticisms of donor policies it has in the past chosen not to engage in what some NGOs term 'campaigning'. A necessary and legitimate criticism of World Vision's approach could be that the lack of a more aggressive or assertive approach to donors is the result of being compromised through using official funds. This challenge should be regularly considered by World Vision staff in their relations with public sector agencies. The problem with this critique is that it posits a simple cause and effect, the inverse of the argument that NGOs will receive less public sector funds if they are critical of donor policies. What is very apparent through working with the staff of both bilateral and multilateral agencies is that these are not monolithic structures and that, while NGO criticisms will vex some within a particular agency, the same criticisms will be welcomed by others within the same agency.

It should also be noted, in regard to 'campaigning', that World Vision has become much more active on specific advocacy issues. There has been an aggressive advocacy work on the issues of a global ban on land mines, the spreading of conflict and the arming of low-income countries. World Vision staff have also become increasingly active on the rights of children, including child labour, protection of street children, removal of children from bonded labour, and the elimination of sex tourism. In a number of cases, this has involved direct actions with (and sometimes in opposition to) government agencies and policy makers. Generally there has been widespread support and encouragement for more forceful actions within the World Vision partnership.

More difficult and daunting issues are globalisation and the New Policy Agenda. In terms of global economic trends, the central question is whether World Vision is addressing the main issues or is merely focusing on transitional or surface problems, related to donor policies. Most of the policy input from World Vision to governments and the World Bank has tended to focus on aid priorities, relatively little attention has been given to wider macroeconomic issues. Some staff work has been done on debt and on the impact of multinational corporations, but this has not led to clarity on how to reform transnational enterprises, governments or multilaterals.

How can an NGO have accountability in relation to international economic trends? In the case of World Vision, some of the key input comes from members of the International Board, who come from such countries as Brazil, the Philippines and Zimbabwe. They bring concerns about global economic shifts to the senior management, representing not only project communities but groups of partner agencies in a number of countries. This has helped initiate a wider process of reviewing World Vision's perspective on global economic trends. An important process has been developed through WV documents such as the 'World in Which We Work' and the 'Global Context Paper' based upon interchanges with a range of groups, including UNRISD, IDS Sussex and the Global Business

Network. There remains a deep concern within World Vision that NGOs, including World Vision, are in danger of becoming little more than ladles in the global soup kitchen (author's expression, but the idea credited to Alan Fowler).

CONCLUSION

It would be dishonest for any NGO to act as if there are no contradictions between receiving funding from bilateral or multilateral donors, and their stated commitment to serving the needs of low income communities. Yet this chapter has argued that possibly a greater difficulty is moving beyond aid reform to action on deeper and more powerful global economic relations. In the case of World Vision, it has been possible to at least partially balance the accountabilities of project work and of policy work on aid issues; however, our capacity to address larger issues remains to be tested. There have been key learnings from the experience in work on aid and other policy matters, including the need for transparency, the acceptance of operational and policy ambiguities, and the need for deepening relationships with other NGOs and some of the staff of official agencies. World Vision has not always had good relations with other NGOs in some countries but engagement in public policy work has been an important bridge for learning and sharing concerns. There are problems and dangers for NGOs in the new world order in terms of what role they are to play and how to avoid being servants of an externally imposed agenda. It will be easy in the near future for big international NGOs (BINGOs) to become dying international NGOs (DINGOs) as external changes create an inhospitable environment or reveals NGO work as marginal in a changing world order.

The problem of how to approach global economic issues is proving more difficult than addressing specific advocacy issues on relief and aid policy. Can NGOs change quickly enough to influence the wider questions? There are opportunities for giving serious attention to the role of NGOs in shaping policies beyond being channels for funds, working on programmes or raising questions on aid. To move further requires new strategies, including new mechanisms for accountability and governance among NGOs, which allow for new forms of relationships with low income communities, based not only on programmes or projects, but upon a critique of present global economic relations. This type of accountability will be new, moving beyond participation as presently understood and demanding a reconceptualisation of economic and political structures. For most NGOs this is new territory, but it is important to consider this as a necessary step that builds upon present policy reform efforts. In the end, it may be that the experience of multiple accountabilities in project work and policy reform is a stepping stone to something larger. Certainly, the challenge for NGOs is to move beyond present aid policy work into the wider, more difficult and more contentious arena of how to reshape the forces that are presently driving the global economy.

10 In Unequal Dialogue with Donors: The Experience of the Sarvodaya Shramadana Movement[1]

Jehan Perera

INTRODUCTION

In 1996 the Sarvodaya Shramadana Movement completed 38 years of continuous evolution as a force that contributes to progressive non-violent
social transformation in Sri Lanka. The Movement has survived eight governmental changes, two bloody youth insurrections (which were countered
by equally horrendous suppressive actions) and a civil war that has been
going on for over 13 years. Furthermore, the Movement was singled out
between 1989 and 1993 by the late President Premadasa for an unprece-
dented attack on all fronts. The Movement had only just commenced reha-
bilitating itself in mid-1993 when an unexpected development took place
from the side of Sarvodaya's main donor organisation, NOVIB of the
Netherlands. With little warning they cut 42 per cent from their planned
grant for 1994/95 and plunged Sarvodaya into a financial crisis. This crisis
has prompted Sarvodaya to rethink its relationship with donors. This
chapter is about possible future directions open to Sarvodaya. Sarvodaya
has been repeatedly subjected to donor evaluations: in this chapter we
evaluate our relationship with our donors.

THE SARVODAYA MISSION

'Sarvodaya Shramadana' means the awakening of all in society. This is
sought through the sharing of labour and other voluntarily given resources
for the personal and social awakening of all beings. In very concise terms,
the mission of Sarvodaya Shramadana is to create a new social order based
on the values of truth, non-violence and self-denial, and governed by the

156

ideals of a participatory democracy. The decentralisation of power and resources, upholding of basic human rights, satisfaction of basic human needs, protection and nurturance of a healthy environment, and tolerance of cultural, religious and linguistic differences should be given pride of place in such an order. The economic principle would be one of a sustainable (no-poverty, no-affluence) society based on the sharing of resources and their prudent use. For Sarvodaya Shramadana, development is the process of awakening individuals, families, rural communities, urban groups, the nation and the world at large. This awakening has six major dimensions: spiritual, moral, cultural, social, economic and political. There should be balanced progress along all these dimensions although, at a particular point of time, one or more of the dimensions may receive greater emphasis.

SARVODAYA'S PROCESSES AND PROGRAMMES

The Sarvodaya Shramadana Movement has developed a large number of processes to achieve these ideals. These processes begin at the individual level, move on to families and communities, and eventually to national and world levels. The ultimate objective is to unfold the new social order envisaged above. The unfolding processes have developed into concrete programmes, for example the Early Childhood Development Programme, the Rural Technical Services Programme, and the Economic Enterprises Development Programme. These programmes need an institutional framework, expertise, physical inputs, human response[2] development, evaluation and constant upgrading. They cannot be achieved without appropriate organisational structures which need to function in the broader existing legal framework of society.

Sarvodaya Shramadana's greatest input for national development comes from the people in village communities. The Movement started with one village in which volunteers from outside the village worked to evoke self-reliance, built community participation and demonstrated how planned action could satisfy basic human needs. This process, based on Shramadana (gift of labour) Camps, spread from village to village. People contributed at weekends and vacations for years until the Movement covered several thousand villages spread over all the districts of the country. The Sarvodaya Shramadana Movement got recognition as a constructive, non-violent, community service cutting across man-made barriers such as caste, race, language, religion and political affiliation. It became a national people's movement for self-development harnessing the creative energy of community participation.

The first phase of this process released in village communities is the awakening of the inherent strength, potential and resourcefulness of the people (Jana Shakthi) for their own self-development. This is followed by training in skills and leadership and the institutionalisation of different groups such as children, youth, mothers, farmers and craftsmen. Creating legally independent village level societies, representative of all these groups is the next step. This kind of democratic participation and organisation enables them to be innovative and adaptive to new technologies while upholding value systems, nurturing progressive traditional norms and freeing themselves from psychological dependencies from outside.

Over 2000 villages (out of a total of over 8000 villages which have had Shramadana experience) have registered societies and democratically elected office-bearers. They hold full responsibility for their self-development programmes. The rest of the Sarvodaya villages are on their way to such registration. Sarvodaya believes that democracy cannot be imposed from above, but that it should be nurtured to evolve from below. It is Sarvodaya's firm and proven belief that the total fulfilment of a human being within a family (which itself is a cohesive part of a larger community) can be achieved by this kind of a participatory approach. What Sarvodaya has striven to do is to convert this belief into a practical working model by progressively introducing appropriate and innovative technologies and structures.

At present Sarvodaya's organisational structure consists of autonomous village societies, clusters of villages (Gramadana Units) and co-ordinating units at the divisional, district and national levels. This is the result of an evolutionary process rather than a grand design from the top. With the Sarvodaya ideal being communities enjoying a high degree of self-reliance, decentralisation and autonomy, emphasis was never placed on control, monitoring and reporting mechanisms. These would have given power to the leadership of the Movement and its headquarters. Unfortunately, it was to be the practice of this decentralised ideal, so important from our point of view, that brought forth the most severe criticisms and penal sanctions from some of our foreign donor agencies.

DONOR SUPPORT OF SARVODAYA'S ACTIVITIES

In the late 1960s the leaders of Sarvodaya Shramadana were invited to share its peoples' participatory experiences with international organisations like the FAO, UNESCO, UNICEF, WHO and also voluntary development organisation like NOVIB in the Netherlands, OXFAM (UK) and

Friedrich Naumann Stifftung (FNS) in Germany. These organisations offered Sarvodaya assistance for its members' projects. Thus started an era of project assistance which took concrete form from 1972 onwards through negotiations with the national structure. These development partners did not conduct their evaluations in the central office of Sarvodaya or in its district centres but went to the remotest villages in the country to see and assess for themselves what Sarvodaya had achieved with the full participation of people.

NOVIB, the Netherlands Organisation for International Development Cooperation, became Sarvodaya's main development partner. In 1969, 1970 and 1971 Van Vlijmen, NOVIB's Secretary-General, invited A. T. Ariyaratne, the founder of Sarvodaya Shramadana, several times to the Netherlands. This was to assist in NOVIB's campaigns for funds and to inform the Dutch public about Sri Lanka's development needs. This was a period during which Sarvodaya helped NOVIB rather than vice versa. NOVIB staff visited Sarvodaya projects every year: they studied, learnt and assisted in the work.

The second regular development partner was the Friedrich Naumann Stifftung (FNS) of Germany. They financed Shramadana Camps, the construction of Sarvodaya headquarters and the Pathakada Community Leadership Training Institute. Helvetas of Switzerland was, and still is, another strong partner of Sarvodaya. The relationship between Helvetas and Sarvodaya going back to 1978 has always been exemplary. Budgets were presented and agreements reached well ahead of time while Helvetas engineers provided much assistance to the movement, especially in the development of the Rural Technical Services Programme.

There were many other organisations that provided project assistance. Some of these were 11-11-11 Campaign (Belgium), OXFAM (UK), OXFAM (USA), Ford Foundation, Risso Koseikai (Japan), UNICEF, Manitese (Italy), IDRC (Canada), CIDA, NORAD, American World Jewish Service, Alton Jones Foundation and ITDG (UK), among others. During this period of co-operation through projects, Sarvodaya was able to disseminate its ideology amongst rural people, educate people for self-development and employment, build structures and institutions from the village level up, and even organise many national and international workshops, seminars and conferences on themes related to participatory development.

Dr Sjef Theunis succeeded G. J. Van Vlijmen as Secretary-General of NOVIB. He made an extensive and intensive tour of Sarvodaya activities in villages and recognised their relevance to Sri Lanka and the developing world in eradicating poverty, powerlessness and conflicts from among the poorest segments of the community. His yearly visits did not begin and end with 'rapid appraisals' of our central office or district centres, as became the case in later years with others. He always visited and studied village projects throughout the country. He decided that Sarvodaya was mature enough to make a corporate plan of its own and to receive programme assistance. Together Sarvodaya and NOVIB worked out an extensive six year programme of development co-operation.

In 1977 a Commission of Dialogue, consisting of scholars selected by both NOVIB and Sarvodaya, was set up to jointly develop, monitor and evaluate Sarvodaya programmes. Both partners teamed from this Commission. It was a cooperative relationship, and not one of a donor and recipient. Both NOVIB and Sarvodaya shared and developed their philosophy together. They empowered each other in the understanding of people's participatory development activities. There were tense periods, such as the time of communal riots in 1983, but the organisations could always iron out differences and misunderstandings. Mutual respect, freedom to make decisions and easy access to each other were the salient features of this relationship with NOVIB. Sarvodaya consolidated its position as a kind of model participatory development organisation. NOVIB played a major financial role in helping Sarvodaya become what it is today.

NOVIB was followed by the International NGO Division of the Canadian International Development Agency (CIDA) whose head spent many days in remote villages and grasped Sarvodaya's bottom-up approach. Subsequently, CIDA became a regular partner of Sarvodaya for project assistance. Later on Helvetas of Switzerland and NORAD of Norway became regular partners contributing project assistance. There were others like IDRC (Canada), USAID and so on, who co-operated with smaller project assistance. With programme assistance from NOVIB and project support from other donors, Sarvodaya was able to proceed up to 1985 on its own lines of evolution towards an alternative development strategy.

THE DONOR CONSORTIUM

With good intentions and high expectations, the idea of a donor consortium was mooted in 1985 by a CIDA consultant. The possibility of long-term planning, a committed three year budget, better remuneration for workers and improvement of their skills and one comprehensive monitoring, evaluation and reporting system for all donors were good reasons for Sarvodaya to agree to the idea of a consortium. The main partner, NOVIB, was happy, as it could share the responsibility of financing Sarvodaya jointly with other donors. Furthermore, Sarvodaya agreed to form a consortium as the organisation was at a point in time where it wished to rapidly expand its proven activities.

The first consortium meeting held in 1986 was attended by 26 partner organisations of Sarvodaya and included ambassadors and high commissioners. There was great enthusiasm and commitment on the part of everybody. Sarvodaya was given the freedom to select a general chairperson for the meeting and a chief guest for the opening ceremony. The whole exercise was conducted in the open, with transparency on the part of everybody. Different sessions were conducted by different chairpersons with complete freedom for Sarvodaya and donors to express their views and opinions. At this meeting Sarvodaya presented its first comprehensive plan and budget for an 18 month period beginning from 1 October 1986 to 31 March 1988. A 'loose' consortium was arranged with four donor agencies NOVIB, CIDA, NORAD and ITDG jointly funding the bulk of the Sarvodaya budget. Helvetas continued to support the Rural Technical Services while other donors supported specific ongoing or new 'projects'. This flexibility was particularly useful in the case of SEEDS (Sarvodaya Economic Enterprises Development Services) which grew more quickly than had been anticipated when the plan was formulated. In 1988 a three year plan on the same lines was formulated. This would have ended in March 1991. However, in 1990, the consortium changed its mind. They decided to have another interim period and requested Sarvodaya to develop yet another Strategic Plan from 1992 to 1995 (as against 1991 to 1994).

As described at the beginning of this chapter, Sarvodaya always had strategic plans, operational plans and budget of its own. Sarvodaya had neither experts nor consultants. Many people from the village level, divisional level, district level and national headquarters were involved in planning and implementation. They worked in the Sinhala and Tamil languages and articulated their thoughts according to their own indigenous value systems. Unfortunately, the foreign experts and foreign-trained Sri Lankan experts who became involved in planning and monitoring activities often found communication with Sarvodaya staff difficult, particularly because of language.

In common with organisations everywhere, there were wastages, misappropriations and malpractices in Sarvodaya. The amounts involved however were small and the defaulting individuals few. While internal and external audit systems were in place and were progressively being streamlined and strengthened as a bottom-up process, the consortium insisted on imposing many complex financial and administrative control systems on the Sarvodaya administration from the top down. They insisted on the production of a corporate plan in the way they saw it. Unfortunately Sarvodaya was not in a position to resist such pressures as this occurred during the worst period of the politically motivated attack against it by President Premadasa. Sarvodaya had no choice but to accede to the demands of the donor consortium before the 1992–5 strategic plan was accepted by them. These impositions and top-down controls by the consortium began to create doubt in the minds of the Sarvodaya leadership. There was hardly any dialogue at the consortium meetings that followed as donor representatives gave every indication of being mere executors of decisions already taken at their headquarters.

After the consortium was formed, instead of reducing the workload of Sarvodaya headquarters' staff (regarding donor demands), it increased this workload to unbelievable proportions. Hordes of evaluators, monitors, experts and consultants had a field day in Sarvodaya most of the year. Some of them were strangers to people's participatory development movements and the ideals that underpin them. Still, Sarvodaya tolerated all this, as the trust factor and long association, particularly with NOVIB, were important considerations. With the severe increase in donor demands from one consortium meeting to another we, in Sarvodaya, were wondering whether the entire consortium idea was in the best interest of Sarvodaya.

There were doubts on the 'northern' side too. The former head of NOVIB, Dr Sjef Theunis, wrote in 1991:

> My former organisation, NOVIB, has never fully understood this initiative. The programmed analyses crushed the people's creativity-structures, the visions. We were ahead of our times. History will be the judge. The chasm between North and South proved to be larger than we had thought possible. In these difficult, even absurd times today, I hope that my brother Ari will obtain his strength from the warmth of tens of thousands of Sarvodaya workers, who have the right to survive.

Despite Dr Theunis's plea, the donor attitude became more bureaucratic and rigid. The Project Director of NOVIB, on a visit to Sarvodaya in August 1993, responded to the organisation's appeals only by making a firm statement that 'We are not interested in philosophy. For NOVIB development is a business. There is nothing idealistic about it. Sarvodaya should conform to a businesslike relationship with NOVIB.' This language was completely new to us. We were making a serious effort to build up efficiency in all departments of our work while not losing sight of our ideals and objectives. Sarvodaya's attempts to open a dialogue with NOVIB were scorned. Decisions were taken in The Hague and simply conveyed to Sarvodaya. We were treated as a subcontractor, not a partner.

The natural expansion of the Movement from village to village was interrupted. The evolutionary process strengthening the organisations at village level and upwards and incorporating them as legally independent entities capable of planning and sustaining themselves was severely affected. While bottom-up processes were working in one direction, top-down systems were imposed by numerous recommendations from monitors. Evaluators, consultants and donors literally took over the policy and decision-making functions trying to convert the Sarvodaya Movement into a mere delivery mechanism. The search for an alternative path to sustainable development Sarvodaya was following was hardly understood by them. The principles of decentralisation, people's participation and bottom-up planning had no value to the consortium. It wanted a powerful and centralised financial and administrative structure. While this exercise had some benefits for Sarvodaya in improving certain weaknesses in administrative and financial management, the overall impact was a disaster as far as nurturing people's initiatives was concerned. Expections of the consortium were shattered. The only beneficiaries of its work were a few expatriates who have now become internationally reputed consultants and experts on NGOs, despite their insensitivity to people's initiatives.

THE EFFECTS OF THE DONOR CONSORTIUM

As a result of the consortium intervention, an organisational structure that had evolved organically was unnecessarily sectoralised, destroying the integrated and cohesive character that was a hallmark of Sarvodaya. For example, the eight districts in the North and East were first separated from the normal consortium programme on the promise that these eight districts would be supported by a separate programme to be funded by two donor agencies. Sarvodaya agreed to this and funds were provided. But the donor-imposed criteria for the selection of the chief executive (that he must be from a particular ethnic group), the way funds were to be transferred to Jaffna and Trincomalee and even the supervision of the chief executive's work were substantially taken out of Sarvodaya's hands and given to consortium monitors. Within a very short time, these monitors began by-passing the executive director of Sarvodaya and the authority of Sarvodaya's Officials Committee. The regular Sarvodaya administration was sidelined. However, when the programme collapsed, the donors put the entire blame on Sarvodaya. The consortium monitors (who were afraid to go to the work sites because of the war situation), gave weak excuses recommending that this programme should be scrapped. And it was scrapped. Accordingly, massive Sarvodaya employee retrenchment had to take place from October 1992 and the entire North and East programme was paralysed. It is only the voluntary efforts of the workers in the North and East that had enabled Sarvodaya to revive its programme to some degree and continue its work.

With regard to the core programmes in other districts, the separation of the social programmes from the economic programmes was the second devastating mistake that donor consultants pushed Sarvodaya into. Earlier, the economic programmes were an integral part of the social programmes and substantial funds were spent on development education and other community strengthening programmes. The chief executive of the economic programmes became the favourite of some of the monitors and donors who assisted him in his attempt to split the organisation ie set Sarvodaya's economic programmes up a new organisation, fully independent of Sarvodaya. The chief executive of the economic programmes was dismissed only after the harassment of Sarvodaya by the Premadasa government was stopped. He soon found a job as a donor consultant on NGOs!

A third area in which the consortium had a major impact was Sarvodaya's Development Education Programme. At one stage, Sarvodaya had about 360 centres where Development Education activities were going on. Today there is only one place. This is the result of the recommendations of the monitoring missions accepted by the donors. A programme for which originally about 70 per cent of our funds were spent became the least important for them and hardly any funds were allocated for this activity, despite Sarvodaya's conviction that such activities were of great importance.

A CLASH OF CULTURES

The Sarvodaya staff are not well equipped in modern business management techniques, monitoring systems and reporting in comparison with the lap-top computer toting consultants who fly in and can produce dozens of recommendations and reports without ever visiting the rural areas. Such consultants are hardly aware of the vast transformation of rural life taking place in all sectors as a result of the efforts of Sarvodaya through motivated, non-professional villagers. Most Sarvodaya educators lack university degrees and the ability to speak English even though they possess years of field experience and common sense. Perhaps, for these reasons, what they could teach was not considered to be of importance by the consultants.

The Sarvodaya staff soon developed an inferiority complex and a fear of the donor promoted consultancy missions. It was a classic example of an uneven confrontation between the dominant materialistic value-system of the 'northern' development paradigm and the humanistic and holistic approach to development of the South. The Sarvodaya management personnel tried their very best to improve administrative and financial management, monitoring and reporting systems. All these were delivered on time, especially during the last three consortia meetings. Unfortunately, these reports were not read or discussed or even appreciated by the donor representatives. Those who chaired those meetings, like the representatives of NOVIB and ODA, were on a different wavelength from the executive director or his chief executives. One of the donor representatives wanted a Sarvodaya worker to show the 'spiritual' contained in his work in a village she briefly visited!

The spirit of partnership was no longer evident from the consortium. While Sarvodaya displayed full transparency and accountability, in the way Sarvodaya understood it, there was hardly any transparency or responsibility on the part of the main consortium partners. It was only directives, one after the other, that we received from them. The consortium recommended and imposed on Sarvodaya a top heavy administration with professionals who were paid much higher salaries than highly experienced non-English speaking community level workers. They requested Sarvodaya to make its volunteers paid workers. For executive officers, vehicles and other facilities were provided. Even the auditors were changed so that much higher fees had to be paid.

The budgets were formulated jointly with the consultants. The consortium, which had agreed to find the required funds in full, now decided to give only about half of what Sarvodaya and the consultants had agreed. Overheads increased while field programmes were cut. The monitoring missions recommended, and the donors insisted, that Sarvodaya should not allow any more villages to join its programmes. They dictated that the 8600 villages that Sarvodaya had reached should be reduced to 3000 in 1992 and 2000 by 1994. This was a condition for approving even the reduced budget. How Sarvodaya was to face those 6600 other communities whose expectations were shattered was of no concern to them.

Sarvodaya believed that the consortium concept was adopted to follow a strategy of 'partners in progress'. Despite the potential advantages of the consortium concept, however, the disadvantages became manifold. The executive director and the other senior officials became preoccupied in implementing proposals and recommendations imposed by the donors as well as various monitoring and evaluation missions and consultants virtually on a daily basis. In a period of less than two years, 123 recommendations were imposed on Sarvodaya. It was humanly impossible to implement all of them. The senior staff of Sarvodaya had hardly any time to look at what was happening in villages. Under the guise of 'professionalism' and 'business development' these donors held sway over Sarvodaya to the extent that the character of the organisation was drastically affected. The meeting of the donor consortium was gradually converted into a business forum where no humanitarian considerations were given attention. Donor representatives, from ODA (UK) and NOVIB, dominated the last two meetings and dictated terms to Sarvodaya. The donors even went to the extent of imposing 'sanctions' on Sarvodaya by adducing reasons such as our inability to meet their 'expectations'. Ironically, this is the same type of language used by the IMF in dealing with the governments of developing countries. The expectations of thousands of village communities as expressed by Sarvodaya were not given any consideration. The Sri Lankan culture of being polite and courteous continues to inform Sarvodaya actions but how long can Sarvodaya accept this sort of intervention?

CONCLUSION

The Sarvodaya Shramadana Movement experience with donors has been salutary. What started off as a partnership based on dialogue had, by the mid-1990s, become a subcontractorship based on commands and sanctions. Although donors in Sri Lanka were keen to work more with NGOs they had adopted a 'development as business' approach that placed them at loggerheads with Sarvodaya, and many other Sri Lankan NGOs. Underlying the problems of recent years has been a fundamental clash of cultures: on the one side the donors, emphasising a top-down approach, centralisation, professional expertise, materialist values, and the short-term; on the other Sarvodaya, emphasising a participatory bottom-up approach, decentralisation, voluntarism, holistic development and the long-term.

Donor approaches to Sarvodaya were riddled with inconsistencies. While wanting to work with NGOs because they have low overheads and are cost effective, donors insisted on paying volunteers, employing highly-paid professionals and the greater use of vehicles! While espousing participation, devolution, social development, stakeholder analysis and so on, donors sought to impose hastily prepared plans produced by visiting foreign consultants. The major contribution that donors initially made to helping Sarvodaya expand its network has been lost in this clash of cultures and donor inconsistencies.

In order to maintain good relations with donors, NGOs need to be able to write professional reports and properly audited statements. Everything should be shown on paper. That is the most important obligation to fulfil. The quality of work in the field matters less to the donors. Basically they do not have much of an idea of what goes on there anyway. Their whistle stop visits to rural development sites can never reveal the realities of development, though the exhaustion they may feel from trekking about in the countryside may salve their consciences.

NGOs must recognise that when they work with donors they enter into a power relationship in which they are the subordinate. They cannot expect to be able to heavily influence donor behaviour, particularly when donors are in a consortium and, by scaring-off non-consortium donors, can become monopoly suppliers of foreign aid. Unless NGOs are prepared to rely on voluntary contributions (from villagers, the middle classes in their own countries and privately supported northern NGOs) then ultimately the donors have the power because they have the money for which there is much more of demand than supply. The temptation for donors (who are ordinary humans after all) not to throw their weight around is almost impossible to resist.

Notes

1. This chapter is based on the Sarvodaya publication, *Future Directions of Sarvodaya*, Colombo: Vishwa Lekha, 1994.
2. The word 'resource' (commonly used in HRD) has been replaced by the word 'response' because we believe that people are not resources to be used, but ends in themselves.

11 Elephant Loose in the Jungle: The World Bank and NGOs in Sri Lanka

Roland Hodson[1]

Growth is vital for poverty reduction, but it is not enough. (Robert McNamara, President of the World Bank[2])

They give you money. They give you all the ideas, expertise and everything else. Your job is to follow the yellow lines, the green lines, the red lines, read the instructions at each stop and follow them. The World Bank is eager to assume all the responsibilities. They don't want to leave any responsibility for the borrower, except the responsibility for the failure of the project. (Professor Mohammed Yunus, Founder, The Grameen Bank[3])

INTRODUCTION

From its foundation 50 years ago the World Bank's[4] primary mission has been the alleviation of poverty. Particularly since the Presidency of Robert McNamara in the 1970s and the World Development Report of 1980 the Bank has been vocal in claiming a lead role in this most difficult task. Although the Bank initially built its reputation on large-scale infrastructure projects and had periods during which emphasis was placed on agriculture and a basic needs approach, the institution came to the conclusion that without the correct economic policy framework no investment would produce the economic growth necessary to reduce poverty.

This realisation prompted a concentration on policy-based lending to induce and assist governments to change economic policies towards a model that includes a reduced state sector and greater market orientation. When this process, commonly called structural adjustment, began to attract strong criticism from Non-Governmental Organisations (NGOs)[5] and multilateral agencies such as UNICEF, the Bank began to look for ways to cushion the poor from the effects of structural adjustment. The importance of this search grew as the Bank itself realised that it had seriously underestimated the time it would take for countries to reorient their policies and begin to see an improvement in the overall economy sufficient to benefit the poor in any significant way.

The Bank's response resulted in special funds being set up in order to assist the poor to meet the additional hardships caused by the adjustment process. Ghana and Bolivia, two of the Bank's early laboratories to test its policies, operated such funds. Later this feature became a common part of the Bank's programme. The aim of these funds was to provide short term employment creation and the delivery of social services to those most affected by structural adjustment. To achieve these goals the World Bank turned to NGOs. At a time when governments were being required to roll back their bureaucracies, the Bank could not rely on the same demoralised institutions to mount crash programmes. In any case the Bank had concluded that reforming the civil services of many developing countries to the point where they could deliver services to the poor cost-effectively would be possible only in the long term, if at all. This conclusion produced a shift of funding away from the state towards NGOs, a pattern which has continued to the present.

As the process of structural adjustment proceeded the Bank realised that even if its clients economies responded well to its prescriptions there would remain within most poor countries a large segment of the population which would not benefit. There were voices within the Bank who felt that the Bank should go beyond the short-term safety nets and fund long-term poverty alleviation projects to assist those not benefiting from economic growth reduce their poverty in a sustainable way. Others felt the Bank had little comparative advantage in designing and managing poverty alleviation programmes and should leave this work to more specialised agencies. Still a third group felt that attempts to address poverty directly would not succeed and the best way forward was to promote education and health services that would help the poor participate more fully in the wider economy.

Whatever the balance of opinion within the Bank may have been at the time, a 'Poverty Alleviation Project' for Sri Lanka was negotiated in 1990 and agreed in 1991. It is that project which is the subject of this chapter.

THE SRI LANKA POVERTY ALLEVIATION PROJECT (SLPAP)

It is widely known that Sri Lanka has performed well in improving its social indicators relative to its per capital GNP through programmes to redistribute land, high levels of expenditure on education and health and subsidies on basic foods. It is less well known that Sri Lanka was well on its way to this achievement at the time of independence. For example, Sri Lanka had a literacy rate in 1900 which exceeded that of Pakistan and Bangladesh in 1975[6] and has enjoyed universal adult suffrage since 1931.

But the universal coverage of these relatively generous social pro-grammes together with subsidies to the state-owned industrial sector created a financial burden that eventually crushed the economy, thus setting the stage for the structural adjustment process. By 1986/7 when the last published Consumer Finance Survey was done, it was estimated that 28 per cent of the households in the country were below the poverty line as determined by the WHO/FAO calorie allowance. The SLPAP was aimed at these households. It was one of the first projects designed by the World Bank to make available large sums through NGOs, not primarily as compensation for the short term effects of structural adjustment, but in an attempt to alleviate long-term poverty.

The essence of the Project was that the Government of Sri Lanka (GOSL) would set up a Trust which was initially to be called the National Development Trust. A total of $87.5 million was allocated to the project over five years with $57.5 million coming from the World Bank, $10 million from the German Kreditanstalt für Wiederaufbau (KfW) and $2.5 million from the United Nations Development Programme (UNDP) for technical assistance. The balance was made available by the GOSL.

THE TRUST FUND AND THE POLITICAL PROCESS

The World Bank planned that the trustees of the Fund would be independ-ent of government and drawn from academe, the private sector and NGOs. However the trust deed called for the trustees to be appointed by the President of Sri Lanka and, de facto, to serve at the President's pleasure. Because of the Government's pervasive influence throughout society, establishing the Trust's independence was inevitably going to be difficult. The first Chairman was the then Secretary to the Treasury who, while being a senior civil servant, was also a close political confidant of the President.

At the time the loan agreement was being negotiated the then President, Ranasinghe Premadasa, insisted that the name of the Trust be changed to the '*Janasaviya* Trust Fund' (JTF). As the word '*Janasaviya*', meaning people's strength, was also the name of the President's own high-profile anti-poverty programme, most voters thought the World

Bank Project was part of the same programme. While this confusion had been foreseen, the Bank staff responsible were faced with either accepting the President's demand for the name change or possibly seeing the work and expense invested in the project preparation come to naught. The President, a wily negotiator, would have been reluctant to lose such a large inflow of funds but he managed to persuade the Bank's representatives that he would not back down. The Bank agreed to his request for the name change.

In August 1994, when the government changed, all trustees were asked to resign and did so. Prior to the election, when one of the leading trustees came out in support of the opposition, he felt bound to resign his position in the Trust. The Bank's intention to create an institution relatively insulated from political pressures had not succeeded. This experience raises a fundamental problem of World Bank assistance to NGOs. World Bank funding is generally in the form of loans to a sovereign state. Although the loans are highly concessionary and are in large measure de facto grants the government still undertakes a long term obligation. Minimising political influence from the government of the day on the use of funds is difficult as legally they have borrowed the money and are responsible for its use. It is ironic that the greater the degree of good governance in the sense of a democracy with a competing party structure, the more likely the case that there will be pressure to politicise the use of donor funding.

THE ROLE OF THE MANAGING DIRECTOR

In a country with a strong tradition of autocratic management whether in government, NGOs or the private sector, the appointment of the Managing Director was an important determinant of how the organisation would function. A prominent public servant, who had been the youngest ever individual to hold the rank of Secretary,[7] was chosen. He had previously been the high profile Chairman of the Youth Services Council, a quasi-governmental organisation. Because of his close connection to the Premadasa government and the then ruling party, he was viewed with some suspicion by most NGOs.

The choice of name of the Trust and the identity of the Chairman and Managing Director sent strong signals that the Trust would have little autonomy. At a time when many NGOs were profoundly alienated from government on a wide range of issues this made it likely that the Trust would find it difficult to establish a good relationship with the NGO community.

THE NGO COMMISSION

The launch of the JTF was followed almost immediately by the setting up of a Presidential Commission of Enquiry to investigate the alleged malpractice of NGOs. It was widely expected that the Commission's Report would result in criminal charges being filed and recommendations made for strengthened legislation to control NGOs. While the Terms of Reference of the Commission were to investigate the NGO sector as a whole, in practice only three NGOs were investigated in any depth. The media, both state and private sector, gave wide publicity to the work of the Commission creating an atmosphere of apprehension within the NGO community.

The principal organisation investigated was Sarvodaya Shramadana (see the chapter by Perera in this volume), by far the largest and best known NGO in the country. In most quarters it was felt that the NGO Commission was a quasi-legal persecution of Sarvodaya as its founder– leader, Dr A. T. Ariyaratne had become a strong critic of the government. Some of the investigative methods used by the police who were assisting the Commission involved arresting Sarvodaya employees under emergency regulations and interrogating them for long periods. The Commission incurred large expenses checking thousands of documents relating to Sarvodaya's work over many years.

In its final report the Commission made no formal findings but gave wide publicity to land sales that appeared to have benefited the Ariyaratne family, along with 28 other allegations. Although no criminal charges were laid, Sarvodaya's reputation was damaged and the Premadasa government's reputation for extra-legal and strong-arm tactics was reinforced. The practical result for the JTF was that it was not possible to work through the largest NGO in the country and many other NGOs wanted to keep their distance.

THE 'JOHN CLEESE'[8] POVERTY PROJECT

Under the Premadasa government relatively little funding from the JTF went through NGOs. Most funding passed through government officers to local organisations who were generally perceived as responsive to local political influence in the implementation of projects. Unable to work with NGOs but required by the World Bank to carry out social mobilisation of beneficiaries the JTF hired and gave elementary training to 1500 university graduates and school leavers. The process of recruiting, training, and managing this cadre of social mobilisers was an administrative nightmare. These JTF staff were often seen by villagers to be in competition with the social mobilisation programmes of other organisations already working under a variety of names.

Despite these difficulties enough of the programme was carried out to allow the JTF to hold at bay its critics in the government and the ruling party who wanted to see the funds disbursed quickly. Throughout this period the JTF management walked a tightrope trying to please the government in one direction and the World Bank and other donors in the other.

This predicament for the JTF eased dramatically when the political space in the country opened up with D. B. Wijetunge's assumption of office after the assassination of President Premadasa on 1 May 1993. In his first days in office President Wijetunge telephoned the Sarvodaya founder A. T. Ariyaratne and signalled that the government wanted a co-operative relationship with Sarvodaya and by implication the NGO community. However the JTF bureaucracy, conditioned by anti-NGO sentiment and not sure how long the apparent new freedom would last, did not respond immediately. The World Bank then made it clear that in the new political environment the JTF would be expected to work closely with NGOs. The World Bank pressed in particular for reconciliation with Sarvodaya and wanted an agreement signed while a World Bank mission was in the country. The result, a hastily prepared agreement calling for large scale funding to Sarvodaya, was signed without an assessment of Sarvodaya's needs and capacities or discussion with other members of the Sarvodaya Donor Consortium.

Towards the end of 1993 the JTF moved rapidly to recruit other NGOs. The immediate priority was to arrange for NGOs to take on contracts to provide a social mobilisation service in a defined geographic area. As extremely short deadlines were set and personnel experienced in vetting NGO capacity were not available the result was that NGOs with a wide range of experience and capacity were given funding.

The terms of these funding agreements included the obligation for the NGO to assume responsibility for the employment of the social mobilisers previously directly recruited by the JTF. The JTF recruitment of these employees had been primarily on the basis of educational qualifications, not usually the best way to select social mobilisers. This condition, of which many NGOs were privately critical, did not deter most NGOs from signing the agreements. With the prospects of untold World Bank riches in sight the NGOs concerned seemed prepared to accept what was offered. The rush to transfer the employment of the social mobilisers from the JTF to NGOs was dictated by the World Bank. A new task manager had ruled that JTF direct employment of social mobilisers was a back door method of increasing employment in the state sector, although at the time of recruitment the Bank did not express any concern.

The JTF bureaucracy did not have sufficient skill, time or inclination to develop equitable relationships with NGOs as partners and to nurse them according to their capacity. Most of the key staff had been recruited from government service or state owned banks with only a few having had experience of working with NGOs. Up to this point the history of the JTF looked like a John Cleese film on how not to run a poverty programme. However towards the end of 1993 a peculiar process started.

THE TURNAROUND

The JTF partners, NGOs many of which no other funding agency would have selected for funding on the scale supplied by the JTF, began to show surprising signs of ability to improve their competence and capability. Some of the JTF appointed social mobilisers, particularly those from families that could provide alternatives, drifted away. This left a group of young people, mostly from poorer rural families, many of whom proved to have more dedication and skill than could have been expected. Their training, while inadequate, had given them enough of a start that many were able to learn on the job, with little supervision or encouragement.

The main task of these social mobilisers was to identify interested target group households and encourage them to form self-help groups whose first activity would be to start a savings scheme. The development community has known for sometime that the poor could and would save but in this case the record of saving was noteworthy given the conditions under which these programmes were carried out.

According to the best available information the average member of the savings groups saved a little less than one dollar per month, a notable achievement given their low household incomes. While the strength and solidarity of these savings groups will have to be nurtured in the years to come, the results are better than the World Bank or the JTF had reason to expect.

THE JTF EXPERIENCE WITH CREDIT

Many members joined the savings groups in the expectation of qualifying for credit. However this credit was not the interest-free or subsidised interest rates common to NGO programmes in Sri Lanka. The credit on offer was at the 'market rate' with reference to the cost of formal banking sector credit. During 1992–4 this rate had been fixed at 21 per cent while inflation was officially in the range of 10–12 per cent. This represented real interest rates of 9–11 per cent. The utilisation of this credit was principally to purchase agricultural inputs. Credit for this purpose in most cases was previously supplied by local shop keepers or cooperative societies. For those with clear title to their land, bank credit was also sometimes available.

The provision of credit probably increased farmers' net income through reductions in the cost of credit but there is little evidence that the availability of this new source of credit produced a significant increase in new non-farm income generating activities. This apparent failure goes to the heart of the project's strategy for poverty alleviation. In designing the project the World Bank assumed that the availability of credit was the main constraint to self-employment and micro enterprise. However the limited experience of the JTF to date suggests that availability of markets for goods and services that can be produced on a small scale in rural areas may be a bigger constraint.

The Grameen Bank experience, on which the JTF was to some extent modelled, has produced evidence from their long-term borrowers showing that while the poor can be relied upon to repay their loans, when approached in the correct way, the availability of credit alone has not significantly raised household incomes. Those borrowers who were able to move away from the traditional forms of self-employment and were able to establish linkages with the urban markets have been most successful in increasing their incomes. The activities that the majority of the poor undertake are low-margin, low-profit activities. From a macroeconomic perspective the provision of new credit to this group is likely to pull in more producers into the market thus putting further pressure on margins and profits. This phenomenon has been witnessed in Sri Lanka.

Within the JTF there was a Human Resource and Institutional Development fund of $14.5 million. This fund was available to be used to train beneficiaries in new skills. But the emphasis of the JTF has not been on transferring new technologies that could allow the rural poor to enter areas of production with bigger margins and higher potential profits. Though other agencies and projects had done limited work in this area the JTF did not succeed in forming effective linkages during its first three years. It is here that the breakthroughs may be more likely to come in significantly increasing the incomes of the poor through self-employment.

THE CREDIT 'CATCH 22'

But even if one accepts that availability of credit is a key constraint in poverty alleviation, the JTF Project suffered from a design fault. The project's assumption was that the major constraint in providing credit to the poor was a shortage of capital. The project design set out stringent rules of past performance in loan repayment rates by credit institutions to be eligible to receive funding from the JTF for credit.

It is a truism of investment management that past performance is not a good indicator of future performance, particularly in a field where good performance is usually based on the competence and leadership of one or two key individuals. In fact it seems that few of the credit providers earmarked in the JTF project proposal met the criteria if strictly applied. Even when they did there was little evidence that these institutions had the capacity to expand lending on the scale envisaged.

The real capital shortage was in new organisations and institutions with an interest in making credit available but with no credit track record. The World Bank project design insisted on two years of good performance in order to get assistance. Without the capital they could not produce a track record and without the track record the new organisations could not be given capital. This 'Catch 22' made it difficult to expand credit provision. After several years of working within this constraint, a new Task Manager for the project did arrange a special permission from the World Bank to bring new credit partners into the programme but the limited scale of this provision meant that it was unlikely that much of the demand for credit that was generated by the social mobilisation work could be met during the lifetime of the project.

RURAL INFRASTRUCTURE

Construction of small scale rural infrastructure such as feeder roads, irrigation tanks and drinking water facilities has long been a core NGO activity in most countries. In Sri Lanka however such work had been carried out primarily by the government using local private sector contractors with political connections. The awarding of these projects was often a part of the political patronage system.

In the early years of the JTF the overriding priority for both the local management and the World Bank was to establish the JTF as a viable institution in the face of pressure from line ministries and other sections of government. The JTF management felt that the only way to do this was through rapid disbursement. The way to achieve rapid disbursement was to feed into the pre-existing system by working through government officials and politically connected institutions at the local level.

During 1994, responding to the new political atmosphere in the country, the JTF rural infrastructure programme underwent a dramatic shift. Local NGOs were given time and funding to work with communities to identify, prioritise and implement small infrastructure projects. The enhanced organisational capacity of local grassroots organisations that emerged may turn out to be one of the more lasting achievements of the JTF. This practice of trusting rural infrastructure construction to NGOs rather than politically connected contractors may come to be the standard approach. Another World Bank project, upgrading rural drinking water and sanitation facilities, worked in a similar fashion. As other donors and the government heed the lessons of these experiences the role of the contractor could be reserved for technically difficult projects beyond the engineering capacity of local organisations.

In addition to enhancing local organisational capacity these infrastructure projects created immediate short term wage employment while building infrastructure that may facilitate micro enterprises in the areas. Target group members working on rural infrastructure projects showed a willingness to save a portion of their earnings, sometimes up to 25 per cent. When sequenced properly, the exception rather than the rule, these infrastructure projects proved to be a good entry point for the wider anti-poverty programme.

COST–BENEFIT ANALYSIS VERSUS PARTICIPATORY METHODOLOGY

The World Bank was interested in evidence that this type of rural infrastructure will produce an economic rate of return. The cost–benefit methodology, in addition to being difficult to apply to such projects, can also be in conflict with the methodology of letting local people set priorities. For example, when questioned about why they have prioritised a particular section of road construction the first answer most often given by participants is that it will be possible to take sick people to hospital in a vehicle. How often such an event actually takes place is not known and even if it were it would be difficult to place a financial value on expediting such trips to the hospital.

It could be argued that in purely economic terms such a road is a poor investment as the existence of the road encourages the poor households to hire transport to take family members to hospital who would often be too old to contribute much to production. However when poor people made this their choice the JTF was responsive on the grounds that people should set their own priorities.

While rural feeder roads can have an economic value in moving products to market, if measured in these terms many of these roads would not be cost effective. There is little evidence that the existence of these roads has stimulated production in the area. However the psychological impact of feeling more connected to the wider society and its services seem to be uppermost in people's minds when selecting road projects.

These considerations illustrate the conflict between funding rural infrastructure according to strict economic criteria and people's wider priorities. This is one of the key issues that emerges when one marries the World Bank 'numbers culture' to the NGO participatory culture.

THE NUTRITION PROGRAMME

As designed by the World Bank the nutrition programme was to be a free-standing component providing on-site cooked nutritional supplements to children up to age five and pregnant and lactating mothers. The project design failed to take into account the social stigma attached to eating in a public feeding centre. The original design also did not give sufficient weight to the costs in time, energy expended and lost wages or home production involved in getting the mother and child to a feeding centre.

The nutrition programme as designed was a classic 'handout programme' in which the food was to be given at no cost to the mothers and children who showed up. While there may be a medical justification for providing on site feeding as the only way to raise nutrition levels quickly, this free handout tended to negate the principle of sustainability and local control that the JTF elsewhere espoused.

The JTF staff, who were opposed to the project design, made sympathetic noises to World Bank missions and then proceeded to carry out the nutrition programme as they saw fit. Instead of on site feeding of imported food, emphasis was put on training mothers to recognise and prepare the most nutritious and appropriate foods available locally. This education process, while time consuming and manpower intensive and while having only a limited immediate impact on levels of under-nutrition, has enhanced local understanding of good nutritional practice while avoiding the problems of feeding centres. However many of the poorest mothers are not able to afford to purchase the correct foods consistently and often lack the time to prepare them.

THE EXPERIENCE OF SANASA

SANASA, known in English as the Federation of Thrift and Credit Co-operative Societies, together with Sarvodaya, is one of the two large national NGOs with a distinct approach and an international reputation. SANASA had been seriously damaged in the 1980s when the government wrote off thousands of housing loans that the organisation had made using United States Agency for International Development (USAID) funding. As a result of this experience the SANASA national level leadership was reluctant to get involved with the project but invited the JTF to approach its district level units who would be free to sign individual agreements with the JTF if they wished. For the national leadership this was a delaying tactic to gain time while it worked out how to avoid the JTF.

However, the national leadership of SANASA did not anticipate the aggressive way the JTF would cultivate the district officers offering incentives such as salary supplements, office equipment and motorbikes and payments to attend meetings. The result was that the discipline and direction that the national level had exercised over the organisation and which had been largely responsible for its success began to break down. This outcome, unforeseen by SANASA, forced the organisation to seek a national level agreement with the JTF which they hoped would reinforce the authority of the centre and its traditional role as guide and conscience of the movement.

This example suggests that when large sums of money are involved and when the staff concerned feel pressure to disburse there is a danger of unintended consequences which can damage an organisation while intending to offer assistance.

FUNDING TO NGOs

Much of the concern expressed about the impact of the JTF has centred around what such a large amount of money would do to the NGOs in the country. The concern about the magnitude of the JTF is part of a wider concern about the rapid increase in donor funding to NGOs worldwide. While the $87.5 million available to the JTF was to be spread over five years and although much of the money will remain unutilised there is no doubt that the arrival of the JTF stimulated a shift in funding arrangements for many NGOs in Sri Lanka.

Prior to the JTF almost all funding for Sri Lankan NGOs came from international NGOs or bilateral donors. America, Canada, the United Kingdom and the Scandinavian countries have been particularly active in funding NGOs in Sri Lanka and elsewhere. With the launch of the JTF there was a major new source of funds for national and local NGOs. NGOs appreciated the fact that JTF funding decisions had short lead times and the demands for proposals and reporting were less extensive than those from other sources of funds. On the negative side NGOs continued to be concerned that political criteria would be applied in evaluating performance.

From time to time local members of parliament would make difficulties for JTF partners by endeavouring to ensure that assistance is aimed at their supporters. The fact that politicians sometimes resist the emergence of alternative sources of assistance is evidence that the channelling of funds through NGOs can increase pluralism in society. It could mean, for instance, that you might be able to get a road built to your village even if the village did not vote for the party in power. This reduction in the dominance of the state, even in a small regard, is a contribution to building what is sometimes called civil society. The overall additional capacity that has been emerging in hundreds of grassroots organisations and scores of NGOs may prove to be a much bigger boost.

While JTF funding was highly prescriptive, following closely the small group formation for savings and credit model, NGOs as a whole did not object. Smaller and younger NGOs seemed to be at a loss for a clear strategy and methodology and welcomed JTF input. Other larger organisations, such as Sarvodaya and SANASA, which certainly have their own strategies and methodologies, also did not publicly object to adopting the JTF model (à la Grameen Bank) perhaps because they had some concern that their 'whole village' approach, which tries to work with the whole village as a unit, had not been fully successful in reaching the poor.

CASH SHORTAGES AMIDST PLENTY

Although in principle the JTF had access to more funding than could be utilised, in practice the organisation suffered recurring cash shortages. The Treasury, through which all foreign aid is channelled, was subject to cash limits to meet IMF agreements. At other times the actual mechanics of getting parliamentary or cabinet approval was a problem. For these reasons the flow of funds to the JTF has been frequently disrupted.

The result has been that NGOs did not receive the funding they had been promised in a timely manner. This caused cancelled training programmes, staff of NGOs not receiving salaries on time and people not receiving loans in time to plant. These cash flow difficulties, endemic in government programmes, are relatively new to NGOs. If the NGO community comes to rely on World Bank funding channeled through government treasuries these problems will have to be solved if major damage to the credibility of NGOs is to be avoided.

Some NGOs, such as Sarvodaya, have perhaps suffered cutbacks in some of their traditional sources of funds due in part to the availability of JTF funding. While the Sarvodaya Donor Consortium had made clear its concern about Sarvodaya's poor performance for some time, the availability of alternative funding has been reported to have made it easier for the traditional donors to cut back.

CAPACITY BUILDING AND SERVICE DELIVERY

The most significant impact of JTF funding has been the rapid growth and expansion of many of the JTF partner organisations. In the NGO world where the 'small is beautiful' philosophy is a sacred tenet this rapid growth is suspect. At a time when some commentators are calling for NGOs to 'scale down in terms of size and growth in order to scale up in terms of long-term impact', this trend will be questioned (Edwards, 1994c). When there is a finite amount of managerial and administrative ability, overfunding causes poor-quality implementation and is an invitation to waste and corruption. A significant portion of the JTF early grants have undoubtedly been for activities whose cost effectiveness is at best unproved and sometimes suspect.

But the surprising outcome is how quickly the NGO sector in Sri Lanka, which is weak compared to stronger NGO networks in other South Asian countries, has been able to respond to the availability of funding. Skills for planning, budgeting, accounting and monitoring performance remain inadequate but have improved. While it will take years for this expansion of NGO activity to consolidate and be properly evaluated the preliminary impression is that Sri Lanka has witnessed a significant leap in NGO capacity. That capacity would expand to match the funding available should not be surprising. The normal market forces of supply and demand apply even to the provision of services in the NGO sector. The skills of planning, budgeting, accounting, monitoring and reporting that the JTF is endeavouring to build up are themselves sometimes disparaged as part of a project mentality to do with service delivery. The argument is that projects and service delivery are not the answer to poverty.

It may be that the day when northern NGOs should be running projects in developing countries may be ending. But it is equally clear that after all the advocacy work has been done, all the relevant information exchanged, the workshops attended, and the networks networked, somebody will still have to give the good news to the poor and explain exactly how it has been decided they are to get out of poverty. In the meantime it seems that the poor themselves have set as their priority what is disparaged as mere service delivery.

The JTF was unashamedly committed to service delivery, not really aware that this approach was considered counter-productive in some circles. While the cost effectiveness of this approach is still to be proven, the preliminary evidence is that however weak the NGOs prove to be they will be more efficient than state delivery. This appears to be the case as the personnel in NGOs realise that the penalty for non-performance is greater for them than for personnel working in the state sector. If NGOs prove not to be more efficient than the state sector then it will certainly be easier to dismantle the NGO managed programmes than it would have been had the same amount of money been invested in building up state programmes. This gives donors greater flexibility and leverage to achieve their objectives.

The concern that such provision provides a 'patchwork quilt of services of varying quality'[9] is true in the Sri Lankan case. The implicit assumption that government provision would be of more equal quality would be hard to verify. On the ground one finds considerable variation in the quality of government services, a phenomenon which often is directly correlated to the distance from the capital.

The fundamental issue is whether government service or NGO employment is best calculated to engender good performance from staff over a span of years. The penalties for bad performance are virtually zero in government service. The penalties for poor NGO performance are weak but the potential to raise them is greater with NGOs. It may be true as Edwards (1994c) and others have argued that rapid growth may distract from the 'depth of learning, accountability and organisational change required to promote high-quality work'. But this perspective tends to indicate a remoteness from the harsh reality of families in serious poverty demanding a way out.

The NGO objective should not be 'quality' for its own sake. NGOs should be looking to make an impact. Impact is the product of quality multiplied by quantity. Raising both parts of the equation is of course desirable but quantity should not be disparaged. High-quality NGO programmes that cannot be replicated are tokenism, often of more benefit to the organisers than the poor.

THE EVOLUTION OF THE JTF

A serious problem has been the managerial limitations of the JTF itself. As there were strict limits on the number and type of personnel imposed by the World Bank, the JTF has been forced to operate as a highly centralised organisation with no regional offices. This made building close relationships with NGOs difficult. The level of supervision that the JTF was able to muster to monitor the use of its funds was low. On site visits were infrequent and most often the JTF staff visiting NGOs did not have the experience and training to recognise problems early and offer advice.

Although the JTF had funding to create a strong management information system this was still under development three years into the project. Data collection and analysis was weak. Financial information was sufficient to pass audit requirements but the limitations to the management accounting system made it difficult to get access to financial information by partner, geographic area or type of activity.

The World Bank Project design set up the JTF in functional divisions with no strategy to promote synergy or integration between the various interventions. This has proved to be a major liability as each Division cultivated its own client NGOs carrying out that Division's sectoral programme. Despite considerable resistance the JTF eventually managed to get the Bank to accept the concept of one NGO carrying out all aspects of the programme in a defined geographic area. This approach had the potential to reduce costs in duplicated offices, staff and travel and obviate the need to parachute NGOs into an area to carry out a particular programme, but was not fully implemented during the first three years of the project.

Despite these serious problems the organisation learned from its experience and continued to improve. The starting point of expertise and experience was low. In an ideal world no one would have entrusted so much money to such an organisation but it has turned out better than could have been expected.

THE PERFORMANCE OF THE WORLD BANK

With the Sri Lanka Poverty Alleviation Project the World Bank made a major step in attempting to tackle directly the poverty of those not yet benefited by the process of economic growth. For this the Bank and the individuals responsible should be congratulated. But due to lack of operational experience in this type of programme, the project design had serious flaws and left little flexibility or local management discretion. Through frequent supervision missions the Bank tried to ensure that the project design was closely followed. The level of micro management of the project at times reached ridiculous levels with 15-member supervisory missions leaving hundreds of pages of notes and instructions, much of it based on an inadequate understanding of the situation.

On the positive side, if the Bank had not been able to use its influence the heavy politicisation of the project would not have been challenged. If the Bank learns to manage and supervise projects better and ensures that essential agreed policies are implemented without taking away a sense of local ownership and responsibility, its capacity for poverty alleviation would be significantly enhanced.

The project has been damaged by a rapid turnover of the World Bank staff responsible for its management. In the period 1993–4 the project had four 'Task Managers', the job title of the Bank staff person responsible for the project. All of the Task Managers had limited or no experience of managing poverty alleviation projects. The World Bank continues to recruit its staff based primarily on their academic qualifications and analytical ability. But for innovative projects such as the JTF, the Bank needs people experienced in team building and project management in similar programmes.

Because of the huge cultural gap between World Bank officials and Sri Lankan NGO staff, the potential for creating miscommunications and resentment is great. A story that forms part of the JTF history and encapsulates this gulf is provided in Box 11.1.

Box 11.1   Do as I say, not as I do

A World Bank official flies to Colombo and lodges at the most expensive hotel in the country. He has a car and driver at his disposal. He calls a meeting of NGOs receiving World Bank funding at very short notice. The NGO leaders travel to the meeting, mostly by public buses, some travelling overnight to get to the meeting on time. In the meeting the World Bank official launches a tirade about the need to be cost-conscious and not to waste the World Bank funding. The NGOs seem resentful and restless but everyone is too polite to point out to him that the silver pen he is using to gesticulate had the letters 'CONCORDE' written down the side. Even provincial NGO leaders can guess where he got it and the level of his travel expenses.

Edwards and Hulme (1994:26) have made a strong case that 'it is the quality of the relationship between the grassroots organisations, NGOs, donors and governments that determines whether patterns of funding and accountability promote or impede the wider goals of all these organisations in development'. In the JTF experience to date, relationships at all these levels have been poor. This, as much as any other factor, has wasted energy and limited performance. The fundamental challenge of how to marry the financing of the World Bank to the NGO culture using a government dominated institution as the intermediary will always be an inexact science but if the Bank can learn from its experience there is no intrinsic reason why it cannot succeed.

CAPACITY, COMPETENCE, COMPETITION AND THE CONTRACT CULTURE

While the capacity of individual NGOs and the sector generally to implement aspects of a poverty alleviation programme has improved under JTF sponsorship, not all NGOs have improved equally. The JTF, not surprisingly, holds a portfolio of partners that range from excellent to poor. In a free market the JTF would discontinue funding to the poorest performers and expand the funding to the top performers. While this process may one day begin it requires a management team secure in their authority and isolated from political pressures. Any organisation whose funding was terminated would run to the local Member of Parliament and claim an injustice. As the process of accessing management capability in poverty alleviation is viewed as being highly subjective only those organisations who have been proven to be financially corrupt were terminated in the first three years.

The allocation of funding based on management capacity alone would favour the larger organisations who have experienced staff with professional skills. Many of the smaller more locally based organisations whose performance is weak may take longer to improve but in the long run may provide a distinctive service that may be of value in the overall development process of the country.

The availability of JTF funding has encouraged the start up of new NGOs of whom it might be said that their initial purpose was to attract JTF funding. Whatever the initial motives of the leaders of these organisations might have been, they should be judged on their performance.[10] The introduction of these new NGOs into the market-place has promoted a small element of competition among Sri Lankan NGOs that may prove to be healthy. Sri Lankan NGOs have been dominated by a few leading individuals and organisations. The JTF has allowed a new flowering of leadership that would never have had an opportunity under previous arrangements.

Some suggest that only NGOs with a track record should be funded. This in effect creates a cartel that allows the established organisations to monopolise funding and makes it impossible for new NGOs to develop. In the long run the older organisations become complacent. While NGOs are uncomfortable with the idea of competition and are much happier talking about collaboration there is no reason why in general NGOs are exempt from the general rule that competition stimulates performance.

However, there are types of competition that would be unhealthy such as running two social mobilisation organisations in the same community. As the social mobilisation process is essentially to encourage self-discipline and self-reliance, two organisations competing for the same members would tend to undermine that process as well as be wasteful of resources.

Many of the new NGOs are headed by individuals with experience of working in the older NGOs, particularly Sarvodaya. It may be that in the long run one of Sarvodaya's most important contributions will be to have developed managers who then left and set up on their own. At least four of the JTF's strongest partners have this background (see Chambers, 1992, for a discussion of the diffusion of NGO personnel).

Some NGO commentators worry about the rise of the 'contract culture' and the apparent loss of autonomy of NGOs (Edwards and Hulme, 1994). With the exception of Sarvodaya, SANASA and a few other organisations, most NGOs in Sri Lanka have always been dominated by their funders who have set the priorities. Only the strongest organisations, with international reputations, can influence their donors and even then the extent is hardly sufficient to speak of autonomy. One can lament that 'he who pays the piper calls the tune', but it is not clear that this problem is getting worse with the entry of the World Bank into the NGO funding picture.

It might be a better world if the World Bank, bilateral organisations and governments were more open to the concerns of NGOs but NGOs also need to learn that they do not necessarily have the best solution to all problems. The NGO sector needs to be as open about their failures as they expect the Bank to be. NGOs do have the right to be part of the debate and it seems that both in the context of Sri Lanka and internationally this is taking place. There is nothing to stop NGOs continuing to lobby for changing the rules of the game while simultaneously taking part. In fact if you are a player you are more likely to get a seat at the table to discuss the rules.

For better or worse the World Bank, as huge as an elephant, is loose in the NGO jungle. We can only hope that in addition to having a long memory, the elephant proves to be a quick learner. If it does, the elephant can help mightily to reduce poverty and build more self-reliant and prosperous communities. If the elephant is not a quick learner however, as our friends in Africa say, a lot of grass will get trampled.[11]

Notes

1. Roland Hodson was employed by the World Bank as an Advisor to the World Bank funded Sri Lanka Poverty Alleviation Project from October 1992 to March 1995. This paper is an insider's account of the project's experience. The views expressed are those of Roland Hodson alone and in no way carry the endorsement of the World Bank.
2. *World Development Report 1980*, Oxford, New York: Oxford University Press. From the Introduction.
3. 'Hunger, Poverty and the World Bank': Keynote Address to World Bank Conference on Overcoming Global Hunger, 29 November 1993, Washington, DC, page 7.
4. Sometimes referred to in this chapter as 'the Bank'.
5. In this context NGOs means non-governmental, non-profit development organisations based in both the North and the South. However, in the rest of the chapter the term NGOs refers to Sri Lankan NGOs.
6. *World Development Report 1980*, p. 89.
7. Highest rank in civil service equivalent to Permanent Secretary in the British system.
8. John Cleese is a British comedian who makes humorous training films showing how not to run an organisation. He is perhaps better known for his role in the TV series 'Fawlty Towers' which shows how not to run a hotel.
9. M. Edwards, 'International NGOs and Southern Governments in the "New World Order": Lessons of Experience at the Programme Level', paper presented at the INTRAC workshop on Governance, Democracy and Conditionality, The Netherlands, June 1993, cited in M. Edwards and D. Hulme 'NGOs and Development: Performance and Accountability in the "New World Order"', a background paper presented to an International Workshop of the same name, University of Manchester, 27–9 June 1994.
10. It would be equally unhelpful to speculate on the motives of the academics who speculate about the motives of NGO leaders.
11. 'When the elephants play the grass gets trampled'. See also Hulme (1994) on 'institutional learning' at the World Bank.

Part III

NGO–State Relationships: Reluctant Partners Revisited?

12 The Associative Phenomenon in the Arab World: Engine of Democratisation or Witness to the Crisis?[1]

Mohsen Marzouk

Arab NGOs and researchers are confronted today by a difficult dilemma: despite a huge increase in their numbers over the last few years and the recognition by national governments (however speculative) of their autonomy, NGOs as a whole have been unable to play a significant role in speeding up the incipient processes of social and political democratisation in the region. Why is this so? Is it because of factors internal to the NGO 'movement', or the political and social situation which prevails in the Arab world (the authoritarian nature of political regimes and the weakness of civil society), or a mixture of both? At the root of this dilemma is the fact that increasing expectations are being placed on NGOs in Arab countries at a time when the nature of NGOs, the distribution of political power, and the economic choices that have characterised the long years without democracy, have not changed radically. Attempts by Arab countries to adapt to the paradigms of the New Policy Agenda outlined by Hulme and Edwards in Chapter 1 (free markets and, where convenient perhaps, political pluralism) have given birth to an apparent opening – a narrow margin of freedom unwillingly granted under pressure – rather than to fundamental changes. In this context, it would be surprising if the expansion of NGOs in the Arab world *did* become an agent of democratisation; thus far, the evolution of NGOs resembles a horizontal accumulation of organisations that has had little decisive effect on the established political and social landscape.

The purpose of this chapter is to demonstrate that the factors which hold back the development of Arab NGOs are part of a wider pattern linked to political and social systems in the region. It is divided into three sections.

First comes a general overview of the processes underlying the current condition of Arab NGOs. The second part of the analysis provides a quantitative and qualitative account of NGOs in the region today. Third, the chapter explores the relationships which exist between Arab NGOs and their political environments. Before embarking on the first of these sections, it is important to clarify the conditions under which Arab NGOs can hope to become agents of social change. Antonios (1994) identifies two relevant indicators:

(a) the very existence of these organisations – provided that they are not controlled by the state – allows for greater diversity in opinions, practices and social actors and thus gives the democratisation process a solid infrastructure;

(b) the way power is exercised in NGOs and the way in which NGOs are related to power structures in society are important indicators. If NGOs themselves are democratic and genuinely representative of marginalised groups, their contribution to the democratic process is likely to be stronger. (Edwards and Hulme, 1995)

To these two indicators must be added a third: the state of democratic evolution in civil society. Civil society is defined here as the field in which public social interactions take place which are not linked to a quest for economic profit, a direct struggle for political power or to the executive power of the state. Civil society is the fundamental space of action for NGOs. NGOs, together with other civic institutions such as trade unions and political parties, make up the basic components and structures of civil society, but civil society is not merely the sum of such structures and institutions. Rather, it is a field for social relationships and negotiations governed by an ever-changing set of interrelationships both within and in relation to the state. These interrelationships are crucial, but what are they and what repercussions do they have for the evolution of NGOs in Arab countries? To answer this question it is necessary briefly to go back into history.

THE HISTORICAL PROCESS: THE STATE, 'MASTER OF THE GAME'

The history of government recognition of the role played by NGOs is roughly the same in most Arab countries. From political Independence to the beginning of the 1980s, NGOs were under state control. Since then, attitudes have become more tolerant. NGOs have been accepted as autonomous and legitimate actors in social life, and in some countries, in political life. This change came about as a result of wider developments in the relationship between state and society.

The First Period: from Independence to the Early 1980s

Immediately after the emergence of Independent Arab nation states, NGOs were considered as vehicles for political mobilisation in support of totalitarian governments based on single-party or military regimes. Organisations for young people, women, writers, journalists, lawyers, trade unions, and others were all forced to comply with guidelines set out in their entirety by their respective governments. In order to set up an NGO prior authorisation was necessary. Custom-made laws granted governments considerable prerogatives to control the organisation, or even manage it indirectly. Governments also benefited from coercive legal powers which gave them authority to disband individual NGOs. The dominant attitude towards NGOs was suspicion. Despite popular, socialist and revolutionary rhetoric, many Arab governments had no qualms about using overt police control. In Algeria, for example, a circular of March 1964 ordered the authorities to undertake an exhaustive inquiry into NGOs 'in order to stop the formation of associations that, under the guise of social, cultural or artistic activity ... could undermine security inside and outside the State' (Babadji, 1991:233). This situation was not specific to Algeria: similar cases were reported in most Maghreb and Machrek Arab countries.

The Second Period: the 1980s and 1990s

The late 1970s were crucial years in determining the economic, political and social choices of Arab governments. The failure of welfare states was almost complete: economies were in crisis; and societies were unbalanced by strong anti-establishment currents protesting against methods of political organisation that could no longer maintain their own unity and hegemonic control. Under internal pressure (from popular protests) and external pressure (exerted by financial creditors), Arab governments found themselves forced to adopt a set of partial reforms which opened new prospects for NGOs in the region. Three changes were particularly important: in the role of the state, the mode of political domination and the choice of economic strategies.

The Role of the State

Since the beginning of the 1980s, the role of the welfare state has been questioned by Arab regimes. The alarming economic situation in most Arab countries left no option other than to conform to the structural adjustment programmes offered by the World Bank and IMF, which required a diminishing role for the public sector and a liberalisation of markets to promote private-sector initiative. As elsewhere, adjustment has had short-term social costs, as in Bahrain where public demonstrations followed the recent removal of subsidies on basic foodstuffs. The state's withdrawal has been concentrated in sectors previously considered as strategic: transport, health care, education and the development of underprivileged communities. The recent resurgence of NGO activity in the Arab world is linked directly to the retreat of the state and the revival of the Liberal creed of which it forms a component (Babadji, 1991).

Political Reform

The reorientation of the role of the state has been accompanied by wider political reforms. Single-party regimes were denounced as an underlying cause of the general crisis, and opposition groups were invited to play a more active role in the public arena. Democracy was elevated, in countless speeches, to the highest rank in the hierarchy of political values. Initiated in the early 1980s, this opening remained incomplete, failing to move beyond the institution of a timid political pluralism which has not fundamentally challenged the old system of political domination. What is more, with the exception of Tunisia, the changes were not accompanied by the departure of the political leaders who had been responsible for previous policies. In fact, these formal improvements were linked to a tactical withdrawal by state interests in the face of the violent popular uprisings that broke out in several Arab countries during the period from the late 1970s to the early 1980s (in Egypt, Tunisia, Algeria, Mauritania, Jordan and Morocco). However, the reforms did enable NGOs to speed up their evolution, sometimes at a very rapid pace. In Algeria, the 1988 riots led to an extraordinary proliferation of committees and organisations. Djeghloul (cited in Babadji, 1991) mentions that 'in two months more associations were set up than in twenty-five years' (see Section III).

Civil Society

In parallel to the withdrawal of the state, Arab civil societies started to demand greater involvement by the population in the management of their countries. Elites were able to speak out in favour of a democratic culture, against the system of domination that had prevailed over the past decades. A global context in turmoil, with the fall of the Berlin Wall and the resulting globalisation of democratic values and liberal economics, furthered this process. Today, changes in favour of a more liberal organisation of society, a more democratic political system, more efficient governance and new rules for the involvement of people in development have entered the discourse and programmes of most public actors, almost to the extent of becoming historical imperatives in themselves. However, these new paradigms have not influenced the practice of state-sponsored development in any serious fashion. The spaces for expression offered to civil society were demarcated by a clear line: 'do not speak against the regime in power'. Since involvement in formal politics was restricted in this way, NGOs and other actors in civil society offered practically the only possible alternative for those keen to become more involved in public life.

The social and political opening up offered by Arab regimes to their populations over the last decade is paradoxical. Although the need for continued moves toward democracy has been admitted, the only alternative offered is a reorganisation of existing structures of state authority. In this context, the evolution of NGOs may be little more than a temporary solution imposed by economic recession and political crisis, which NGOs themselves help to manage and mitigate. Instead of reflecting a genuine evolution of civil societies, this process may divert societies from the road to their fulfilment. The result may be an NGO sector which is deformed, unable to become a real engine of democratisation.

THE EVOLUTION OF ARAB NGOs

Within the context of a superficial adaptation of Arab systems to new global realities, NGOs have grown rapidly over a short period of time. The result is a kaleidoscope of organisations which are very heterogeneous in terms of their activities, orientations and relationships with government. A broad classification would include:

1   traditional caritative organisations, usually with a religious base. In some countries (such as Syria) these organisations have been taken over by the state; elsewhere they have acted as a springboard for the formation of more radical NGOs;

2   mass organisations and their derivatives (see below).

Figure 12.1 Number of NGOs in Arab countries, 1988–93

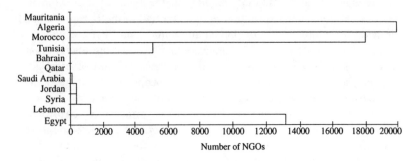

Number of NGOs

Source: Kandil (1994) and El Taller (1995).

3   NGOs in the conventional sense of the term, subdivided into interme-
    diary humanitarian and development agencies, and membership
    organisations.

Quantitative Development

In terms of size and number, the growth of NGOs varies greatly between
different countries in the Arab world (see Figure 12.1). These variations
have their roots in different political situations. In countries which have
experienced political liberalisation over the last few years, the number of
NGOs has grown rapidly, for example in Algeria, Morocco, Egypt and
Tunisia. Elsewhere (in the countries of the Arabian Gulf, for example),
the continuation of relatively closed political systems has restricted NGO
development.

    The sheer speed of NGO development in the region shown by these
figures may indicate that this process is not the fruit of a natural maturing
of Arab societies. In less than a decade the number of NGOs in some Arab
countries has nearly doubled, as shown in Table 12.1.

Development NGOs are a Minority

Among the thousands of NGOs which are legally registered, the number
of active organisations is very small. 'It is difficult to distinguish in the
current proliferation those that are durable from those that are short-lived'
(Babadji, 1991:235). The most influential organisations remain those
closely linked with governments, having emerged or continued from pre-

Table 12.1 Quantitative evolution of NGOs in four Arab countries

Country	Number of NGOs (1980s)	Number of NGOs (1990s)
The West Bank and Gaza	272 (1987)	444 (1992)
Jordan	221 (1980)	587 (1992)
Egypt	11 471 (1985)	13 239 (1991)
Tunisia	1 886 (1988)	5 186 (1991)

Source: El Taller (1995).

vious mass organisations of women, students and others. Closer to parastatals than true NGOs, they have historically been organisations for monitoring and mass mobilisation for the benefit of the regimes in power. As a rule, their orientations reflect government programmes. In some Arab countries, these organisations are changing their plans and adopting a new discourse which places them in the position of NGOs (in the modern sense of the word) in the eyes of foreign funders. However, this conversion does not seem to have seriously challenged either their role or the nature of the relationships they maintain with the authorities.

New associations, which are the closest to the definition of NGOs used in this book and elsewhere, are a recent phenonemon. They reflect the democratic aspirations of the Arab present, are prepared to fight for their autonomy, refer to Liberal as well as Islamic ideology and values, and constitute potential agents of social change. Their activities include:

- a new conception of the struggle for the integration of women in the development process;
- the protection of the environment through education and awareness raising;
- participatory social development;
- the integration of young people and marginalised groups into the development process;
- the protection of human rights.

These NGOs are clearly in a minority in all Arab countries. In Tunisia, for example, women's organisations and development NGOs represent only 2.5 per cent of the 5186 associations recorded by official statistics (see Table 12.2).

Table 12.2   Tunisian associations, by category, 1992

Category	Number	Percentage
Women	2	0.09
Sport	822	15.85
Scientific	115	2.21
Charitable aid, social	509	9.81
Development	126	2.42
Club type	400	7.71
General	41	0.79
Cultural/artistic	3 171	61.12

Source: Boularès (1993).

Lack of Coordination

A further weakness of Arab NGO development is the fact that it is so scattered. Seldom do associations have common structures for action. Despite their increasing numbers, they do not meet the requirements of a *movement*: mass-based programmes, sustainable internal dynamics and, as a result of the interaction between these two components, a driving intellectual or ideological force. The word 'movement' here does not refer to a single standard approach, but to a collective dynamic in which members pursue common objectives and draw their motivations from more or less similar references. The only credible experiences of NGOs working together in this way have been in Lebanon and Palestine, where state authority is weak, if not non-existent. In Palestine, the Israeli occupation and the absence of a recognised government allowed more space for NGO activities to develop on a large scale in basic services (such as health and agriculture), and encouraged Palestinian NGOs to forge themselves into a strong network with common principles and a code of practice. It is significant that Palestinian NGOs only started to fear for their autonomy after the Israeli-Palestinian peace agreements were signed in 1993. In Lebanon, the weakening of the state following the long civil war (as well as the heterogeneous make-up of the community) have laid the foundations for large-scale action by NGOs which are currently developing common action through networks such as the Lebanese NGO forum and the Collective of Lebanese NGOs.

Poor coordination among NGOs is a major handicap in the face of the strength of political elites in the Arab world. NGOs lack the unity that would allow them to represent a real force in civil society, able to mobilise large sements of the population to exert pressure for change. Why do these structural weaknesses exist? Preliminary research by El Taller suggests that the most important factors lie in the nature of the *political environment* that surrounds NGOs in different Arab countries.

NGOS IN THEIR POLITICAL ENVIRONMENT

The general attitude of Arab governments toward NGOs rests on a contradiction. Most have adopted a new discourse and have reviewed legislation in a more liberal direction, while simultaneously maintaining authoritarian control over political power. Legislation allows governments to exercise control over NGOs on a continuum between informal sanction, legal penalties and dissolution. However, the reverse is also possible. In Egypt, for example, the government adopts a more liberal attitude toward NGOs: the restrictive laws inherited from the 1960s which regulate the NGO sector have not been changed, but they are being implemented with more reserve – a 'kind of acrobatics which leaves more room for manoeuvre ... though with conditions' (Antonios, 1994:7).

Arab regimes are using new strategies and official recognition to encourage NGO expansion, replacing old methods that have been undermined by past crises. When NGOs are tolerated, it is because their aims do not oppose, or may even support, those of the state. However, official attitudes are not always negative, with NGO–government relations varying along a spectrum from mutual ignorance, through complementarity (for example in service-provision), to outright confrontation. Different regimes are aware of the opportunities provided by NGOs and they encourage a wide fringe of associations 'under supervision' which 'enable them to support and reorient NGOs toward actions which are subsidiary or complementary for the Administration' (Ghazali, 1991:250). Such NGOs have no intention of opposing or influencing 'technical or political orientation or decisions in their fields of action; moreover they can act as bodies that absorb, use or simply neutralise the human resources that they gather. As such, NGOs can represent a link in the existing chain of regulating mechanisms, a "locking device" which allows the implementation of one-way control over the flow of new demands from the people who have been mobilised' (Ghazali, 1991:250). In this sense, Arab regimes may act as a brake on the development of NGOs in the region. It is revealing to note that only where the state is weak (as in the examples of Lebanon and

Palestine cited above) have NGOs been able to play a significant social and political role.

Attempts to co-opt Arab NGOs politically do not only come from the regime in power, but from other political actors, including the Opposition. For these actors, NGOs are perceived as instruments that can be used to expand political support and influence. The origins of this attitude lie in the excessive politicisation of public life in the Arab world. The most striking examples of this process are the Islamic movements which, by establishing their own organisations and infiltrating others over many years, have managed to cement an impressive network to be used for their own purposes, for example the Islamic Liberation Front in Algeria and the Islamic Brotherhood in Egypt. Such movements are essentially populist political parties with an autocratic style and a political agenda very different to the newly-emerging Arab NGOs.

The repercussions of excessive politicisation are clear. Instead of promoting democratic culture and behaviour within their organisations, NGOs reproduce the same authoritarian structures that govern Arab political and social life in general. This occurs for two reasons. First, as Antonios (1994:11) notes for Egypt, 'an overwhelming majority of associations are managed according to traditional models that do not encourage real involvement'. They use the same models of authority that prevail in society generally. The overwhelming majority of Arab NGOs surveyed in El Taller's (1995) research exhibited centralisation of power, strong hierarchical tendencies, weak internal democracy (with general assemblies not meeting regularly), and poor internal communications. Second, the NGO sector has become a means of social and political advancement which offers a greater chance of success than traditional routes, which have become saturated because of the ossification of most Arab political systems.

WHAT ARE THE PROSPECTS FOR THE FUTURE?

Is this a lost cause? Could it be that Arab NGOs are unable to respond to the requirements of an irreversible democratisation of Arab societies? There is some evidence (some of which has been cited in this chapter) to suggest that the answer to both questions is 'yes'. However, the reality is more complex than this. Arab societies, despite all the problems that hinder their development, hold out sound opportunities for emancipation and the evolution of civil society. The negative characteristics of many Arab NGOs cited above are not terminal. Of course there is a difference between the *acceptance* of democratic rules and their *implementation*, whether within a specific NGO or more broadly in the realm of state–society relations. But the very fact that social and political democratisation is recognised as a need is a step forward. This applies in the first place to Arab political powers. While it is true that Arab regimes adopt the democratic discourse at least in part as a cosmetic exercise, cracks are appearing in the political system as a result of this acceptance. Arab NGOs could be the first to benefit from the changes which are occurring as a result of this process. Unlike traditional political and trade union actors, NGOs can (if they make the necessary effort) draw their legitimacy from a new type of social or community representativeness, based on genuine participation.

The present dilemma in Arab countries can be summed up in the following paradox: on the one hand, states are so weakened that they have become unable to perform effectively in providing services and guaranteeing the welfare of their citizens. On the other hand, Arab societies, although they are undoubtedly evolving, have not yet reached a level at which non-state actors are able to fulfill these functions. In order to escape from this impasse, two paths are being followed simultaneously. The first is institutionalised, ordered and systematic; it is led by the state (from within the state) which has opted for a new discourse and a new practice which advocates democracy and liberalism. The second path is disorderly, radical and often violent. It comes from the deprived social strata and marginalized intellectuals who rely on the popular ideological references provided by Sharia Islam. In the face of these movements, Arab states in crisis become less and less able to prevent the haemorrhageing of their authority or to oppose radical change. The resolution of these dilemmas will depend on the ability of all the actors in the Arab world, including NGOs, to turn this stagnant, crisis-ridden situation into a transition towards a real democratic change. The key question for the next decade is how best to go about this immense challenge.

Note

1.   The original term used in this chapter to describe the broad range of non-governmental institutions in the Arab World was 'associative phenomenon'. For the sake of brevity, this has been replaced throughout the text by 'NGOs', meaning the full range of non-governmental actors in civil society and not simply intermediary NGOs.

13 NGO–State Relations in Post-Mao China

Jude Howell

INTRODUCTION

Following the consolidation of Deng Xiaoping's power in December 1978 the reformers were able to embark upon a radical programme of economic reform. The key elements of the new development strategy included the decollectivisation of agriculture, the nurturing of a private sector, price liberalisation and the opening of China's doors to global capitalist forces. Whilst leading industrial countries were lamenting the devastating impact of global recession upon their economies, China was celebrating a GDP growth rate of 13.4 per cent in 1993 (Levinson and Wehrfritz, 1994).

These dramatic changes in the Chinese economy have set in motion a process of social transformation. New socioeconomic groups such as rich farmers, traders, entrepreneurs and Chinese managers in foreign companies have begun to emerge. The relaxation of controls over urban migration has encouraged millions to seek their fortunes in the coastal cities, creating a new underclass of petty criminals, prostitutes and beggars. With opportunities to attain economic wealth outside of the formal state structures and to achieve managerial positions without first climbing the Party ladder, society has become more complex, fluid and dynamic. The negative side of this dynamism has been the widening gap between poor and rich. As dissatisfaction with increasing regional inequalities has found expression in incipient separatist movements, the central government has desperately been seeking ways of redressing these imbalances.

It is within this context of rapid social and economic transition that new forms of intermediary organisations have begun to emerge. These include organisations such as the Self-Employed Workers' Association, the Association of Township Enterprises and the Women Mayors' Association. These operate in the space between the Party/state[1] and society, articulating the interests of newly emerging socioeconomic groups and reflecting the increasing diversity and complexity of society. They represent the seeds of a potentially flourishing NGO sector in post-Mao China.

The chapter begins by exploring both the rise of new intermediary organisations in China as well as the arrival of foreign NGOs for the first time since Liberation. I then examine the relationship of these organisations to the state and the reasons underpinning current state tolerance for these new institutional creatures. Although foreign NGOs have only limited operations in China, given the potential for their expansion, I reflect upon the crucial issues of legitimacy and accountability. Finally, I consider the prospects for foreign NGOs in scaling up their activities as China gradually moves towards a 'socialist market economy'.[2]

THE EMERGING NGO SECTOR

The liberation of China in 1949 brought an end to both foreign missionary activity and local welfare, sectoral and cultural associations. In order to assert its control over society and mobilise participation the Chinese Communist Party (CCP) set up mass organisations such as the All-China Federation of Trade Unions, the All-China Women's Federation and the Communist Youth League.[3] These served as transmission belts between the CCP and society, communicating Party policy downwards and theoretically transmitting grassroots opinions upwards. Dormant during the turbulent days of the Cultural Revolution (1966–76), these mass organisations gained a new lease of life with the onset of a radical programme of economic reform in 1978. Despite their efforts to reform their structures, to find new ways of reaching members and to create a new image, they have still remained closely aligned to the Party/state.

The introduction of market forces in post-Mao China has not only restructured society but also opened up spaces outside the immediate control of the Party/state where newly emerging socio-economic groups have begun to organise. Whereas in the pre-reform period the CCP and its appended mass organisations monopolised the arena of sociopolitical participation and control, in the post-Mao era there are an array of organisations, providing fora of association, representation and participation. Examples include the Association of Private Entrepreneurs, the Qigong Society, the Foundation for Underdeveloped Regions in China and the Disabled Federation. The Ministry of Civil Affairs refers to both the old mass organisations and these new post-Mao organisations as 'social organisations' (*shehui tuanti*), which are distinct from Party or government agencies. By October 1993 there were reportedly over 181 000 such organisations registered with the Ministry of Civil Affairs.[4]

The rise of these new social organisations has in turn been paralleled by the tentative appearance of foreign NGOs engaged in both relief and development work. The disastrous floods in the summer of 1991, the worst this century, claiming 1600 lives and causing US$7.5 billion worth of damage, had the salutory effect of drawing overseas funding into China and providing an entree for foreign NGOs. This was the first time in post-liberation China that the CCP had requested international relief aid. Although it did not receive the US$200 million it had asked for, the large donations from Hong Kong, namely US$79 million, were an indication of the potential resources available (Mosher, 1991:10).

It is difficult to estimate accurately how many foreign NGOs currently operate in China as there is no formal system of registration and NGOs tend to concentrate their activities in one province of China. However, discussions suggest that there are around 15 foreign NGOs currently operating in China, excluding multilateral agencies such as UNICEF.[5] The British Save the Children Fund, for example, has education, health and water projects in Yunnan, Anhui and Tibet; Oxfam has rural development projects in Yunnan and Guizhou; the German Friedrich Naumann Stifftung has training schemes in Harbin and Changsha; and Peace Corps sends English language teachers to Sichuan province.[6] Given the scale of China, the role of NGOs in the delivery of welfare services in the mid-1990s is minimal.

NGO–STATE RELATIONS

Given the multiplicity of referents and usages attached to the term NGO in Western development discourse, it is not surprising that in Chinese and in cross-cultural exchanges the term likewise takes on a variety of meanings. Government officials as well as representatives of social organisations frequently refer to social organisations as NGOs in their discussions with foreigners. This is partly because they are perceived to be distinct from the Party/state and partly because officials and representatives are aware that foreign donors often prefer to channel their money through NGOs. The anomaly is highlighted in the fact that the Women's Federation, which is a mass organisation closely aligned to the CCP, chaired the NGO forum at the UN International Conference on Women.

However social organisations are not a homogeneous category. On the basis of their sources of funding, staffing arrangments, organisational goals, structures and membership criteria we find that social organisations differ in their degree of autonomy from the Party/state, the history of their origins and their relationships with their members. We can thus identify four broad types of social organisation, namely mass organisations (*qunzhong tuanti*), semi-official organisations (*banguan banmin tuanti*), popular organisations (*minjian tuanti*) and illegal organisations (*feifa tuanti*). These can be placed along a continuum of autonomy, spontaneity and voluntariness, with the mass organisations at one extreme and the illegal organisations at the other. By autonomy we understand that the organisation can devise its own policies, determine its own structures and relies upon its own efforts to raise money. It is thus independent from the Party/state. We describe an organisation as spontaneous if it has grown from below. Membership is voluntary if members can join and leave at their own will.

Given the historically close ties between the mass organisations and the CCP as well as the fact that cadres are paid by the state and vertically integrated into its structures, it would be generous indeed to describe these as NGOs. Although there are clearly tendencies for greater autonomy within both the All-China Federation of Trade Unions as well as the All-China Women's Federation, these still remain closely wedded to the CCP.[7] Even though the mass organisations engage in welfare-type activities, using voluntary labour, their organisational structures, sources of revenue as well as their methods of participation still bear the hallmarks of the Party/state.

In their efforts to reform and find alternative sources of funding, the mass organisations have sponsored the setting up of secondary associations. The Communist Youth League, for example, founded the China Teenagers' Association, which in turn initiated the Project Hope scheme.[8] By raising funds in Hong Kong and elsewhere, the project has enabled individual children to go to school and in some cases entire schools to be supported. Without the front agency of the China Youth Association the Communist Youth League would find it very difficult to raise money overseas. Similarly the Women's Federation set up the China Children and Teenagers' Fund to raise money overseas for educational projects and the official Chinese Protestant Church created the Amity Foundation in 1985 to carry out development work and raise funding from abroad. The Foundation has initiated a range of projects including training courses for rural health workers, translation of the well-known 'Where there is no doctor' and flood relief assistance. All these ventures are an attempt to orient these organisations towards the grassroots, sever links with the Party/state and become more autonomous.

Next to the mass organisations along the continuum we find the semiofficial organisations, such as the China Wildlife Conservation

Association, the Foundation for Underdeveloped Regions in China and the Friendship Association of Women Enterpreneurs. These earn the title 'semi-official' because they receive some funding from the state, some of their office workers are transferred from government departments and some of their leading council members are state cadres. Furthermore the state has played a key role in their foundation, not only encouraging them to set up but often providing them with the necessary starting funds and ongoing support. For example, the Shanghai Women's Federation provided considerable assistance to the Shanghai Association of Women Engineers when it first got underway. At the same time they are also often a product of pressure from below. This was the case with the Xiaoshan City Individual Labourers' Association which grew initially out of the needs of individual labourers to organise and in response to encouragement from the State Council.[9] Membership of these organisations can be voluntary but in some cases, such as the Private Entrepreneurs' Association, it is automatic upon registration of the business. The semi-official social organisations are complex, hybrid structures, embracing a diversity of Party/state and grassroots relationships.

More spontaneous, voluntary and autonomous than the semi-official organisations are the popular organisations such as the Calligraphy Association, Qigong Society, women's salons and various literary societies. These correspond closest to the notion in development discourse of 'membership support organisations' (Farrington and Bebbington, 1993:5), where members elect their leaders to manage the organisation. However there are also a very few 'grassroots support organisations', where non-state professionals provide services for a particular client group. Examples include Buddhist and Christian associations which have set up schools and hospitals.[10] Both sub-types rely on their own funds, raised from donations and activities. Financial constraints are a crucial determinant for the lifespan of these organisations as well as the range of activities and services they can provide.

Illegal or unrecognised organisations include both those which would not seek state recognition such as secret societies and those which have not been permitted to register such as democracy and women's salons.[11] Advocacy groups challenging government policy, religious organisations such as the China Christian Association and alternative interest group organisations such as the National Autonomous Federation of Students fall into this category. These are the most autonomous, voluntary and spontaneous precisely because they operate outside the state legal and administrative system. They set their own goals, manage their own affairs and raise their own money. The evacuation of democracy dissidents in the aftermath of the 4 June killings relied crucially upon the support of the secret societies and sympathetic state officials.

From the above typology of social organisations in China it is clear that the claimed NGO sector is not only more heterogeneous than first appears but also enjoys a range of relationships to the state. The close involvement of state cadres in the activities of the semi-official organisations makes these cross-breed institutions, which fit comfortably neither into the category of NGO or state. Unlike many Asian and Latin American countries, China has few NGOs in the development field which have been set up from below and are able to control their organisational structures. Moreover, there are no pressure groups seeking to represent the interests of vulnerable or poor groups and very few advocacy groups, which are able to openly pursue policy issues such as environmental damage.[12]

Like the new Chinese social organisations, foreign NGOs have to attach themselves to a government department which, as well as having a supervisory function, will also mediate on their behalf within the administrative web. MSF, for example, registered with the Ministry of Agriculture whilst the Friedrich Naumann Stifftung, a German NGO allied to the German Liberal Party, is linked to the State Statistical Bureau and the Ministry of Agriculture. The choice of government department can be crucial to the success of a foreign NGO's work. Whilst some interviewees in foreign NGOs argued that a strong government department could make a significant contribution to getting NGO projects underway by providing key introductions and essentially lending its prestige to the NGO, others also pointed out that a weak government department could be a bonus in that NGOs could carry on their work with minimum interference.

Thus we can see that there is an array of relationships between intermediary organisations and the state, varying in terms of legality, degree of state control and extent of state financial and administrative support. Current state tolerance for this growing intermediary sector is in part informed by a recognition that these organisations can perform useful functions on behalf of the state. Whilst politically-oriented social organisations such as the Beijing Autonomous Workers' Federation were banned after the tumultuous events of 1989, those operating in the economic, cultural and social welfare spheres have been allowed to continue, precisely because they can complement if not supplement the state.

They can, for example, serve as a 'bridge between the state and the people',[13] that is, provide a new indirect channel through which the Party/state can impart policy to enterprises, households and individuals; horizontally link dispersed economic actors and otherwise isolated professionals and social groups; enable consultation in policy-making;

coordinate sectoral policy; and regulate the market (Howell, 1993b and 1994). Furthermore, some semi-official social organisations have begun to take on social welfare activities. For example, the Self-Employed Workers' Association uses some of its membership fees for death or sickness of its members or in helping households in dire economic straits. In the state sector this would have been the responsibility of the work unit. As self-employed workers and private entrepreneurs do not have their own work unit with the accompanying benefits and prerogatives and a national social welfare system is not yet in place, the role of social organisations in providing such support is crucial in protecting members' well-being. In the same vein welfare-oriented social organisations as well as foreign NGOs assist in guaranteeing minimum welfare provision for some at a time when the central government is attempting to reduce the state budget.

FUTURE PROSPECTS FOR NGOs

Having established that China has few development-oriented NGOs which have grown from below or which are set up by non-Party/state professionals, it would seem that foreign NGOs seeking to initiate or fund development projects in China will have to operate mainly with government departments such as local levels of the Ministry of Agriculture and semi-official social organisations such as the Foundation for Underdeveloped Regions in China. However there are signs that a more buoyant NGO sector could develop in the course of the next decade. Let us then consider the factors favouring such an optimistic scenario.

First, the desperate need to reform state-owned enterprises, of which one third are reportedly loss-making, has accelerated discussion about the setting-up of a national social welfare system. In order to deal with the problem of overstaffing and low labour productivity in state-owned enterprises the reformers have given the go-ahead to managers to lay off workers. The introduction of bankruptcy regulations in the late 1980s symbolised the official sanctioning of a policy to 'smash the iron rice bowl'. Attempts to implement this have met with considerable resistance from workers, leading sometimes to violent clashes. When lay-offs were announced in a factory in Liaoning Province, for example, workers physically attacked the factory cadres. As the work unit in China is both a site of production and reproduction, dismissing a worker is not just an issue of wage loss, but also a matter of housing, pensions, access to schooling, medical care and other subsidies. The need to make unemployment more acceptable to workers has stimulated numerous experiments in insurance schemes, pensions arrangements and social security. Researchers in government think-tanks such as the Chinese Academy of Social Sciences have turned their attention to the welfare state models of Britain and Sweden. Moreover, recent statements by China's top leaders underlining the urgency of developing a national social welfare system illustrate the priority given to this issue by the CCP.

It is within this context of a search for a national social welfare system that the prospects for NGOs, both foreign and domestic, have to be understood. As the economy becomes increasingly driven by market forces, the old systems of sociopolitical control and welfare provision are beginning to break down. Aware that they have become increasingly out of touch with their members and indeed discredited because of their close ties to the CCP, the mass organisations are desperately trying to reform and free themselves from the continuing dilemma of trying to serve simultaneously both the interests of the CCP and their members. Similarly the old systems of security such as the cocoon-like work units which catered for the social and welfare needs of their employees are no longer viable in an economy where the goal of profit wins the day. The reformers are therefore open to alternatives.

The second factor favouring a more flourishing NGO sector is the escalating budget deficit.[14] In the reform period the Party/state has ironically grown enormously. The number of employees in the Party, government and mass organisations reached the grand figure of 34.65 million in 1992, 80 per cent more than in 1980.[15] Despite efforts to implement new taxation regulations, state revenue has continued to trail behind expenditure. As a counter-measure the reformers have since the early 1990s proposed an overhaul of state structures, which would entail, among other things, a streamlining of staff. Recent attempts to reduce the size of the administration have encountered considerable resistance, which again underlines the need to establish a national social welfare system.

As part of this restructuring of the state, the reformers are envisaging a greater role for social organisations in the delivery of social welfare services. As a senior official in the Ministry of Civil Affairs succinctly put it: 'The government cannot totally manage health, culture, social welfare and education. In the future China will have a big society and a small heaven. Social organisations will play an important role.'[16] Thus the rapid proliferation of the new social organisations has altered the institutional structure mediating between society and the Party/state, laying the seeds of a potential civil society. As a result the institutional fabric of the state and society has become more complex, creating a more favourable environment within which development-oriented social organisations, either foreign or domestic, could flourish.

A third and related factor making for an optimistic scenario for NGOs is the alternative source of finance that NGOs can provide at a time when state coffers are emptying too fast for comfort. The willingness of the Chinese government to let aid agencies assist with relief work during the catastrophic floods of 1991 in southern China reflected in part a need for financial help. The amount of money that was raised in Hong Kong signalled to the government that there was a large pool of resources which could be potentially tapped in future. The current tolerance for foreign NGOs in China reflects a recognition of the need for alternative sources of funding, as in many other low-income countries.

The greater openness of the Chinese economy and the concomitant expansion of social ties provide favourable conditions for enhanced foreign NGO activity. With increased exposure to different social welfare systems through international exchange and conferences such as the 1995 International Women's Conference we can expect government officials to be more receptive to foreign NGO initiatives. However, given the strength of the Chinese economy and ideological concern about the dangers of overreliance on external financing, it is likely that the Chinese state will continue to maintain a cautious stance towards foreign NGOs.

Other favourable factors for foreign NGOs are the reunification of Hong Kong with China in 1997 and its ethnic and geographic proximity to China. Hong Kong has a long tradition of social work and an abundance of NGOs. The floods of 1991 provided an opportunity for some of these to gain experience of working in China and to forge links with government agencies and social organisations. As 1997 approaches, these organisations are rapidly expanding their ties with China, in part to secure themselves a niche for the future, as the business sector has already done. We can expect that the reformers will welcome these moves, as again Hong Kong NGOs will bring in resources and enable the state to shed some of its functions. In the long-run they could also provide an alternative source of employment, which would be a stabilising factor in society given the trend towards rising unemployment.

Whilst there are numerous factors favouring an expansion of the NGO sector in China, it is important also to consider the constraints upon this development. The prospects for foreign NGOs operating in China will depend crucially upon the fate of the new social organisations.

Given the current concern of China's top leaders for the problem of 'social disorder', manifested in increased crime, drug-smuggling, prostitution, peasant riots and factory strikes, we can expect the CCP to be keeping a watchful eye on illegal social organisations, and in particular, those which might constitute a potential threat to their power. The response of the CCP to illegal political and advocacy organisations will be a significant barometer of its overall position towards popular and semi-official social organisations.

The contradictory tensions implicit in the Party/state's desire on the one hand to shed some of the state's functions to semi-official or popular social organisations and on the other hand to maintain social control will also determine the boundaries of these organisations' activities. To the extent that semi-official social organisations are able to raise more of their own money and so gain increased independence from the Party/state, it will become more difficult for the Party/state to control them. If these organisations should gain a consciousness of themselves as an 'alternative sector', working in opposition to the Party/state and on behalf of an amorphous 'people' or indeed on behalf of specific interests, then it is likely that the Party/state will attempt to regulate their activities further. We can therefore expect the Party/state to continue to encourage organisations that are prepared to take over state functions of service delivery or to act as intermediaries between newly emerging socio-economic groups such as entrepreneurs and the Party/state. However, organisations that seek to mobilise people in opposition to the Party/state through consciousness-raising processes or to pursue advocacy and lobbying strategies are likely to be nipped in the bud.

Whilst the future trajectory of China's new social organisations will have repercussions for the prospects of foreign NGOs, there are also other factors which will shape the role foreign NGOs are likely to play as China moves towards a socialist market economy. We can expect the Party/state to continue to be suspicious of the activities of foreign NGOs. This is partly because of a lack of experience with foreign NGOs, partly because of an ideological concern that some of these organisations may be seeking either to proselytise the Christian faith, or promote democracy or organise opposition to the CCP, and partly because of a long-standing suspicion of foreigners which dates back to the Opium Wars of the nineteenth century.

Given the tragic events of Tiananmen, the current media focus on China's poor human rights records, dissatisfaction with China's management of the International Women's Conference, as well as unrest in Tibet and Xinjiang provinces, some foreign NGOs may still opt for political reasons to stay clear of China. For the near future foreign NGOs will have to be prepared to work with local government and Party officials and to confine their activities to funding and service delivery. Those that seek political goals such as the empowerment of the poor, consciousness-

raising through literacy campaigns or projects aimed at democratic participation are likely to be frustrated in their efforts.

However, foreign NGOs should not take a dim view of the prospect of
working closely with the Party/state or with some semi-official social
organisations. Given the high degree of Party/state permeation of the
economy and society in post-liberation China as well as the gradualist
approach to reform, it is not surprising that the Party/state is still much in
evidence. In a semi-reformed economy there are indeed benefits to having
links with the Party/state, such as obtaining access to resources which are
administratively allocated, gaining prestige and having channels through
which members' or clients' interests can be represented. The Self-
Employed Workers' Association in Xiaoshan City, Zhejiang Province, for
example, started life as a grassroots organisation. As members needed to
have links with various government departments to obtain information,
raw materials, licences and so on, the organisers decided to invite several
senior officials from relevant government departments such as the Water
Board or the Electricity Department to sit on their council. In this way the
association could build up its network of contacts (*guanxi wang*) which it
could draw on to resolve or obviate conflicts between the Party/state and
members.

Furthermore it is important to remember that Party/state officials differ
in personality, competence, the issues they are concerned about and the
interests they seek to represent. Increased decentralisation in post-Mao
China has reinforced the tendency of local officials to place local interests
above central priorities. In recent years 'localism' has proved a serious
headache for central government, which has found it difficult not only to
increase financial contributions from the regions but also to guarantee the
implementation of central policies.[17] Hence local Party/government
officials, keen to improve the local economy and well-being of its permanent residents, are likely to welcome initiatives to stimulate local economic growth.

Given also current attempts to streamline the state, older cadres are
looking for alternative employment. Social organisations, consultancy
companies and business enterprises provide such an opportunity. Cadres
we interviewed who had made the leap into social organisations frequently expressed the view that they enjoyed greater autonomy and
room for manoeuvre than in their previous state positions. With their
network of connections and patronage links with the Party/state as well
familiarity with its structures and concerns, such former Party/state
cadres could be a useful resource for NGOs, which lie outside the
administrative system.

Furthermore some of the older cadres were involved in voluntary organisations and even educated in missionary establishments in pre-Liberation China and so have a concept of grassroots, voluntary activity. The organisation 'Industrial Cooperatives' (*Gonghe*), for example, was set up in pre-Liberation China to promote industrial cooperatives in rural areas. The emergence of thousands of new social organisations has provided the context for its revival in 1987. Although its council members are largely made up of well-known, senior officials, some of these were previously engaged with this organisation. It is likely that the leading body of this cooperative movement will strive towards greater autonomy, drawing upon its historical traditions in pre-Liberation China.[18]

CONCLUSION

This chapter set out to explore the emerging NGO sector in post-Mao China, drawing attention to the diversity of NGO–state relationships. As the extent of foreign NGOs in China is still very limited, the discussion of accountability and legitimacy reflected upon issues for future concern. As China moves further down the road towards a 'socialist market economy' and the state becomes a slimmer body operating more at the macro level, we can expect the currently emerging intermediary sector linking the Party/state and society to become more dynamic. To the extent that social organisations take off and are more able to determine their own destinies, the possibilities for foreign NGOs working in China will expand. Not only will the idea of an NGO sector have become more acceptable, but there will also be more autonomous organisations around, with which foreign NGOs could initiate links. However, this scenario is still somewhat optimistic. For the near future foreign NGOs can expect to deal mainly with semi-official social organisations, which have the potential to become more autonomous structures, depending in part upon their success in raising their own funds.

Notes

1. The term Party/state is used here to underline the high degree of fusion between the Party and state in China. Although the reformers are attempting to separate out the Party and the state, the two remain closely wedded with Party cadres occupying nearly all responsible positions in the state administration, army and government.
2. This article is based upon interviews conducted with foreign NGOs in Hong Kong in October 1992 and June 1994 and Beijing 1993. I would like to

express my gratitude to representatives of The Save the Children Fund, Oxfam, Amity Foundation, Friedrich Naumann Stifftung and World Vision in Hong Kong and China for discussing their work in China with me. It also draws upon work by Professor Gordon White and Ms Shang Xiaoyuan and colleagues at the Chinese Academy of Social Sciences funded by UNRISD and ESRC. The author takes sole responsibility for all views expressed in the article.

3.   Other organisations included the Federation for Commerce and Industry, the Association for the Popularisation of Science and Technology, the Overseas Chinese Association and the Peasant Association (only till the mid-1950s).

4.   Of these 181 060, some 1460 were registered as national social organisations, 19 600 as branch and local organisations at provincial level and over 160 000 were registered with county authorities: interview, Ministry of Civil Affairs, Beijing, October 1993 and *China Daily*, 7 May 1993, p. 3.

5.   Also according to a UNDP official there are about 100 organisations sending EFL teachers to China.

6.   Other organisations include the World Wildlife Federation/Fund, which in October 1993 was considering setting up an office in China, the German Friedrich-Ebert Stifftung, Brothers to Men, VSO, MSF-France (health project in Tibet), Project Hope USA, WUSC, Japanese Overseas Volunteers Programme, Ford Foundation, GTZ and CIDA. CARE used to operate in Yunnan but withdrew. Its projects were taken over by Oxfam.

7.   For a more detailed discussion of the changing role of trade unions in post-Mao China, see Howell (1993a, ch. 6).

8.   I am grateful to Michael Crook of CIDA, Beijing, for drawing my attention to this.

9.   The term 'individual labourers' refers to self-employed workers who rely mainly on their own labour, family labour or on a maximum of eight or so employees.

10.   Examples of the work of Christian associations include the Xinde Foundation in Changsha, the Agape Social Service in Changsha, Gaoli Church Clinic in Weifang, Shandong and Yancheng Church Clinic in Jiangsu. For further details of support to private health clinics and schools see *The Amity Foundation Project Proposals 1993/1994*.

11.   Some 'women's salons' are permitted while others have been dissolved. For example an informal women's salon of twenty people met regularly at the Beijing Institute of Geology until their activities attracted the attention of the Public Security Bureau.

12.   In October 1993 an environmental pressure group was in the throes of setting up. Of concern to its founding members was how to manage the authorities in a way that would not result in the closure of the organisation. Petitions have also been organised by leading intellectuals on the environmental consequences of the Three Gorges Dam.

13.   See Xue Muqiao, 'Establish and develop non-governmental, self-management organisations in various trades' in *People's Daily*, 10 October, translated in Foreign Broadcast Information Services, 1988/201.

14.   Xinhua News Agency, 29 June 1993 in *Summary of World Broadcasts*, FE/1727 B2/1 29 June 1993.

15. Xinhua News Agency, 25 July 1993 in *Summary of World Broadcasts*, FE/1760 B2/2 6 August 1993.
16. Interview with senior official in the Ministry of Civil Affairs, Beijing, September 1992.
17. Tangtai, Hong Kong, 15 August 1993 in *Summary of World Broadcasts*, FE/1777 B2/1 26 August 1993.
18. I am grateful to Derek Bryan and Jenny Clegg for their comments on the character and history of Gonghe. Gonghe stands for *gongye hezuoshe*, which means Industrial Cooperatives. It is often transcribed as 'Gung Ho'.

14 The State–NGO Relationship in Sri Lanka: Rights, Interests and Accountability
Ranjith Wanigaratne

THE NATIONAL SETTING

Since independence in 1948 government strategies in Sri Lanka have successively moved from a 'right of centre' liberal democratic stance (the United National Party) to a 'left of centre' radical democratic stance (the Sri Lanka Freedom Party). Up to 1977 the overall results might be summarised as achieving high human development levels with low rates of economic growth (Isenman, 1980).

In 1977 the incoming UNP government initiated liberal economic policies that marked a break with the past with reforms 'designed to move economic management away from intervention and controls' (Ministry of Finance and Planning, 1981:1). These changes were associated with a spurt in economic growth which averaged 6.2 per cent per annum 1978–85.

The phase of high economic growth was also manifested upon an agrarian structure and distribution of wealth and power that inhibited a wider distribution of benefits of growth. Thus in this growth phase, segments of the population with prior access to wealth and power were better able to exploit the advantages offered by the rising GDP more than the poorest sectors of the population.

Whereas in the preceding low growth phase of 1970–77 the highest 10 per cent in the national income ladder accounted for 30 per cent of the total income, this position increased to 34 per cent by 1981 and to 49 per cent by 1985. On the other hand, the share of the lowest 40 per cent which accounted for 15 per cent of the total income in the low growth phase of 1970–77, underwent only a slight increase to 16 per cent in 1981, in the subsequent high growth phase. Thereafter, its share declined to 7 per cent

216

by 1985, the beginning of a succeeding lower growth phase. The early years of 1990s showed a continued deceleration of GDP growth to a 5 per cent growth in 1991, 4 per cent in 1992 and to rise once again, this time to nearly 7 per cent, in 1993, as the economy recovered from the recession of the late 1980s.

The economic adjustments that were initiated by the government on the advice of the World Bank in the post-1990 period included a programme of privatisation, rationalisation of the public sector, deregulation of tariff systems to remove protectionism, and withdrawal of a state subsidy on fertiliser and other goods. The government also sought to bring the poorest segments of the population into the mainstream of economic development through providing them access to land and sources of income through measures such as the Mahaweli Development Programme, integrated rural development programmes, micro-enterprise schemes and manpower training.

An alternative set of policies were concurrently introduced to cushion economic hardships faced by the poor arising from structural adjustment policies of the 1990s. Among the welfare programmes the more permanent ones were the Food Stamps Programme, the *Janasaviya* Programme, the School Midday Meal Programme, and the Janasaviya Trust Fund which supported, complemented and supplemented the *Janasaviya* Programme through financing self employment projects and grassroots organisations and non-governmental organisations initiated enterprises.

The *Janasaviya* Programme established in 1989, and operational islandwide in six rounds, benefited about 265 000 assetless families by 1994. It aimed at providing basic food and living needs, asset creation, improvement of human capital through manpower training and group activity, thrift and savings, self-enterprise creation, and a range of other development initiatives. However, despite a resumption of higher rates economic growth in the 1990s, especially after 1992, and the introduction of 'safety nets' to reduce negative impacts of economic growth, the country continues to be plagued by high unemployment, low productivity, low incomes, landlessness, malnutrition and other constraints which keep about 30 per cent of the families in absolute poverty. Of a labour force of 6.5 million persons in 1991 nearly 1.2 million (18 per cent) were unemployed. This was only 8 per cent less than what it was 14 years ago in 1977 (1.3 million), inspite of economic growth oriented policies that were implemented in the intervening period. The total number employed in 1991 was also 61 per cent higher than what it was 20 years ago in 1971 (747 000 unemployed persons). The backlog of educated unemployed is about 350 000 and about 125 000 are being added to the labour force who are looking out for work.

THE EVOLUTION OF GROs AND NGOs IN SRI LANKA

Early Developments

Grassroots organisations (GROs), spontaneously generated as a response to felt needs of society, have been a part and parcel of the Sri Lankan culture from ancient times. They were usually associated with religious institutions (cultural values), irrigation, agriculture and artisan production (economic values) and civil society more generally (civic values). The continued existence of these grassroots organisations over long periods, often inspite of radical changes in the central government, indicated their resilience to short-term national political and economic stresses. Their independent evolutionary character not only safeguarded them during times of war, disorder and other radical circumstances but also made them amenable to gradual change over long periods of time.

This system of grassroots organisations weakened in the eighteenth century and thereafter owing to several factors. A series of decisions were taken by the British during the period of their occupation of the island and by the national government after independence in 1948 to centralise the management functions of the country within a number of departments and ministries. The indigenous systems of grassroots organisations which supervised and co-ordinated land, irrigation, food production and village level administration were taken over by the line agencies of the central colonial administration. This position continued in the post-independence times up to the present.

The indigenous GRO development was thus narrowed down to religion and religious institutions-based cultural development. Yet even these indigenously evolved grassroots organisations were placed under heavy externally induced stress. In this case Christian missionary activities supported by the central administration through its patronage moved into welfare and social development activities. A new set of church-based NGOs emerged with the establishment of the Baptist Mission in 1802, the Wesleyan Missionary Society in 1814, Church Missionary Society in 1818, Young Men's Christian Association and Young Women's Christian Association in 1882, the Salvation Army in 1883 and a number of other organisations and educational institutions run by such organisations. A nationalistic revivalist movement emerged in the late nineteenth century as a reaction to British colonial domination over the indigenously evolved economic and sociocultural institutions. The Buddhist–Hindu–Muslim reaction to the activities of Christian churches and NGOs resulted in the creation of rival religious organisations such as the Buddhist Theosophical

Society in 1880, Mahabodhi (Buddhist) Society in 1890, Young Men's Buddhist Association in 1897, Ramakrishna (Hindu) Mission in 1899, Vivekananda (Hindu) Society in 1902, All Ceylon Buddhist Congress in 1918, Muslim Education Society in 1890, and many federated NGOs which managed educational institutions based upon the Buddhist–Hindu–Muslim ethic. Through active lobbying many of the educational institutions were eventually linked to the line agency managed school education system (Samaraweera, 1973).

After independence these religion-based NGOs received some measure of state patronage, which by the 1990s resulted in the formation of separate state ministries in charge of Buddhist, Hindu and Islamic affairs. On the other hand, the Christian NGOs focused on establishing linkages with international donors. The colonial governement sponsored cooperative formation and these institutions remain important, especially in rural areas. There are both independent cooperative movements, such as the Federation of Thrift and Credit Societies (SANASA), and state-controlled co-operatives, particularly the multi-purpose cooperative societies (MPCSs).

Post-war Period: 1946–50

The relationship between the NGOs and the state in the late 1940s is linked to two far reaching pieces of legislation promulagated in 1948 in response to recommendations of a Social Services Commission that was appointed in 1946. These laws provided for the establishment of (1) a Department of Social Services (DSS) charged with, among other activities, the responsibility over social welfare services provision to women, children, elders, paupers and wage labour, and (2) a Central Council of Social Services (CCSS) to coordinate all voluntary social service organisations in the non-governmental sector.

The rationale behind the establishment of the Department of Social Service and the Central Council of Social Services in the late 1940s seems to be the consideration (perhaps arising from the carry-over effects of the revivalist movement of the late nineteenth century) that 'if any organisations are given complete freedom without any state intervention they tend to overstep the limits that they have to observe... They also must be protected from mis-appropriation of funds (from either local or foreign donors) by their employees or others. Therefore any right-thinking person would agree that there must be a mechanism to control and supervise these activities' (de Silva, 1981: 29). In essence the issues of state supervision, accountability and transparency of internal management mechanisms of non-government organisations and tinkering with them were considered legitimate functions of the state.

Rural development societies (RDSs), which sought to develop village based social infrastructures such as community halls, bridges, wells, village roads and irrigation channel construction and maintenance, through a combination of 'free labour' (*shramadana*) and state funding directed by a national level management body, the Department of Rural Development, were established in 1947. The rural development societies were created spontaneously by village communities to develop local level social infrastructure. They were assisted in registering themselves with the Department of Rural Development through its village level Rural Development officers. The executive committees of the RDSs were popularly elected by the general membership as with the case of cooperatives. Separate societies were formed for women (*mahila samiti*) to look after thrift and credit mobilisation, child education and welfare, homegarden development and women managed village industries, and other aspects. The national publicity given to the cooperative movement and rural development also gave further impetus to GRO formation around cash, labour and material assistance needs of village communities. By the early 1950s both co-operatives and rural development societies were well established throughout the country.

At the community level pooling of resources formerly took place to cater for the various village functions (for example, harvest festivals, alms-giving ceremonies, exorcising ceremonies), religious–cultural needs and exigencies (for example, grave illness or death of a person). As monetisation of the economy increased pressures arising from cash scarcities compelled the transforming village societies to evolve more formal organisations to systematically mobilise resources to cater to such situations. Products of the GROs formed in this way are found in the funeral assistance societies (*maranadhara samiti*), temple, church and mosque societies, and mutual aid societies (*anyonyadara samiti*).

Taken together the state-managed cooperative societies, rural development societies, and thrift and credit societies developed side-by-side with spontaneously generated GROs. The amalgam of spontaneously generated and state-induced, assisted and directed GROs have worked alongside government line agencies towards satisfying economic, socio-cultural and organisational needs of the people. Their combined activity pervaded all walks of life of the people as well as all regions and sub-regions, towns and villages in the country. The endogenous nature of social services provision and mobilisation of people in development oriented activities, which dominated the first half of the 20th century continued into the latter decades of the century but with diminishing strength. Increasing economic pressures in the post independence (after 1948) period also saw a shift of GROs into an increasingly monetised climate, where voluntary action for satisfying and improving the individual and common needs and the facilities tended to get entangled with cash and cash needs, paving the way for international donors to enter the indigenous GRO system.

Government–NGO Relations in the 1950–78 Period

The relatively buoyant national economy of the 1950 decade permitted some optimism in state intervention in social welfare to ensure a minimal living standard to all sectors of the population. Thus in the 1950s and even in the 1960s about 40–50 per cent of public expenditure was directed towards social welfare. The institutional development needs and the demand for essential services which catered to education, housing, health and sanitation, food and other living needs of the people were satisfied through a combination of state line agencies, state assisted/guided GROs and spontaneously generated and self-maintained GROs. In this scenario there was very little scope for the establishment of national NGOs or Northern NGOs in providing social welfare 'nets', mobilisation of 'underprivileged' and 'marginalised' groups and their 'empowerment'.

The few NGOs which emerged during the 1950–60 decades, such as the *Sarvodaya Shramadana Movement* (1956), CARE International (1956) and the Family Planning Association (1953), were financially supported by external donors. They were viewed with some suspicion by the state bureaucracy. This marginalisation of NGO activity found support in the radical social democratic elements in party politics which were in ascendence in the late 1950s and beyond, in the Marxist and neo-Marxist elements of the intellectual community and in the priests and social elites.

The assistance extended to the above NGOs by international sponsors such as Konrad Adenauer Foundation, Frederick-Ebert Stifftung and the International Planned Parenthood Federation (IPPF) assistance, were also fired by geopolitical considerations, which combined altruism with objectives of preventing the spread of communism or the emergence of authoritarian regimes. Both donor assistance and externally financed NGOs, such as *Sarvodaya*, met with suspicion. This condition continues to pervade political and bureaucratic attitudes in Sri Lanka towards NGOs, their activities and their supporting donor agencies. The state attitude towards NGOs in particular, continues to be underlain by fears that (1) the machinery of government is being manipulated, undermined and its decision-making power is being whittled away via the medium of NGOs to serve global geopolitical ideologies and objectives; (2) divisive elements in Sri Lankan society are being fostered through NGO intervention; (3) social change is segmentally and artificially accelerated for market incorporation of communities or retarded to maintain a stasis and isolation of given communities (for example, indigenous ethnic minorities and locations) for 'historical preservation'; (4) external ideologies are being transplanted and perpetrated within the evolved indigenous society; (5) pressure groups of all forms are being created, which link up with divisive political interests in the country.

NGO activity and support from NGO donors in Sri Lanka were marginal in the 1950s and 1960s and up to mid-1970s. However, the growing inability of successive governments to stem the deterioration of the economy saddled with a heavy social welfare burden and low economic growth, and resultant increase in unemployment, low incomes, poverty and the marginalisation of whole regions of the country created an environment that favoured a greater role for NGOs.

The Post-1978 Period: Government–NGO Relations

Since the shift to economic liberalisation in 1978 the role of the private sector and of NGOs in development has become more important in state policy. The deepening of income disparities, amidst rising economic growth, and marginalisation of poor and the near poor due to systematic removal of subsidies in the 1980s gave impetus to a mushroom growth of NGOs both assisted by local private donors as well as by international agencies.

The governments of the 1980s sought to cater to the social welfare demands of the people without sacrificing investment in economic growth. They were manned by a bureaucracy which represented an amalgam of colonial and post-colonial training and upheld the notion of state-run welfarism, and social and institutional development of the country. Old fears of the loss of decision-making power remained. Segmented political interests, radical intellectuals and other diverse interests continued to uphold endogenous change for their own narrow partisan reasons, even while recognising the ineffectual nature of the state machinery and the worsening poverty and unsettled conditions in the country. These continued to support the notion of a higher state control over the development process, including the activities of the NGOs. Inevitably, tensions between the state and the emerging NGO sector increased and governments sought to supervise NGOs.

NGO Co-ordinating Agencies

The Central Council of Social Services (CCSS) was upgraded in the 1980s to serve as a state directed umbrella organisation of NGOs and GROs, itself forming links with the International Council of Social Welfare in Vienna, USAID and the World Bank. Currently, about 258 NGOs are registered or affiliated with it, some of which have benefited from external funds channelled through it. Sri Lankan development NGOs formed the National NGO Council (NNGOC) in 1981 to serve as an umbrella organisation for both village level NGOs and NGO federations and affiliates. At the beginning of June 1994 it had formed network links with 159 NGOs operating in the island. The Board of Management of NNGOC consists largely of retired members of the Sri Lanka administrative service, which brings this umbrella organisation and member NGOs not only the required administrative capacity but also brings the NGOs within the orbit of influence of the national policy makers.

Legal Controls over NGOs

A related strategy to bring NGOs in line with government policies was through the passage of several legislative enactments. The increasing involvement of international agencies in the setting up of NGOs in the country, and the lack of financial and administrative management accountability in many local NGO counterparts of external NGOs led the government in the early 1980s to attempt to legislate about NGO formation. This came about through the Voluntary Social Service Organisations (Registration and Supervision) Law No. 31 of 1980. Under this law all social service organisations in the country were to be registered with the Department of Social Services.

This law provided for

the registration with the government of voluntary social services organisations; to provide for their inspection and supervision; to facilitate the coordination of activities of such organisations; to give governmental recognition to such organisations which are properly constituted; to enforce the accountability of such organisations in respect of financial and policy management under existing rules of such organisations to the members of such organisations, the general public and the government; to prevent malpractices by persons to such organisations; to regularise the constitution of voluntary social service groups which have not been legally recognised; and for matters connected therewith or incidental thereto. (Voluntary Service Organisations Act No. 31, 1980)

Active lobbying against the implementation of this 'draconian' law by Sri Lankan NGOs, while preventing its full operation, nevertheless, brought into focus several issues: (1) the mushroom growth of NGOs and their activities may result in generating potential sociopolitical pressure groupings which may be manipulated by sectoral interests to destabilise governments; (2) many of the NGOs received funds from external donors, whose objectives of funding may also involve elements of political intervention besides service provision; (3) duplication and overlap of functions performed by NGOs by line ministries would result in a waste of resources and a distortion of the national development process; (4) formulation of NGO projects on social development often without understanding or concern with state policies on external donor assistance or with state policies on development may lead to unacceptable situations for a sovereign state; (5) the need to dovetail various programmes and projects of NGOs into the overall development plans of the government to make a widespread and a lasting impact upon the social and economic development of the country.

In spite of continuous lobbying by NGOs against the 1980 Act the government was able to maintain some measure of control over the NGOs to register. Pressure was brought to bear upon NGOs by the government through the control over their foreign exchange receipts and over the NGO applications for purchase of capital items from abroad.

The government of the post-1983 period too has not entirely relinquished its former position of attempting to ensure NGO accountability and co-ordination. Under Section 5 of the Public Security Ordinance (Chapter 20), a set of regulations entitled 'Monitoring of Receipts and Disbursements of Non-Governmental Organisations No 1 of 1993', has been promulgated. It prescribes that (1) every Non-Governmental Organisation in receipt of money, goods or services, from foreign or local sources, in excess of Rs50 000 per year shall be registered with the Director of Social Services; (2) every Non-Governmental Organisation in receipt of a total sum of money, or the equivalent of a sum of money, in excess of Rs100 000 in any year, whether as a donation, gift, contribution, income, or otherwise, shall sumbit to the Director of Social Services, before a prescribed date each year, a statement of accounts certified by a qualified auditor for the previous year. Non-compliance with the regulations is punishable by imprisonment for a term not exceeding five years and to a fine not exceeding Rs50 000 (*Government Gazette Extraordinary*, 22 December 1993).

While these regulations made both the administrative accountability and financial accountability of an NGO to Government a requirement, registration with the government was possible along several paths. The NGOs could register themselves as people's companies under the People's Company Act, as cooperative societies under the Cooperatives Act, as agricultural service organisations under the Agrarian Services Act, and as voluntary production or service organisations in the rural sector under the Voluntary Social Services Act. Each of the acts placed them within the management and financial supervision of different state agencies. On the other hand, qualitative differences in the provisions attached to the separate acts provided the necessary flexibility to the NGOs to choose that which most suited their individual organisations. As the choice of modes of legal registrations, their simplicity and speediness imply, the government's attitudes and policies towards the NGOs appear to have been relatively liberal in comparison to some Asian countries.

PRESIDENT PREMADASA AND NGOs

In 1988 President Premadasa came to power. Despite his liberal policy position he committed his government to massive poverty alleviation programmes and, in particular, the *Janasaviya* programme. This was followed by free school meals programmes and the *Janasaviya* Trust Fund. In effect, NGOs were squeezed out of their main business (poverty alleviation). By the end of 1990 the NGOs has no particular role to play except in assisting the state. Since the management of the programmes was through the bureaucracy, the ability of NGOs to contribute in a significant way was marginalised. The continued marginalisation of the NGOs and the accompanying process of delinking of their beneficiaries continued over the early 1990s. A further complication was added to this deepening schism between the government and the NGOs through an externally financed and NGO-fomented spate of forced and induced religious conversions. The old issue of cultural revivalism and nationalism–culturalism surfaced again, with the Buddhist and, this time also, the Catholic laity and GROs associated with them protesting against improper and wrongful practices, including forced conversions of poor and depressed communities by Christian fundamentalists using NGOs as cover for their evangelical work. In addition, the issues of democratisation, human rights, the Tamil separatist conflict and the refugee issue, which surfaced in the 1989–94 period, were championed by the NGOs. NGOs and their activities were pushed directly into the political arena.

The Premadasa government began to view NGOs as a political force, which it sought to neutralise. Of the NGOs, the most powerful in terms of organisation, coverage, length of time of existence and support of international donors was *Sarvodaya* and its charismatic leader Dr A. T. Ariyaratne. Over the years both liberal democratic and radical democratic party governments had sought to weaken the role of *Sarvodaya*. By 1990, NGO activity in general, and large-scale NGOs such as *Sarvodaya* in particular, were seen as a 'thorn in the flesh' of the government. The Premadasa government (which was characterised by centralised and personalised decision making) appointed a former Supreme Court judge to head an NGO Commission to report on NGO affairs.

NGO Commission Report Findings

The Commission reported in 1993 but its findings were not published at the time of writing (late-1994). Extensive 'excerpts' were 'leaked' to the press, however. Overall, the Commission found that by and large the NGO scene in Sri Lanka in the early 1990s was 'somewhat chaotic, anarchical and in disarray'. The bulk of NGOs were traditional welfare NGOs, with a sprinkling of so-called 'third generation' NGOs. While there was a regulatory regime on paper, as prescribed by the Voluntary Social Services Organisation (Registration and Supervision) Act, it was in abeyance. The Commission found that NGOs enjoyed an almost total freedom. Consequently, it advised a reactivation of the regulatory machinery in order to bring order back into NGO affairs and a spirit of competitive co-operation in the NGO–government relationship, rather than antagonism.

The Commission found that there was no record, official or unofficial, of the exact number of NGOs operating in Sri Lanka. Many were operating without the state authorities being aware of their existence. There was also no record of the exact amount of foreign financing and resources coming into the NGO sector nor was there a record available to the authorities about the manner of disbursement of such funds. As a result the responsible government agencies had no idea of NGO performance.

The Commission observed that 'voluntariness', the cardinal value on which practically the entire NGO case is placed, did not purely mean being non-governmental. It in fact implied selflessness, altruism, compassion, a sense of dedication and service for its own sake without expectation of reward for oneself. Even in some NGOs with high ideals, under the cover of 'voluntariness' some persons were found to be making use of their own positions and office, obtaining money, property and other benefits. Evidence pointed towards the diversion of funds in Sri Lanka and abroad in private accounts. The acquisition of property and the misuse of the property, vehicles and facilities of the organisation for personal gain was noted. A 'new phenomenon' of benefits in the form of acceptance of air tickets, scholarships and expenses for children's education abroad, medical expenses and so on was noted. These were found to be solicited and often demanded by local counterparts ('Special Reports', *The Sunday Times*, 26 December 1993).

Some of the organisations professing to be democratic were found to be so only in name or form rather than in actual operation. Unethical conversions of children, the poor and the disadvantaged and backward communities, of Buddhists, Hindus and Catholics, unable to withstand enticements of cash and other materials offered by fundamentalist sects, were revealed. The Commission itself was subjected to criticism by high religious dignitaries in the country for not concentrating its sole attention to this matter to the exclusion of all other matters. The Commission observed that unless this 'burning issue' is effectively and resolutely stopped it may even lead to a disruption of the existing religious harmony in the country.

The Commission, however, saw a need for a voluntary and independent sector to articulate the views of the people and to buttress the democratic processes in the country. It observed that the government policies and actions indicated that it was well aware of the problem of poverty, and that the most appropriate approach to ameliorate it would be through a 'bottom-up', participatory process of voluntary community actions, which would be difficult for the government to achieve on an island-wide scale by itself.

The Commission recorded that, of 47 International NGOs reported to be operating in Sri Lanka, only 40 had signed memorandi of understanding (MOUs) with the Ministry of Plan Implementation. It observed, however, that although the NGO Liaison Unit of the Ministry was established to facilitate foreign NGO activity, the Ministry had also become the focal point for local NGOs. The Commission was critical of this NGO Liaison Unit for its low profile and lack of publicity and suggested its revamping.

By and large the NGO sector has shown a resistance to government oversight. Even the work of the Commission was viewed as unwarranted and unnecessary. Many of the NGOs 'claim a right to be where they are and to do what they are doing and regard their domain as a no-go area for the government', the Commission reported.

The NGO Commission's Recommendations

The Commission recommended that the government should endeavour to provide NGOs with the necessary environment to pursue their ideals and objectives within civil society, since it considered it legitimate for an NGO to take up matters of public and topical interest in the fulfilment of its larger role. However, it was noted that issues such as human rights should not be used for political purposes for confrontation with the government, but as pure human rights issues. This matter had to be viewed differently in the case of foreign-based and foreign-funded NGOs having close connections with governments and institutions abroad. The Commission observed that Sri Lanka has been subjected to foreign intervention in its internal affairs. If assistance has to be sought abroad it should be sought, in the first instance, from the Asian region in preference to the West. Such linkages should be with tried and tested organisations, which have a reputation for fair dealing and impartiality.

The Commission also recommended that since the government–NGO relation is a two-way relation, a goverment statement of its policy towards NGOs should be provided. (This was done in May 1994, by the President of Sri Lanka). From the NGO side there should also be a similar statement of policy, which can only come about through NGO umbrella organisations which can give a national voice to their membership. If only a section of the NGOs decide to work with the state, rather than the total mass of the NGOs, the NGO sector may suffer a split. Therefore the responsibility of federating of NGOs into an umbrella organisation to preserve the NGO integrity and freedom of action lies with the NGOs themselves, rather than with the government.

Sarvodaya, as the largest NGO in Sri Lanka, was reported to be active in 8000 out of 22 000 villages of the island. It was reported to possess a volunteer force of 10 000, and besides income from other sources it was reported to receive external aid from a European Aid Consortium to the tune of about Rs220 million a year. It declares that its work is established upon an ideology and method which originates from the indigenous society. The Commission was unable to unravel its organisation and administrative structures, nor to make a proper assessment of its work without a deeper study. It therefore recommended the need for an independent body, a separate Commission, to study the structure and organisation of *Sarvodaya*, *Sarvodaya Sangamaya* (organisation) and the *Sarvodaya* movement and to assess and evaluate the large claims made on behalf of *Sarvodaya* by its executives.

Specific Recommendations of the NGO Commission

1   A comprehensive policy declaration is needed The government should be prepared to grant a place to people's organisations to enable

the people to advance and protect, within the democratic framework their legitimate and collective interests and aspirations through peaceful and lawful means. This would include their right to reasonable participation by consultation mechanisms at different levels of economic decision making which the government shall endeavour to facilitate. It would also mean expanded scope for private initiative for development and welfare activities.

2   Those GROs and the NGOs in receipt of an annual income less than Rs150 000 and owning properties within the Metropolitan area of a value less than 1.5 million or 1 million outside and with other assets in cash/securities not exceeding Rs250 000

(a) will be exempted from incorporation or compulsory registration;

(b) such exempted GROs and NGOs can, however, voluntarily secure incorporation or registration if they consider it advantageous to do so. Subject to above the GROs, NGOs and international NGOs are compulsorily registered;

(c) local NGOs are also given a place in our proposals. Apart from their welfare and development activities which they should continue, they should endeavour to give every assistance to the grassroots organisations (GROs) to evolve into better organisations. In their own regard, they should try to become more democratic and representative of the community;

(d) international NGOs are also welcome in this country. The Commission expects them in future to move away from project aid but to continue assistance in money, materials and other assistance to the NGO sector and the country. In their role to assist the GRO sector, the Commission considers it best if they collaborate with local NGOs rather than go it alone.

3   The appointment of a 'Commissioner for NGOs' and a Secretariat to attend to NGO activities.

4   A new and comprehensive legal enactment in respect of NGOs containing, inter alia, provision for

(a) compulsory registration of NGOs;

(b) formation of NGOs;

(c) certain supervisory powers in respect of NGOs, including the monitoring of foreign funding and the supervision of children's homes, homes for the aged, hostels and so on run by NGOs.

(d) The establishment of a NGO fund to help needy and deserving GROs and local NGOs. This fund would consist of monies granted by the state, and contributions made from the NGO sector, particularly contributions made by foreign funding NGOs in the circumstances set out in the report. The state shall not make use of this fund. It should be used solely to fund needy and deserving GROs and local NGOs, in terms of principles, rules and regulations made by an NGO advisory council.

5   Providing for co-ordinating mechanisms at all levels for government/NGO co-operation.

6   Finally, the Commission recommended that the government provide, encourage and assist the NGO sector to bring about the following developments:

(a) the formulation of a code of conduct;
(b) establishment of a research and training centre. This could be done in consultation and collaboration with the government;
(c) establishment of an information centre and data bank;
(d) the upgrading in skills of GROs;
(e) establishing networks and organisations representative of the NGOs to facilitate dealings with the government.

POSTSCRIPT

With the assassination of President Premadasa and with the coming in of a new President, the confrontational attitude of the government vis-à-vis NGOs was replaced by a more conciliatory position, with open invitations extended by the government to the NGOs to assist government efforts at development. Project and financial management training is being sponsored by state agencies for the benefit of NGOs and the government is exploring ways of channelling donor funds to NGOs.

Seemingly, the government is making amends for the 'no-win' confrontational stance of preceding governments. At the same time it seeks accountability, and a transparency of organisations and their workings and to inculcate a deeper understanding of development aims, policies and programmes of the government among the NGOs and their donors. Nevertheless, regulations prescribed by the Voluntary Organisations Law of 1980 and the Gazette Notification of 1993 coupled with the open invitation made by the government to the NGOs (a 'hard–soft' policy stance), reveals a continued presence of the traditional desire of Sri Lankan governments to induce the NGOs to toe the national policy line and not stray away from the state prescribed function for the NGOs largely of attending to social welfare needs.

The NGO sector since the early 1980s apparently lost sight of two cardinal realities of Sri Lanka's development: (1) that the elected government is the sole source of legitimate power and authority in the country; and as such (2) NGOs as facilitators of democratic processes and instruments of articulation of aspirations of the people had no legitimate existence without a prior recognition of their role by the government. Individual and sectoral interests developed within the NGO sector following upon their mushroom growth over the 1980s. These interests were partly a result of the diverse objectives of external donors who by directing funds and technical assistance to NGOs, sought a transformation of the sociocultural and economic base of the country that bypassed government. The transformation where it occurred was partly localised and divisive, maintained by intensive direction of funds and attention and is largely unsustainable. The transplanted pockets of so-called 'participatory development' maintained by external funds, catering quite often to alien development paradigms, remained aloof from the historically evolved domestic sociocultural base.

The historically evolved 'quality' of the domestic sociocultural base was also subjected to a threat of fragmentation and marginalisation. In the 1990s this marginalisation process, particularly on account of a spate of induced and 'forced' religious conversions of poor groups by NGOs of fundamentalist Christian sects, has resulted in a resurgence of the old nationalist revivalist movement spearheaded by the Buddhist, Hindu, Islam and Catholic laity, mobilising public opinion against fundamentalist NGOs in particular and externally funded NGOs more generally.

NGO formation continues to be seen by many local 'counterparts' as a source of income, employment and benefits. This is to a large extent determined the mushroom growth of NGOs in the 1980s, and the continued resistance of many NGOs to government moves to inculcate a sense of accountability and transparency of their organisations.

It remains to be seen whether NGOs in the country will move into the realm of national policy lobbying and programme formulation and implementation in promoting social welfare in active co-operation with the government, or whether they will continue to be preoccupied with localised issues and projects based upon ideals and concepts often in conflict with the historically determined sociocultural realities of the country. Now that government has extended a hand of friendship, with expectations of a more mature and disciplined response from the NGOs to join it in developing the country, the ball is in the NGO court, so to say, to move into a path of constructive cooperation to realise a set of common goals for the greater good of the people of Sri Lanka. The choice now lies with the NGOs of the country and their external donors.

15 NGOs and Development in Brazil: Roles and Responsibilities in a 'New World Order'

Margarita Bosch

The last few decades have brought significant changes in the political, economic and social landscape of Brazil. Neo-liberal policies have been introduced in the economy, with the emphasis on open markets, cuts in the public sector, structural adjustment, deregulation and privatisation. Democracy has been re-established, accompanied by decentralisation and constitutional guarantees regarding wider participation in public-sector management. In this landscape, two conflicting views of citizenship have emerged: one, a communitarian vision, is based on solidarity between peoples in civil society; the other is a more traditional, liberal conception of citizens bonded to the state. This first view sees in Rousseau's thinking on community the opportunity anew to substantiate and channel the energy that transforms and emancipates. The basic values underlying the communitarian model are: (1) building on the horizontal obligations that exist between citizens; (2) developing a new political culture based on participation and concrete solidarity; (3) a new quality of private and community life, based on autonomy, self-regulation, decentralisation, participatory democracy, co-operation and production based on social value. This vision goes far beyond the liberal conception of citizenship, though it does not deny the importance of the political advances secured thus far in Brazil. But as Chaui (quoted in Lefort, 1983:11) states 'democracy is a process of invention because – far from being the mere conservation of rights – it is the uninterrupted creation of new rights, the continuous subversion of what is established, and the permanent re-institution of society and politics'.

This communitarian vision of citizenship has helped to focus attention on new forms of social exclusion in Brazil which are continually created by market systems, based on gender, race and other factors. Representative democracy is the maximum possible level of political participation afforded under capitalism. However, this level of participation is not fixed; it can be increased and adapted through the development of more complex forms of participation. Capitalism will adapt to these new configurations to produce a new, post-capitalist social order. During the next few years in Brazil, new criteria for political participation will be established which will combine elements of both representative and participatory democracy. This process will involve four major changes:

1   the redefinition and broadening of what is defined as political;
2   the democratisation of social, economic, and cultural relations;
3   the global repoliticisation of social practices; and
4   the creation of new ways of transforming current structures of exploitation and domination into shared relations of power.

NGOs IN THIS NEW CONTEXT

NGOs have acquired an increased visibility in Brazil since the 1970s. They constitute a group of organisations formed by people linked either to the church, or to political activism with a Marxist slant. They do not represent corporate interests but have historical links with traditional social movements, in addition to the movements that appeared during the years of military dictatorship. As a result they represent activists from a wide range of concerns: human rights, women, race, ecology, Aids, street children, and many others. Brazilian NGOs have developed a variety of projects and programmes that aim: (1) to provide material support and services to co-operatives, production and income-generating groups and communities; and (2) to perform political tasks that – through popular education, the creation of awareness, and the provision of advisory services to popular organisations – support the development of citizenship and strengthen the autonomy of grassroots groups. Supported almost entirely by foreign non-governmental funding agencies, Brazilian NGOs have not historically cultivated relations with government and, far from substituting for the state, have maintained a constant opposition to it:

> Throughout their history they have tended towards confrontation with the state, always from a distance. Brazilian NGOs are the least inclined to try and replace the state, unlike their counterparts elsewhere in Latin America and in other continents: Bolivian NGOs, for example, have responsibilities on a virtually governmental level in agriculture, technical assistance and health. We find NGOs in Asia with 3000 employees...even

30,000 people. NGOs of this kind in India, Bangladesh and other regions, have welfare duties on a par with the 'Legião Brasileira de Assistência' (the 'Brazilian Legion for Assistance', a nationwide governmental body) or a Department of Agriculture or Health. Brazilian NGOs have no significant links with the market, having a relatively small investment in activities directly connected to production. Small-scale development experiences have already been exhaustively questioned, criticized and abandoned by most NGOs. There has been some going back, for example, to work centred on alternative technologies in agriculture. But even these are not conceived by NGOs as economic or productive projects divorced from politics and education; on the contrary, they are taken up as political and educational projects. (Durao as quoted in Landim, 1993.)

In the Brazilian context, NGOs see themselves as part of the world of politics, activism and human rights, in the struggle for the construction of citizenship and the democratisation of the state, be it in a supportive role, advising popular movements in urban and in rural areas, or acting as new social and political protagonists that seek to influence public polices. The development of a stronger identity among Brazilian NGOs has been based on a distinction from, or even opposition to, social welfare (Landim, 1993). The history of welfare organisations in Brazil, derived from religious affiliation and an orientation towards people as clients, is one of the reasons for the rejection of welfare by current NGO leaders. The tension between the provision of material services on the one hand, and the struggle for civil rights and influence over government policies on the other, has been particularly intense, with 'assistencialism' ('welfare') being the 'evil spirit' to be continuously exorcised by NGOs in their work.

A small number of Brazilian NGOs maintain a high profile through the status they have in society, by having prominent intellectuals in their ranks, or by operating ambiguously in conflicts and/or alliance with political parties, churches, universities, trade unions and sectors of government (Fernandes, 1985). However, the struggle for civil rights has given rise to a specific type of NGO committed to social transformation and the defence and promotion of human rights. These NGOs seek to develop and promote social organisation among grassroots groups in order to overcome the problems of poverty faced by the vast majority of the population. The main features of their work are:

- their target populations are groups excluded from their basic rights;
- their methods give priority to building horizontal relationships with people and organisations, offering advisory services, education on

legal rights and the linking of community organisations with broader social movements. New social movements in Brazil tend to work through non-hierarchical and decentralised structures in conjunction with the media, publicising protests and demands to increase the impact of social mobilisation;

- they are autonomous from government and political parties.

In the legal area, they seek:

- the implementation of laws which reflect a new social order;
- to guarantee equal access to justice for all;
- constitutional changes through wider participation at constituent assemblies;
- the creative application of existing laws, both in legal actions, and in the political struggle to promote new rights;
- to promote an understanding that the law is connected to issues of power.

In relation to this last point, two tendencies within the NGO community exist in permanent tension: the first group of NGOs seek equal access to justice, to the state apparatus and to the political process in general. These NGOs use the law creatively and promote constitutional and legal reforms to advance social gains. They tend to work directly with communities and grassroots groups. The second group seek channels of power outside the state and political parties, aiming to strengthen the ability of communities to develop new forms of regulation and new rights that can meet their interests more effectively. NGOs in this arena tend to work with social movements in their search for a new model of society, characterized by new power relations.

Four sets of influences have been important here:

- a more professional approach among left-wing activists who seek to work with the new social movements, bringing a greater political awareness to daily life, and moving from a basic needs to a basic rights focus in their work;
- the influence of the Church and of the Theology of Liberation in the search for a new model of society based on ethical values of equality, freedom and social responsibility;
- social mobilisation and legal organisation in the struggle for land, housing, sanitation, health and education;
- the influence of Northern NGOs in supporting the development of democracy, both ideologically and through the financial support they provided during the period of dictatorship in Brazil.

TWO CASE STUDIES

Walter Rachid: Victory in Court, Indifference from Government

Walter Rachid was born on 21 November 1983, in the city of Olinda, Greater Metropolitan Area of Recife, state of Pernambuco. He died at the age of nine on 31 July 1993. The cause of death was certified to be 'multiple failure of body organs as a result of post-transfusional Aids'. Rachid belonged to the lower middle class, a part of the Brazilian population which, although having a place to live, has no access to proper education and health services. In 1986, he was taken to hospital by his parents for the treatment of bronchopneumonia. While in hospital his condition worsened as the result of a succession of medical errors, resulting in deep anaemia which required a blood transfusion. The blood was contaminated, though the disease was only discovered in 1989 when, ill with TB, Rachid was HIV-tested and diagnosed as positive.

After failed attempts to get help from the government, Rachid's parents initiated legal action through the Federal Judiciary Support Service,[1] with a cautionary lawsuit against INAMPS – the Brazilian federal body in charge of medical assistance within the welfare system – as well as the Pernambuco Health Department. The aim was to establish the legal right to a guaranteed level of medical, hospital and social assistance.[2] The solicitor hired by Rachid's parents had to abandon the case, so a team from the Brazilian NGO CENDHEC ('Centro Dom Helder Camara') took over responsibility. The judge granted a preliminary ruling[3] determining that INAMPS and the Pernambuco Health Department were bound to ensure all assistance to the patient's needs. Soon after the ruling, CENDHEC's solicitors proceeded to a lawsuit aimed at consolidating this judgement on a permanent basis. In this process, the media was a very important ally, denouncing the indifference of the government repeatedly. Two other options remained. The first consisted of a criminal lawsuit for manslaughter to be carried out by the Public Prosecution Office, with CENDHEC's solicitors acting as assistants to the prosecution. The second was legal action by CENDHEC on behalf of Rachid's parents to seek compensation for moral and material damages and losses caused by medical negligence at the time of their son's treatment.

Rachid's case is described here for three reasons: first, to illustrate what the fight against AIDS means in Brazil today; second, to illustrate the low standards of care available for AIDS patients: there are no hospitals, no specialised professionals, no domestic assistance and, above all, no sensitivity to the problem; third, to illustrate the absence of a public legal defence system in Brazil and the role of an NGO in addressing this lack. According to the Constitution this service should be organized by the states, but very few do so. The state of Pernambuco, for example, has been waiting for five years for the validation of its Public Defence Office. CENDHEC'S Legal Help Centre aims to do the work that would otherwise be performed by government. CENDHEC managed to go beyond the formal legal procedures to promote public discussion over the case, which helped in overcoming the limitations of one agency acting alone. When undertaken on a collective basis, cases such as this will help towards the construction of a better health service and a coherent and efficient legal defence system to care for those in need. CENDHEC feels that this is the most effective contribution it can make as an NGO toward the securing of basic rights in Brazil.

Brasília Teimosa: the Right to Education

Brasília Teimosa is a low-income community in Recife with a population of 16 913 inhabitants, 90 per cent of whom have no waged income. Only 23.6 per cent of the adults that have jobs have their labour rights guaranteed through the signing of the relevant papers. There are nine schools in the community: six belonging to the state network, one to the municipal network, and two are community schools. The community is known for its fighting spirit and high level of organisation. During 1957 and 1958, at the time of President Kubitscheck's government, Brasilia was being built. Immigrants from the hinterlands of Pernambuco established themselves in a tidal and swamp area situated in Pina, a suburb of Recife. The reaction from the City Hall was rapid. The shacks were pulled down. A war of endurance followed: the immigrants rebuilt during the night what municipal council workers destroyed during the day. Hence the name Brasília Teimosa ('Stubborn or Obstinate Brasília'). Eventually the immigrants' stubbornness proved effective and the area was granted official recognition. Project 'Teimosinho' or 'Little Stubborn One', set up by the Residents' Council in 1979, has since won many improvements for the area.

CENDHEC had already been providing the community with advisory services on land rights and from 1993 a popular education project was set up to support people in their demands for the right to community-run education programmes. The project consisted of four components: (1) showing that education is a collective and de facto right guaranteed by the Federal Constitution as a state obligation which, if fulfilled inadequately, can be legally demanded by the community; (2) teaching the use of legal tools with which the community can demand educational services from the state; (3) advising the population on the opportunities which exist to take part in the drafting of and control over the implementation of public education policies; (4) stimulating the creation of a residents' organisation to push forward the struggle for basic schooling.

After a year's work the following results had been achieved:

- two community lawsuits against the State Education Department, demanding the construction of a new building for the oldest school in the neighbourhood which operated precariously in a single hall, divided by wooden panels;
- a demand for the refurbishing of all the state schools in the neighbourhood. This was led by the headmasters and teachers of these schools, by the members of the Neighbourhood Association, and by parents and pupils;
- a commission to monitor school work representing the schools, the Residents' Council, parents, pupils and CENDHEC;
- a proposal to set up a School Council in each public school in the area.

Initially, state schools feared control by the community, but little by little the community, headmasters and teachers started to join together. At the beginning of 1994, a counterpart team was formed of headmasters, teachers, members of the Residents' Council, and Student Guilds. This group formed a permanent committee that gradually took over responsibility for negotiations with the Education Department, and for monitoring the work, becoming less dependent upon CENDHEC in the process. The community now takes responsibility for demanding collective and de facto rights, and learning to make use of the legal means available in the Federal Constitution and the Brazilian Statute of the Child and Adolescent.

LESSONS FROM THE CASE STUDIES

The Role of CENDHEC

CENDHEC's interventions are deliberately carried out at different levels, with maximum advantage being taken of the synergies which exist between them:

- with communities and their organisations (neighbourhood councils, student guilds and so on), providing advisory services to help prepare people for the full and autonomous exercise of their citizenship;

- in relation to the Education and Health Departments, advising communities on how to maximise the impact of their demands, and supporting legal action, if necessary taking those responsible to court;
- engaging in actions designed to underscore and publicise the government's legal responsibilities in protecting the rights of children and young people, and pressurise the Prosecutors' Office to fulfil its constitutional role as Inspector of the Law;
- with the public in general: as a member of the 'Pro-Education Movement', a network of organisations for the improvement of public schooling; networking with other NGOs that constitute the 'State Forum for the Defence of Child and Adolescent Rights'; in the 'National Forum for the Defence of Child and Adolescent Rights', monitoring legal proposals in the Congress and maintaining a dialogue with members of parliament.

CENDHEC has demonstrated that these roles, and the linkages which have been developed between them, provide effective channels for NGO action in Brazil (though significantly no funding is received from bilateral or multilateral aid agencies, only from northern NGOs).

Expanding the Roles and Scope of Action for NGOs in Brazil

In recent years it has become clear that interventions in the social and political field call for significant internal changes in NGOs. Relationships with beneficiaries/members have become more demanding and more specialised competences are required. Specifically, NGOs require:

- legal, political and social knowledge, particularly in collective and de facto rights;
- the ability to link specialised knowledge with political interventions in government, and to mobilise the media and other channels of social communication;
- broad knowledge in the legal field, which is essential for the creative use of alternative applications of the law;
- involvement in organised civil movements, occupying strategic spaces for intervention in wider fora, social movements and thematic networks.

The development of NGOs in Brazil over the last 20 years has been influenced by political, social and economic changes on both the domestic and international fronts. In economic terms, the most significant changes have been the increasing deterioration of living conditions for the vast majority of the population, reaching levels of absolute poverty for 32 million people in Brazil; and the bankruptcy of the state and its inability to supply basic needs in health, education and housing.

In social terms, the rise of social movements and networks, and their increasingly high profile in the public sphere, has been very important. In the political arena, the return to a democratic regime (with all its implications) and rising demands for public participation in the administration, have clearly been critical. These changes have forced NGOs to redefine their means of intervention, moving from isolated projects to a systematic vision of wider social and political problems, which in turn demands a stronger linkage between actions at the micro and macro levels. A critical analysis of NGO performance suggests that Brazil has good professionals, and strong capacities to formulate and propose ideas for public policy reform, and for domestic and international networking. In the national context, NGOs have grown in legitimacy and credibility. In the media, NGOs are increasingly present: they appear in the political pages of major newspapers, and participate in phone-in programmes, interviews, and debates on specific themes or issues. Government representatives have also shown growing interest in calling for the participation of NGOs in secretariats and as technical staff. This has created some ambiguity on both sides. Government departments have a pragmatic attitude toward NGOs, seeking specialized and low-cost labour. The NGOs, in turn, see this as an opportunity to acquire inside knowledge and experience of government strategy and policies.

In relation to civil society, NGOs have advanced in their ability to establish links with different institutions, extending these ties to the trade union movement, the professional sectors, class organisations and thematic networks. They have joined forces with campaigns for ethics in politics, for external control of the Judiciary, and for the monitoring of various Inquiry Committees. The most relevant example is their decisive contribution to 'Ação da Cidadania Contra a Fome, a Miseria e pela Vida' ('The Citizen's Movement Against Hunger'). This campaign originated during a seminar of Brazilian NGOs in 1993 and aimed to demonstrate that misery and hunger are problems that **can** be solved by civil society. It initiated a huge number of local committees and networks around the country and linked them together into a permanent framework for mass social action. A poll by the Brazilian Institute of Public opinion showed that, by the end of 1993, 21 million people had made a contribution to the campaign by giving food or clothes and 2.8 million had joined one of the campaign committees.

CONCLUSIONS: EXPECTATIONS AND CONCERNS FOR THE 1990s

CENDHEC'S experience shows that it is possible for NGOs in Brazil to play a positive role in securing basic rights and promoting broader participation in the political process. However, it also gives rise to some concerns about the social and economic transformations that are influencing the work of NGOs, and NGO–state relations, in contemporary Brazil. First, how can new roles and responsibilities for putting participatory democracy into practice be accomplished? In particular, how can NGOs maintain a balance between their independent profile and the need to respond to increasing demands from the government sector? Second, how can participatory democracy and decentralisation be secured at a time of cuts in public funds at the national level, conditioned by Brazil's position in the global economy? Third, advances are being made in social and political rights, but without equivalent progress in regulation, implementation and monitoring. How can NGOs help to close this gap? Fourth, in the field of international co-operation, how can NGOs address the 'New Policy Agenda' of economic liberalisation and political democratisation used increasingly by northern donors to govern aid transfers, when they see this agenda as running counter to their own goals – the construction of democracy and the strengthening of civil society? In addition, how can aid to countries such as Brazil be preserved in the face of competing priorities from Africa and Eastern Europe? Many northern NGOs, for example, have already decided to cut back on their support to partners in Brazil. Finally, how can NGOs and donors overcome the vision of co-operation based solely on the basis of funding, and move towards a new style of co-operation that values common objectives for a real 'new world order', rooted in international solidarity and in shared projects for a new democratic society?

Since 1991, ABONG (the Brazilian NGO Association) has been stimulating reflections on international co-operation, both nationally and internationally. By way of conclusion, what follows is a summary of the key questions which emerged from the meeting of ABONG and co-operation agencies held in Recife in 1993, which attempted to lay out some common ground for North–South co-operation in the 1990s. These questions must be answered if closer partnerships are to be formed and maintained under the New Policy Agenda (described by Hulme and Edwards in Chapter 1).

● How can market liberalisation and adjustment policies which foster inequalities within and between rich and poor countries be addressed?

- Multilateral efforts are required to disseminate – in the North and in the South – NGO concepts of evaluation, the impact of co-operation and the work of NGOs.
- NGOs must reinforce the conviction that the problem of development is a shared one, requiring shared agendas and shared commitment to break away from conservative orthodoxies.
- Careful planning of meetings, consultations, exchanges, the construction of joint agendas, and the definition of funding priorities is required in order to find the right combination of multilateral and bilateral exchanges.
- Transparency within partnerships must be promoted to ensure an adequate flow of information among agencies, and in overcoming administrative and financial difficulties.
- Latin American NGOs and International NGOs need to define together a joint strategy to secure continuity of support over time.
- Funding policies that emphasise the macro perspective in project support and institutional programmes and which provide longer-term funding should be encouraged.

The key issue in all of this is the recognition and negotiation of *shared* agendas among NGOs and donors, rather than the *imposition* of agendas from the outside. This is a key task for the next five years.

Notes

1. In Brazil, a special Court of Law exists to adjudicate over all matters involving the Federal Public Administration.
2. The Brazilian judicial process encompasses three components: 'process of knowledge', in which one aims to prove one's rights; 'executive process', where the result of the 'process of knowledge' is served on the defeated party; and 'cautionary process', which aims to secure the existence of the other two processes through preliminary rulings.
3. A preliminary ruling can be granted by a judge at the outset of a case to gurantee the object of the dispute, thereby avoiding the termination of the suit as a result of time limits.

16 Mice among the Tigers: Adding Value in NGO–Government Relations in South-East Asia

Richard Mawer

This chapter examines the issues which emerge from Save the Children's UK's work in South-east Asia over the past 11 years in the field of disability. In particular, the chapter looks at the ways in which Save the Children-UK (SCF) has added value to project activities by using a large number of diverse government, donor, NGO and community contacts to influence government policy and practice through a range of mechanisms dependent on the degree of access to policy makers. It is based on two case studies from contrasting contexts: Thailand, a middle-income country open to outside influences; and its much lower-income and more isolated post-communist neighbours. The case studies represent a more positive form of interaction between NGOs, governments and donors than many others described in this book, but one which is highly dependent on context and the nature and quality of relationships established between the different actors.

I SCF's WORK IN CONTEXT

While most countries in South-east Asia are experiencing high levels of economic growth and associated social turmoil, they display different political and economic contexts, from well- established integration into the global economy, to post-communist restructuring after many years of isolation. At one extreme, Thailand has achieved economic growth rates averaging 11.7 per cent between 1988 and 1990 (Economist Intelligence Unit, 1994). However, the democratic governments which have alternated with military regimes have not brought radical changes in development policy nor major shifts in political power. Wide gaps exist between government legislation and rhetoric, and implementation on the ground: for example, decentralisation has brought little local control over budgets, and so far has had little impact (Hirsh, 1994; *Thai Development Newsletter*, 1994).

By contrast, Laos, with almost 20 years of uninterrupted communist rule, has remained among the world's most economically underdeveloped and isolated countries. The 1990s have seen a marked process of economic liberalisation, but within existing authoritarian political structures. The opening of markets has been accompanied by a search for ideas from the outside world, with a strong desire to 'catch up' balanced by a real fear of the destabilisation that this openness will inevitably bring (Makabenta, 1995).

In Thailand, NGOs emerged from two principal roots: long-established 'Khunying' ('grand lady') charitable foundations; and student political activists who, after being defeated in the 1973 military coup, retreated to community-based activism (often after a period of active engagement in communist insurgency). NGOs born out of direct opposition to government tend to maintain a confrontational attitude, making constructive dialogue difficult. These difficulties were reinforced by the important role played by NGOs in the overthrow of the military-dominated government in 1992. Although some Thai NGOs are still controlled by autocratic leaders with limited target-group or staff participation, NGOs are increasing in numbers, professionalism and influence. In Laos, local NGOs do not exist. The Lao Women's Union and Youth organisations continue to 'follow the party line', and cannot be described as genuine social movements. However, at the provincial level they are relatively autonomous and can be very active.

SCF's approach varies widely in these different contexts, according to the strength of local organisations and SCF's particular history and contacts. In Thailand, NGOs are relatively strong and SCF has little high-level access of its own to policy makers. This requires different ways of working than in Laos, where local NGOs do not exist and SCF advisors have senior ministry officials as direct counterparts. With a relatively small budget in both countries, SCF has been involved in the last eleven years in a large number of projects spread over many sectors: health, social welfare, NGO development, disability issues and HIV/AIDS. Projects have been run in partnership with both NGOs and government, and in one case, by SCF itself. Does this spread of projects and sectors reflect a lack of focus and strategy, or a way of increasing influence and adding value through interconnected and mutually-reinforcing activities? To answer this question two case studies are presented below.

THE DEVELOPMENT OF COMMUNITY-BASED
REHABILITATION (CBR) IN THAILAND

SCF's work in Thailand in the early 1980s included attempts to improve the functioning of government institutions for children. After several years of training input, it became clear that changing from task-oriented to child-oriented ways of working, and maintaining levels of staff enthusiasm, could not be sustained without greater commitment and resources from senior levels of management (Tolfree, 1995). While institutions were unlikely to present a suitable environment for children's development, their very presence encouraged abandonment, especially for children with disabilities. Some parents were convinced that their children would be best cared for by professionals, and saw no way of assisting them to develop in a family or community setting with limited professional inputs.

Therefore SCF investigated the potential for CBR initiatives in a Bangkok slum area. Unable to find interested local NGO partners, and perceiving it necessary to build up on-the-ground CBR experience in Thailand, SCF decided to implement the project directly and use it to encourage others to test out similar methodologies. As a result of previous multi-sectoral work and its credibility with several ministries and NGOs, SCF was able to assist in introducing CBR to a wider audience in Thailand via a National Workshop organised in collaboration with Christoffel Blinden Mission in 1988, which had senior government, United Nations, international and local NGO representation. The Thai government's rehabilitation services showed considerable imagination in bringing the concepts of CBR to the attention of Ministry of Public Health (MoPH) staff and SCF supported them by financing training seminars in two provinces. But as elsewhere in the world, the Ministry's perception of CBR was medically-dominated, focusing on those who could be 'cured' using a 'top-down' approach.

SCF therefore investigated other ways of working. In Chiangrai Province SCF worked at both community and district levels in collaboration with two local NGOs in order to capitalise on existing contacts and initiatives. SCF provided training in CBR techniques, project management support, and some funding, but just as important was the link it provided to government and other CBR experience with Thailand and abroad. In Nakhom Panom Province, SCF worked in partnership with the Provincial Ministry of Public Health, looking to gain insights into how CBR ideas and practices might be integrated into government structures. Again it was the link with NGO experience that provided a significant counterweight to the government's approach to CBR.

These experiences and partnerships taught SCF that in order to be effective and sustainable, more emphasis had to be given to the educational and social aspects of rehabilitation; the constructive roles that disabled children and their families and organisations can play; the importance of involving them and their communities in programme design and evaluation (rather than simply in implementation); and the need for strategies to promote the attitudinal changes that are prerequisites for these changes. The challenge was to move the medical interpretation of CBR towards a multisectoral approach, which required a real shift in relationships between professionals, volunteers, 'clients', families and communities. Sponsorship by SCF of a senior Ministry of Public Health trainer to attend the Institute of Child Health's CBR course in London helped to strengthen links with allies in the Ministry and encouraged them to move the CBR agenda into these more difficult areas. A wider CBR training curriculum was developed for government health and social welfare staff. Building on past cooperation, SCF was approached by the Department of Public Welfare not only to help initiate their CBR activities, but also to link them with related Ministry of Health initiatives from the planning stage.

CBR has also gained wider recognition in the 1992 Disability Act. SCF's experience from the different (but never isolated) projects with which the agency has worked directly, and from the national network of NGOs working with children with disabilities and the associations of disabled people and parents encouraged by SCF, will feed into the implementation of the Act via representation on the CBR Sub-Committee.

WORKING WITH THE UNESCO RESOURCE PACK ON 'SPECIAL NEEDS IN THE CLASSROOM' IN LAOS, THAILAND AND VIETNAM

This UNESCO initiative aims 'to develop and disseminate a resource pack of ideas and materials that can be used by teacher educators to support teachers in mainstream schools in responding to pupil diversity' (Ainscow, 1994), adapting teaching techniques to enable teachers to react positively to differences, problems and impairments within a framework of teachers' responsibility to try and ensure 'Education for All' within their communities. A pilot study developed by an international team was trialled in eight countries during 1990–91, and experience incorporated into a rewritten Resource Pack (Ainscow, 1993; UNESCO, 1993). A subsequent regional workshop provoked interest from the representative of the Teacher

Training Department from Thailand, who initiated planning for a National Workshop in Bangkok in January 1992.

SCF had been working on Special Education, and in particular Integrated Education (IE), in Thailand for some years through projects with a local NGO to integrate visually impaired children into mainstream schools in 12 provinces, and in a government hospital, integrating children with mental impairments into two Bangkok primary schools (Klinmahorm and Ireland, 1992). These projects were closely related to SCF's CBR work, but it was clear that, while individual teachers co-operated in admitting children with disabilities to their schools, the Ministry of Education was not interested in becoming a junior partner in what was seen as primarily a Ministry of Health initiative. Therefore redefining integrated education as a separate focus to the CBR work was seen as a sensible strategy. The goal was to interest and link together the different government departments concerned and the initiatives they were undertaking, usually independently of one-another.

SCF saw the UNESCO proposal as a useful way of advancing this strategy. The agency financed the translation of the Resource Pack into Thai, and used its contacts to include SCF staff and government partners in a two-week training workshop which brought together 20 teachers from three teacher-training colleges in Thailand, Laos and Vietnam. The SCF Education Advisor in Laos, who was working on curriculum development within the Education Ministry, had been able to interest senior government officials in the IE approach and progressively incorporate IE perspectives into teacher-training courses. With virtually no disability professionals to draw on (or upset!), teachers and trainers in Laos have readily risen to the challenge. In Vietnam, using the contacts built up in upgrading special education teachers in Ho Chi Minh City in recent years, SCF was able to introduce the concepts behind the Resource Pack to senior representatives of the Department of Education, leading to the piloting of the package in three schools.

In a related venture (not linked directly to the UNESCO Pack) in Anhui Province in China, SCF worked through pilot kindergartens to integrate very young children with disabilities into mainstream provision. It soon became clear that changing teaching techniques to include children with mental impairments into the class benefitted all the children and staff. Innovations included changing the traditionally teacher-dominated classroom to one in which children worked in small groups, and encouraging more imaginative play and greater pupil–teacher interaction. Teachers gain from using team teaching methods and from focusing on children as individuals with differing needs. These ideas spread rapidly throughout the school to other classes which had no 'special' children, and the approach has proved so popular with teachers and administrators that the project has now scaled-up to ten pilot kindergartens spread throughout the province, and into Chinese Government policy (UNESCO, 1994; Tolfree, 1995).

However, in Thailand, which has considerable experience in segregated special education, the UNESCO project has made very slow progress. It has been blocked by the Special Education Departments fear of loosing control and influence; by the Primary Education Department's reluctance to move into a difficult area at a time when they are also assuming respon-sibility for some aspects of secondary education; and by the Teacher Training Department's desire to 'leave this to the professionals'. Only in one province (where SCF has been able to follow-up and establish con-structive personal relationships between the different government depart-ments) has real progress been made.

These different contacts enabled SCF to expand a national initiative into a sub-regional one, and bring into the educational debate the years of experience that NGO and government staff had accumulated. This was further developed in a workshop on IE for SCF staff and partners, govern-ment, NGO and United Nations representatives from Laos, Thailand and Vietnam held in 1993 (Save the Children Fund – (UK), 1993).

IMPLICATIONS FOR NGO–GOVERNMENT RELATIONS

Ways of Working

While these case studies may indicate a steady progression within a well-planned strategy, this is not the case or the intention. They are written from hindsight, with many tactical shifts having occurred, capitalising on opportunities and attempting to overcome obstacles as they presented themselves. The key factors in the case studies are the mutually support-ive and reinforcing interactions that increased the overall value of each one, whether based on project experience or individual contacts. Training for staff from one project used resource persons from other projects, thus building on practical experience; links are created between NGOs and government departments who do not naturally relate or learn easily from each other; reviews are conducted by representatives of a range of organi-sations to ensure that lessons are learned more widely. Many of these interventions have minimal cost but can have considerable impact. A number of issues and questions emerge from the case studies, relating particularly to how to maximise the potential for NGOs to influence governments:

1   Having a wide range of partners within the programme area has the potential to be most beneficial, especially when direct access to policy makers is not readily available. This applies to levels of working (national, provincial, district and community), as well as to organisations, (government, NGO, community). How can agencies ensure that the resulting 'cocktail' is constructive rather than explosive? Clearly, the answer will be country-specific, and demand considerable on-the-ground presence and contacts to illuminate how lessons learned from working with government can influence policy makers; whether mechanisms already exist to feed NGO experience into government systems; and whether NGO influence is likely to be more, or less, influential than other contacts or media pressure. In particular, as relations between governments, NGOs and community organisations are being reassessed in the light of the 'New Policy Agenda', an understanding of historical interactions, current roles, and future perspectives, is necessary.

2   Even in countries where government and local NGOs are available, there will be circumstances where it is advantageous for international NGOs to implement projects directly. Such situations include:
    (a) cases where it is necessary to gain the initial attention of NGO and government policy makers via direct community-based experience;
    (b) the read to increase the credibility of training inputs and networking activities;
    (c) occasions when NGO partners are unwilling to develop sustainable models for government;
    (d) occasions when prospective partners are not yet ready to accept responsibility for a project: for example, when there are groups of disabled people who lack confidence and organisational capacity.

3   Supporting or creating networks of similarly focused organisations can be very productive and cost-effective in influencing public attitudes as well as government. However, NGOs must avoid the tendency for networks to become fora for the exchange of rhetoric rather than formulating complementary activities. In Thailand, the level of involvement of members in the conception of the network has been the key factor in determining subsequent levels of participation, commitment and financial contributions. Clear initial agreement from the members covering the role of any coordinator and his/her degree of

proactivity, and the level of representation and financial inputs from member organisations, is essential if collective ownership is to be established. Splitting up into activity groups focusing on a particular region or subject area has also proved successful.

4   Many of the most important NGO interventions described above have very low or no costs, but require small amounts of funding at short notice for workshops, training and visits. Readily available funds and flexible procedures are required to take maximum advantage of opportunities as they arise. NGOs need greater access to this kind of funding but donor demands for increasingly detailed and tightly controlled financial and project planning and monitoring documents do not facilitate this process. Declining levels of voluntary income among international NGOs will encourage even tighter financial earmarking. What is required is a move toward broader programme funding rather than current project-specific approaches. Moves toward regional rather than purely national programmes could also increase flexibility.

5   The value of chance encounters and opportunistic interventions should not be overlooked. Intellectual argument and/or money is not the only way to influence government and NGO leaders; establishing personal relationships is vital. This requires a clear understanding of cultural norms by NGO staff; it may also necessitate the ability to drink toasts (or be able to refuse without causing offence) and a compatible sense of humour!

Working with Government

In a multisectoral area like disability, working with government poses particular problems since the different ministries involved vie to establish leadership, gain recognition and secure funding. Ministries may be unwilling to co-operate and the issue may be a low priority anyway. Even within ministries, different departments may be reluctant to co-operate. For example, special education personnel, while possessing the expertise, may not wish to assist integrated education as they see this as deprofessionalising their speciality and undermining their authority. These obstacles can be particularly frustrating in areas where outline legislation has been enacted but detailed legislation is awaited (for example, 'Education for All'). Government can then publicise the legislation while little changes at ground level.

In countries where governments have sufficient authority, resources and skills to initiate change, using high-level access at central level may be the most appropriate way to introduce new ideas. However, this is not always the most productive approach. The introduction of the UNESCO Resource Pack in Thailand has made very little progress since it was imposed from above with little understanding at the level of the teacher-training colleges.

NGO Roles

While NGOs in Thailand have played a vital role in developing services initially and in changing attitudes toward disability, they face a number of obstacles which prevent them from developing the capacity or outlook required to become providers of services on a large (regional or national) scale. The development of local NGO capacity and links between NGOs has long been a major aim of SCF programmes. This has been addressed through a series of training programmes for middle management on project proposal writing, monitoring and evaluation techniques, financial management and fundraising for middle managers of primarily child-focused NGOs. The aim has not only been to improve skills in project development and strategic planning, but specifically to create a more democratic management structure less dependent on charismatic leaders, and more open to the opinions of beneficiary groups.

However, many Thai NGOs lack a strategy to scale up the impact of their work and feed their experience into government in order to develop sustainable solutions; these areas are not priorities for them. This is due either to their basic distrust of government's motives and intentions, or to a desire to provide the best possible ('western standard') services, stemming in part from their charitable rather than developmental roots. This has led to a real reluctance to allow standards to fall in order to improve coverage or to allow for increasing integration into government services.

As conditions become conducive to working in Indo-China, international funding is increasingly being withdrawn from Thailand. NGO fundraising in-country has been increasing and is now seen as a priority, but progress is slow. Developing sustainble services on a larger scale is not presently realistic without a growing dependence on government finance. Such funds are increasing, with government contracting out the more sensitive and problematic areas without giving up overall control. But where government has the funds to finance virtually country-wide primary health and education services (as in Thailand), or while possessing few funds has the political will and organisation to develop the quality and availability of these services (as in Laos), is the growth of NGO service provision an appropriate goal? Is it not preferable to encourage NGOs to use their particular talents and energy in developing pilot experiences from which they can influence government strategy? Such strategies are more likely to lead to sustainable services in the future.

The Government–NGO Interface

A key role for SCF has been to create bridges between NGOs with very different viewpoints, between NGOs and government departments who have little natural affinity, and between different government ministries and departments within them. SCF has also been active in developing networks (such as agencies working with children with disabilities) and encouraging them to use their combined weight to influence government through workshops and representation on committees, and to shape public attitudes through the press, TV and radio. This bridging role requires a complex dance, maintaining contacts with both local NGOs and government without becoming too closely identified with one group or the other. Increasingly, government and NGOs in Thailand are becoming aware of each others strengths as well as weaknesses, and tentatively establishing the groundwork for collaboration and partnership, either at a local/district or national level. The potential for creating 'all-win' situations does exist, though it may be eroded by the trends outlined in Chapter 1 of this book.

Relations with Multilateral Donors

The major relationship with multilateral agencies in these case studies has been with UNESCO, where there does appear to be a particular complementarity between the strengths and weaknesses of the NGOs and donors involved. UNESCO is able to gain the attention of government, and exert peer pressure on other policy makers in the international arena. SCF (and other NGOs) do not automatically have this high-level access but usually have the on-the-ground contacts to understand the 'real' situation, and how this differs from government rhetoric. They can use their in-depth understanding to feed into government planning. UNESCO is obliged to work through formal government hierarchies, and can find itself working with partners with no real interest in (or even conceivably hostility to) projects. NGOs have the flexibility to assess levels of understanding and interest among different players and work with those who are most enthusiastic and best placed to exert influence. While neither SCF nor UNESCO have access to very large-scale funding, UNESCO has the added burden of lengthier planning and approval procedures. SCF has greater flexibility in finding the small sums often required to finance training, meetings, and visits. While this complementarity has been utilised constructively in the case of Integrated Education, it is unlikely that similar relationships can be formed so easily with the more powerful multilateral agencies who may have a clearer desire to determine directions and influence agendas, whether with government or NGO partners. This is more likely to be the case in a country such as Laos which has less experience of official aid and which may have great difficulty in refusing offers of assistance even when deemed inappropriate (LaFond, 1995).

CONCLUSIONS

SCF has managed to further aspects of the Convention on the Rights of the Child relating to disability by encouraging the development of community-based rehabilitation and integrated education initiatives in South-east Asia. This has been achieved by working directly with governments where high-level access is possible and appropriate, or by working through inter-related initiatives with NGOs, CBOs and local government. By developing a large number of innovative and interrelated NGO and government projects, and then providing mechanisms to network between them, considerable added value has been obtained at relatively low cost. This approach demands considerable on-the-ground experience and a flexible and opportunistic approach.

Local NGOs possess considerable advantages in these ways of working. As they increase their professionalism, and draw general lessons more effectively from their project experiences, their capacity to influence, as well as provide services more widely, will grow. Increasing their linkage and networking roles will improve their effectiveness, creating constructive partnerships not only between NGOs, but also with governments and official aid agencies, based on an understanding of each other's strengths and weaknesses. In South-east Asia, whether in countries which are able to finance some level of nation-wide service provision, or in those with fewer funds but which retain the organisational capacity to develop the availability and quality of services, developing pilot projects and influencing governments will be a more productive use of the energy and freedom of NGOs than the pursuit of larger-scale service provision. However, for these roles to be played effectively requires that international agencies recognise the advantages of the kind of strategies described in this chapter, and are prepared to support them with the appropriate level and pattern of assistance.

Part IV

NGOs, the Poor and Disadvantaged: Returning to the Roots?

17 Between Co-option and Irrelevance? Latin American NGOs in the 1990s

Jenny Pearce

The debate about the role of NGOs in Latin America has taken a more cautious direction as the 1990s have progressed. Whereas the 1980s saw a ripple of excitement with the 'discovery' that the negative impact of the retreat of the state from economic development could be moderated by the dynamism of the myriad of organisations outside the state committed to grass-roots development (for example, Korten, 1987; Annis, 1987; Clark, 1991), the 1990s have seen rethinking on both the appropriate role of the state and the specific competence of NGOs.

The diversity amongst NGOs and the unevenness of NGO capacity has been acknowledged; empirical research to test the first enthusiastic embrace has revealed that NGOs must also face some hard questions about their accountability, legitimacy and effectiveness (for example, Bebbington and Thiele, 1993; Carroll, 1992); the danger of co-option into the neoliberal agendas of governments and international bodies has been recognised (Edwards and Hulme, 1994); and the belief that NGOs are necessarily more successful in overcoming poverty than state agencies has been challenged (for example, Arellano-López and Petras, 1994). The potential of NGOs to play a role in democratisation processes, in effective service delivery and in the fostering of a more people-centred development has not been seriously questioned. But precisely how this potential can be realised given the multiple relationships with which NGOs are involved has become more contested and controversial than ever.

This chapter argues that this is a critical point for NGOs in Latin America. They have been drawn into a project of capitalist modernisation and political liberalisation in the region by official bilateral and multilateral funding agencies and governments, and identified as significant actors in that process (see Chapter 2 by Blair in this volume). While some are only too willing to respond and many new NGOs have been established to seize the opportunities, many remain fearful of the implications. Serving the state and big external donors can and often does contradict with social transformatory projects involving the empowerment of the poor. The latter often involves outcomes which are not easily measurable in terms of the efficiency and effectiveness criteria donors usually adopt to protect their 'investment'. As the Latin American private sector becomes stronger, more independent and dynamic the courting of NGOs as service providers by international donors may diminish. But nor do NGOs wish to remain peripheral, underfunded and irrelevant.

NGOs today are caught between the macro-level political imperatives and their micro-level social/developmental roles. This is a time-honoured problem for them, but the nature of the political imperatives has changed dramatically in recent years and fundamentally shifted amd extended the boundaries within which NGOs have hitherto worked, opening up the realm of choice of role and direction as never before.This chapter begins by exploring the changing context in which NGOs operate in Latin America, in particular the evolution of the region's 'associational cultures'. NGOs are just one part of a broad range of groups and organisations struggling to define and redefine the parameters in which they can operate, and understanding the way these parameters have been changing in recent years is a prerequisite for assessing the present debate on NGOs. Divergent models of associational development are on the agenda and increasingly NGOs are having to make choices about where they stand in relationship to these models; the NGO community is likely to further divide and sub-divide as a result.

Perhaps the key challenge for NGOs is to define the criteria on which they will make their choices in the future. This involves establishing an identity and confronting two of the major issues which the opening up of choice has highlighted: legitimacy and accountability. Legitimacy relates to the *right* to represent and the *consent* of the represented. As unelected, self-appointed bodies, which make claims to represent the poor and under-privileged, NGOs often have to build their legitimacy through their effectiveness as organisations. How effectiveness is to be assessed and in particular who is to do the assessing become crucial questions. There are rival claimants to this role often with rival criteria: the donors, the state and beneficiaries. Where NGOs derive their legitimacy from and who they are accountable to, ultimately involves political decisions which NGOs will differ about. But clarity on both may be one way that NGOs still committed to social change can avoid the risks of either irrelevancy or co-option, of either being dragged into the 1990s to fulfil the agendas of others or remaining stuck in the old agendas of the 1970s. NGOs must acknowledge the problems of the past and make choices concerning their new identity for the future. This must include well-articulated objectives, a decision on where to seek legitimacy given the competing possibilities and agreed mechanisms of accountability.

A BRIEF DISCUSSION OF DEFINITIONS

The issue of defining what is meant by NGOs has been a subject of endless discussion (see Carroll, 1992; Bebbington and Farrington, 1993; Pearce, 1993, among many others). Nevertheless, it still seems necessary to offer a clear definition of the terminology to be employed. This is because the term 'NGOs' could be used and often is to encompass an extremely wide range of organisations from social movements and pressure groups through to sports clubs and other forms of civil association. In Latin America the question of distinctions is particularly important, as there is a relatively long tradition of social and political organising of all kinds, and the region is notable in the South for this history and specificity.

In the course of the debate on definitions, it has become common to distinguish membership from non-membership organisations, 'primary grassroots organisations' from 'intermediary support organisations' and international from national organisations (Carroll, 1992:11). Carroll identifies grassroots support organisations (GSOs) and membership support organisations (MSOs) as the focus of his book on indigenous or national NGOs in Latin America who 'tend to serve, represent and work with several primary groups. In other words they operate on the next level above the primary grassroots organizations and seek to assist and support them' (*ibid.*:11). I share Carroll's definitional focus on organisations committed to grassroots social activism, but my own definitional concerns have been to distinguish between intermediary development organisations and 'popular' organisations or movements, and I would not put a membership organisation such as a labour union within the same category as a support organisation, as does Carroll. My distinctions are based on differences in social composition, institutionalisation and accountability.

Intermediary development NGOs, the concern of this chapter, are typically composed of middle-class, educated and professional people who have opted for political or humanitarian reasons to work with (or on behalf of) the poor and marginalised. Popular organisations on the other hand are composed of people with specific identities and interests, arising from class, gender and/or ethnic origins or cultural background, who have come together out of their own need for collective representation, organisation and struggle (Pearce, 1993:222). The latter are organisations rather than institutions and unlike intermediary development NGOs often 'rise and fall' in response to the external political climate and levels of membership commitment. Intermediary development NGOs are subject to institutional imperatives if they are to establish their permanence and credibility, and these are enhanced by the importance of external funders. While popular organisations do receive external funding, many international donors have been reluctant to channel funds directly to such organisations as there would just be too many for the funds and monitoring capacity available, as well as risks of corrupting and dividing such organisations (see Hodson in this volume for an example of the divisive forces that such action can unleash). But dependence on external funding often results in organisations becoming accountable to their funders rather than beneficiaries, reflecting their funder's agendas rather than setting their own in consultation with beneficiaries. In theory (though in practice this is often highly problematic), popular organisations are accountable to their memberships or constituency.

The distinctions outlined above are not hard and fast, in practice they blur at the edges quite a lot. Direct funding of popular organisations does take place; where there are highly bureaucratised leaderships (often the case with Latin American labour unions and peasant organisations) such organisations are just as likely to reflect the interests of governments and/or political parties as those of their members; many NGOs are as fragile as some popular organisations and some are set up and run by actors from the latter. But we would still retain the analytical distinction, not least because of the danger we have alluded to elsewhere that in lumping the two together, the question of agency in development and social and political change becomes confused. NGOs are 'politicised' while popular organisations are 'depoliticised' (Pearce, 1993:222). The former are elevated into increasingly professional protagonists of development and change while the latter lose their distinct character as active and conscious social agents, representing particular social interests and political choices. In the process of category construction too, an objectified 'grass roots' emerges, recipients of aid and support from the more institutionalised agencies who take on the task of mediating between them and the structures of political, economic and technical power. In this chapter, therefore, we will refer specifically to the role of intermediary development NGOs, organisations which offer a broad range of support and service functions to the poor and dispossessed of Latin America.

NGOs AND LATIN AMERICA'S EVOLVING ASSOCIATIONAL CULTURE

Ian Smillie has pointed out that different countries have different organisational cultures in which voluntary action develops. He points to the differences between the developed 'corporatist' culture of Norway, Sweden, Finland, the Netherlands and Austria, where voluntary associations act as interlocutors between their members and government, the 'weak and unsuccessful corporatism' of the UK, France and Italy, and the pluralism of the USA and Canada, where voluntary associations help to ensure that no single interest or interest group will prevail over others on a particular issue. Recognition of the variation in the Northern NGO heritage he suggests:

> is important to an understanding of Southern NGOs. Even though some have been established with the help of Northern NGOs, these Southern organisations emerge from different traditions entirely – cultural, religious, ethnic; pro-government, anti-government, anti-statist, political, apolitical. Some are even government-organised. To view a Southern NGO community through a Northern lens therefore – to assume, for example, that Peruvian NGOs can or will behave like Swedish NGOs in relation to government – could be an error with costly consequences for both the NGO and its supporter. (Smillie, 1993:18)

This reminds us that NGOs are part of 'associational cultures', or patterns of interactions between organisations and the state which vary widely across societies and change over time. It has become commonplace in contemporary discussion to refer to the realm of civil association outside the state as 'civil society'. That term is an immensely rich one in Western political thought. It has stimulated and continues to stimulate a variety of conceptualisations of the relationship between the state and its citizens. In the development literature, it has often been adopted in a rather hasty way. Gordon White has explored the complex web of meanings around contemporary usage of 'civil society' and its association with the democratisation processes in the South in recent years (White, 1994). I am using the term 'associational culture' as a more open-ended term with less normative connotations, which does not assume or deny the existence of a 'civil society', or ask what *ought* to be the role of associations and groups, but focuses much more on the historical sociopolitical environment in which associations are nurtured or stifled or controlled.

The nature of this environment, like political systems as a whole, does undergo challenge and change. This is particularly true of the South where the boundaries between the appropriate arena of the state and that of society has rarely been legitimated and accepted by all the citizens of a given polity exercising equal rights and an equal voice. The legacy of centralised colonial rule, authoritarian government and state-led development have taken their toll on the capacity of citizens to organise independently of the state. As a result, the associational cultures are often fragile, crudely reflective of the structures of power within society and their relationship to class, ethnicity and gender, and the differential access to state influence these allow. They are also extremely vulnerable to external control and manipulation. The notion of a legitimate sphere of autonomous private association protected by legal and institutional guarantees has been a rare phenomena in the South.

Until the paradigm shift of the 1980s away from state-led development, much of the associational dynamism of Latin America centred on the struggle of different social sectors to have the right to organise at all. In the first half of the twentieth century, forms of association had all developed in a context of conflictive class relations, with the state intervening to repress, coopt or mobilise in projects ranging from military dictatorship, to corporatism, to populism. In the Cold War years, competing strategies of reaction, modernisation, reform and revolution created a highly charged political climate. This fostered organisational development of all kinds, but the region's age-old traditions of state cooption and repression and party clientelism intervened to hinder autonomous forms of popular organising.

The mechanisms involved varied between countries; a schematic overview would point to the following characteristics in some selected countries. In Chile, with its strong multi-party tradition, these were the means by which associational forms were captured and colonised as they emerged. In Colombia, it was two traditional and predominant political parties who attempted to control all forms of associational life. As armed and unarmed opposition groups of the left emerged to challenge those parties from the 1960s onwards, they often reproduced the techniques of manipulation and control of the traditional parties, and many of the new social organisations and NGOs which began to emerge were soon embroiled in the antagonisms of rival political forces. State repression and party manipulation combined to allow only a very fragile space for independent social organising.

In Uruguay, the overwhelming presence of a state whose legitimacy derived from an early tradition of welfarism established in the first two decades of the nineteenth century, restrained the emergence of social organisation until the 1970s and 1980s. In Peru, social organising, hithertoo closely associated with the evolving party system, was given impetus by the reforming state of the 1960s, particularly that of the Velasco regime (1968–75) and aimed at social mobilising 'from above' (Carroll *et al.*, 1991). But with the demise of that project, the Church, university professionals and political parties of the left began to promote new forms of socio-economic organisation. Once again, the parties competed for control of what was seen as potential 'base' for their political projects.

In Brazil, the state promoted a corporatist project of control on sectoral organising in the 1940s, which had a long-term legacy. This began to be broken in the 1960s as another powerful institution, the Catholic Church, launched systematic programmes of popular education and social organisation following the radical re-thinking emanating from Vatican 11 and the Medellin Conference of 1968 and contributed to a vibrant associational development in the 1970s and 1980s. The struggle of the trade union movement to free itself from state control was one of the key processes of those decades. In Central America, social organisation emerged as an integral part of struggles for social and political change in the 1970s in a climate of relentless state and elite hostility. Most organisations were caught up in some way with the various political options for change.

A comprehensive survey of the process of associational development in Latin America is not possible here, but for the purposes of this chapter it is important to stress the heavily politicised character of its early stages. It was also deeply coloured by the fact that the state was the central arena of economic agency and a great deal of associational activity based on particular social interests was directed towards influencing or transforming the state. Business associations saw the state as the locus of patronage and protection essential to the ability of manufacturing industry to survive; landowner associations saw the state as the means to preserve their power and influence in the face of the imperatives of political and economic change. Those associations linked to popular projects for change also saw access to or control of the state as the means to re-direct development towards the needs of the poor majority.

Intermediary development NGOs were one specific form of associational development which were often established precisely because of the fragility of the associational cultures in the region. In particular they aimed to address the difficulties experienced by the poor in making their voice heard and the need to support their organisations or help them organise. They were additionally characterised by their access to external funding and therefore their ability to institutionalise themselves in ways not open to other groups.

It is widely accepted that NGOS emerged as a category in the 1960s, and the history has been fairly well documented (for example, Bebbington and Thiele, 1993). The expansion of US development aid programmes to Latin America led to the emergence of a number of US-funded relief, welfare and technical support organisations. At the same time, the Catholic Church began to rethink its spiritual and social role, with greater emphasis on the latter, giving rise to Church sponsored and linked welfare groups and cooperative associations. In the radicalised and polarised atmosphere of the 1960s and 1970s, a third cluster of NGOs emerged. This group was composed of radical, university-educated technocrats, intellectuals and political activists. Often they were excluded from opportunities in higher education and turned to the voluntary sector just as overseas funding agencies began to expand their operations in the 'developing world'.

The vast majority of NGOs born in this period were caught up in 'political' projects of one kind or another, whether it was US efforts to promote reform or counter-revolution, the Church's concern to encourage social action and collective responses to poverty and defend its own institutional presence or the left's concern to bring about fundamental social and political change. The state usually tolerated these associations more than popular organisations, as they brought development assistance and carried out some welfare functions to sectors of society the state had no interest in reaching itself. It maintained institutional control, however, through the ubiquitous bureaucratic procedures whereby all associations had to gain prior permission and go through lengthy procedures to register as corporations (*personeria juridica*). And where these organisations came into conflict with the state, there was no hesitation about using police and military repression to destroy offices and equipment and arrest workers. This would happen particularly at times of social mobilisation and political conflict. The relationship between associational life and the state as the Cold War years wore on was tense and often conflictive, in which the legitimacy of the state was questioned by many organised social groups, while the state did not accept the legitimacy of independent social organisation or provide the framework of rights which promote and protect such organisation.

As well as being an epoch of dangerous political antagonisms, this was also a creative period, in which NGOs committed to social change experimented with a variety of techniques of popular education, 'conscientisation', empowerment and participatory development. David Lehmann has characterised the 'ideology' of these experiments, influenced by the teachings of the radical Church as much as left-wing ideas, as 'basismo', reflecting their concern with building confidence and organisational capacity amongst the poorest sectors of the population (Lehmann, 1990). It was gradually accepted by 'progressive' national and international NGOs that other functions, such as credit to the poor, technical training and other services, should be accompanied by social promotion and organisational work. Many radical NGOs were actively encouraged in this by external development agencies, and for many their legitimacy in the eyes of these agencies derived from their engagement and commitment to radical change. It could be said that in these years, such legitimacy was more important than the accountability of NGOs to funders and beneficiaries alike. Evaluations of the effectiveness of the popular education and other social organisational work was not as rigorous as it might have been as a result. But the context in which this was taking place was such that there was a widespread belief that social and political transformation was on the agenda, and at different moments, such as the Velasco period in Peru, the Allende years in Chile, and the Sandinista years in Nicaragua this was given meaning through the real experiments which took place at the political level.

Further legitimacy was derived from the crucial role many NGOs played in supporting other associational activity during the dark years of authoritarian government and civil war. The 1960s and 1970s had seen continuous growth in grass-roots organisation and NGOs in many countries of Latin America, but associational development became extremely difficult as military governments committed to centralised states and control over all forms of social and political activity gradually came to dominate the Southern Cone countries of Brazil, Uruguay, Argentina and Chile. During the 1980s, insurgency and counter-insurgency swept the rural regions of the Andean countries of Peru and Colombia and the Central American republics of Guatemala, El Salvador and Nicaragua.

The chronology of these processes varies throughout the region, but almost everywhere, the 1980s represented a watershed in the associational cultures of Latin America. Military governments gave way to civilian ones, interventionist states gave way to retreating states committed to structural adjustment and neo-liberalism, armed insurgencies sensed their political as well as military weakness and began to negotiate with governments or face marginalisation. These changes would have important implications for the development of NGOs. Authoritarian governments had weakened the party systems, and particularly parties of the left. Often NGOs were the only survivors, particularly where they enjoyed Church protection, while the rise of social movements led by new social actors (women, shanty-town dwellers, black people, indigenous people) reflected both the decline of old economic structures and political influences and extended the nature and frontiers of collective action and organisation.

Unlike the more ephemeral, non-institutionalised social movements, the NGOs were often able to survive these years intact and even strengthened. Hojman has pointed to the role NGOs subsequently played in the negotiated transition to civilian rule in Chile and their influence in the civilian government which then emerged:

> Non-governmental organisations (NGOs) played a fundamental role in Chile's economic, social, intellectual and cultural development during the 1970s and 1980s...NGOs played a central role in guaranteeing a successful transition, both by supporting, encouraging and offering a platform to the democratic opposition to the miltary regime, and by developing and putting forward theoretical interpretations and policy proposals which would eventually constitute a fundamental component of the incoming democratic government programme. (Hojman, 1993:7)

In Central America, one commentator has ironically pointed out: 'only two institutions have consistently flourished in the Central American crisis: the military and the NGOs' (Lewis, quoted in Biekart, 1995:64–5).

In the course of the 1980s therefore, Latin America's 'associational culture' began to enter a new phase as political spaces opened up as never before and economic restructuring resulted in rethinking the role of the state. The extent of this change should not be exaggerated; Latin America's 'old order' has always died hard and in fact the old structures of power and patterns of behaviour embedded as much in society as the state continued to exert influence. But a new political space had opened up, and many organisations sensed that there was an opportunity to shape the evolving associational culture as never before.

In the process of redefining its relationship to the economy, the state, increasingly run by technocratic modernisers or 'maverick' politicians unhindered by traditional party allegiances, also began to redefine its relationship to society and its organisations. Powerful external agencies such as the World Bank, began to identify NGOs as efficient deliverers of services in the wake of a diminished state, the shedding of its social welfare functions and a private sector still too weak to replace it fully as the main agent of development. By the end of the decade the 'New Policy Agenda' for official aid had been clearly articulated in the dual objectives of economic liberalisation and political democratisation with a central role for NGOs in both (Edwards, 1994).

On the one hand therefore, NGOs confronted a radically different external environment in which they were positively encouraged from quarters which had shown no previous interest and on the other, a transformed internal environment. This was not only true of the state, but many social groups with whom they had worked had been badly affected by national and international events. In particular, there was the impact of the defeat of the radical political movements which had taken on the state since the 1960s, the discrediting of socialist ideas, the legacy of state terror and repression on many activists, the serious weakening of many traditional forms of popular organising such as trade unions, and in some countries, the demobilisation of many of the newer forms of collective action which had risen to prominence in the early part of the 1980s. In the vacuum, the 'NGO' had not only survived but had grown in importance and numbers, increasingly identified as an agent of development rather than social transformation.

The Inter-American Foundation identified 11 000 NGOs in Latin America and the Caribbean by the early 1990s (Carroll, 1992:2). Many of these are NGOs of a new type, described by Bebbington and Farrington as 'non-politicised yuppie NGOs...rooted in the economic displacement of middle class professionals from both public and private sectors' (Bebbington and Farrington, 1993:202). Two specific Latin American examples of this growth are the cases of Bolivia and the countries of Central America. In Bolivia, the implementation of neo-liberal programmes was accompanied by a massive growth in poverty alleviation programmes funded by bilateral and multilateral donors and channelled through NGOs. The number of NGOs grew from 100 in 1980 to 530 in 1992 (Arellano-López and Petras, 1994:559). In Central America, it has been pointed out that apart from two earthquakes in the 1970s, there was virtually no development aid before 1980. But by 1987 the aid figures had tripled to US$1.7 billion (Biekart, 1995).It is not surprising that the debate on the role and future of NGOs has intensified as a result.

CHANGE AND CHOICE: LATIN AMERICA'S ASSOCIATIONAL CULTURE IN THE 1990s

This chapter has focused on the macro-level political picture rather than the role of NGOs in the development process as such. This is not suprising given that NGOs were elevated in the course of the 1980s into actors in a political project. This project consisted of the capitalist modernisation of the Latin American region and the associated development of political pluralism, effective, accountable government and a dynamic, free market economy. This was part of a systematic and transparent policy on the part of a number of international financial institutions and bilateral donors throughout the South and has resulted in the huge increase in aid flows through NGOs in the last decade. According to UNDP, NGOs today reach an estimated 250 million people globally compared to an estimated 100 million in the early 1980s, and their rising budget of US$7.2 billion is equivalent to 13 per cent of net disbursements of official aid (UNDP, 1993:93). While this is still a relatively minor part of such disbursements, it is significant and it is growing.

As political conditions and economic paradigms changed, NGOs were confronted by diverse models of Latin American associational development with which to engage, resulting in confusions and divisions. Part of the confusion is that NGOs have been claimed by a variety of different literatures which construct the collectivities within societies in different ways and often using a different vocabulary. One writer's interest group is another writer's grassroots organisation, movements are often confused with organisations, older forms of class-based associations are written off in favour of identity-based groups, NGOs are used to describe some or all of these. Behind the vocabulary is often a social/political construction, conflicting models on how state-society relations ought to be structured. Here I will refer to just three particular models worthy of disaggregating, all of which have different implications for NGOs: pluralism, David Lehmann's conceptualisation of '*basismo* as if it really mattered', and the 'empowerment' model.

Pluralism is concerned with the desirability of the diffusion of power amongst a range of associations within society as a means of counteracting the threat of the concentration of power within the market and by the state. NGOs in this model play an important role as one alternative power centre amongst others in pressurising and influencing government to meet the needs of the particular constituency they represent. This model lies implicitly behind much of the discussion on 'civil society' and 'governance' by official aid donors. Such a vision leads logically to NGOs playing a mediating role between their social constituency and the state, and suggests they should emphasise their institutional effectiveness and capacity building skills rather than empowerment and mobilisation roles. Within the literature on democratic transition in Latin America, it is often assumed that social movements may have played a role in bringing down authoritarian governments but democracies cannot survive under the constant pressure of people's mobilisation around their interests and needs. This view is expressed clearly by Przeworski:

> If reforms are to proceed under democratic conditions, distributional conflicts must be institutionalised; all groups must channel their demands through democratic institutions and abjure other tactics.

Regardless of how pressing their needs may be, the politically relevant groups must be willing to subject their interests to the verdict of democratic institutions. (Przeworski, 1991:180)

David Lehmann has developed a hybrid model which combines some features of pluralism while retaining the capacity for resistance and empowerment embodied in the 'grass-rootsism' or *basismo* of many Latin American NGOs and popular organisations:

> We thus return, after admitting that many of the aspirations of its ideologues are hopelessly unrealistic, to a strong defence of grassroots activism, be it of secular or religious inspiration. Indeed, the argument is strengthened by the narrowing of its scope and the definition of spheres in which it can be effective. These can be classified in two broad categories: one that of everyday resistance to oppression in which size and duration are not of the essence, and the other...requiring larger-scale organisation, more professionalism and more linkage with grass roots support organisations and with the state itself, so as to fulfil the requirements of institutional competence and sustainability which are essential to a 'basic needs' approach to development. (Lehmann, 1990:212)

This vision does describe the response of many NGOs in Latin America who do not wish to abandon their involvement in popular struggles but wish to strengthen their leverage at the state level too. But many have questioned the compatibility between the two objectives, and have emphasised the risks involved in 'scaling-up'.

The 'empowerment' model hangs onto the notion that the pursuit of social transformation is still the major goal of popular organising and that NGOs should remain as facilitators of that process and not be co-opted into the agendas of either the state or official donors. There is no clear understanding of what such transformation entails any longer, and increasingly it involves a challenge to deep-rooted social oppressions as much as the state-led ones. It understands that democratisation processes in Latin America are as yet extremely uneven and fragile and still characterised by systematic efforts to control associational development through age old traditions of *caudillismo*, clientelism, verticalism, *machismo* and the persistent domination of white and *mestizo* peoples over indigenous and Afro-Latin Americans. Nor has a rights-based state been consolidated in the region, so that many social groups remain excluded and marginalised from the political system and contestatory methods are still the only means of articulating interests and needs.

The initial enthusiasm for NGOs concealed the differences between these and other models, and the term 'civil society' was seized upon so readily that it encouraged all to believe they were engaged in the same project. Yet the importance of 'civil society' lies not in its use as a descriptive term for some observable reality but precisely in the way it has been used historically to construct different conceptualisations of the relationship between the state and the associations and groups of society. There are evidently many areas of common cause between each of the models outlined, such as the struggle for civil, political and human rights and accountable and effective government. However, the 'pluralist' approach had such huge financial backing that it could not fail to emerge as the dominant paradigm, taking with it many NGOs who felt unable to resist the opportunities offered for influence and resources. In the process, the differences with the other models have gradually emerged and deeply divided not only the NGO community itself, but often NGOs from popular organisations, and national NGOs from international donor NGOs.

An example of divisions within the NGO community is Chile, where the return to civilian government has resulted in a schism in the NGO community between those who opted to support the liberal economic model of the government (the majority) and those who did not. The former have benefitted from close access to the government, often in advisory roles, and access to funding increasingly channelled through the government. The ability and willingness of NGOs to maintain their autonomy from government and political parties has been questioned, though they have opted not to seek an official forum for representation within the government for fear of total absorption (Echenique, 1994:112). Studies have also shown the obstacles to participation in policy definition as opposed to implementation (Bebbington and Thiele, 1993:224). The rest of the NGO community, numerous small NGOs mostly lacking connections to the political parties in government, have remained marginal to the mainstream economic and political developments in the country, but are maintaining their roles as empowerers and supporters of popular organisations and poor communities. Chile now has at least two clearly differentiated NGO communities, with a few NGOs falling between the two extremes.

Biekart (1995) has shown the divergences which have emerged between national NGOs and the international donor NGOs. His research on the impact amongst Central American NGOs of the changing nature of aid in the wake of the peace processes and as a result of the New Policy Agenda showed that 'Central American NGOs have taken a quite defensive and reactive position against the revision and restructuring of aid policies from Northern NGOs' (ibid.). The response of some NGOs is to seek to bypass the Northern international NGOs in favour of direct funding from official donors, though Bebbington and Riddell have found a completely opposite response in Ecuador and Guatemala (Bebbington and Riddell in this volume). Elsewhere in the region, popular organisations have asked themselves whether they need NGOs at all, given that these organisations have access to funds, infrastructure and salaries which they gain through claiming to act on their behalf. Why cannot they apply for their own funding?

Many of the tensions and divisions within the NGO community reflect real problems and dilemmas; questions are being asked that simply were not asked in the past. But it seems likely that NGOs will gradually align themselves behind the different models, reinforcing the heterogeneity of the non-governmental sector and, as some researchers have concluded, its 'potential of performing many different roles. The new opportunistic NGOs may be willing to be contractees of the state, older radical NGOs may be more circumspect' (Bebbington and Thiele, 1993:214). A great deal will depend on how the state conceives its relationship to associational life in particular countries. As David Lehmann has pointed out, a change in the corporatist tradition of prior legal recognition of associations 'would send the legal establishment into paroxisms, for the recognition of a right to establish organisations without prior permission would constitute a fundamental change in the Latin concept of the state' (Lehmann, 1990:209). But such a change would be precisely the kind of signal that Latin American governments are prepared to respect an autonomous sphere of social organising and reduce the suspicions of many NGOs about government intentions when it offers them a relationship.

Only detailed empirical research will be able to assess the implications for performance and effectiveness of the path different NGOs adopt. Whether, for instance, NGOs can sustain their perceived advantages, such as closeness to the 'grass roots', participatory culture, innovative capacity and value base as they 'scale up' and take on a parastatal role has become one of the crucial areas of debate and one of the first questions to be subject to empirical scrutiny. The conclusions have varied and are worth recording.Tom Carroll, who has published one of the few in-depth comparative studies of NGO performance in Latin America, offers perhaps the most optimistic conclusion:

There are GSOs that do not appear to lose their valuable traits when they take on large-scale jobs mediated by government. The same may be said for some MSOs with a strong social commitment. True, scaling up places great strains on their organisations. With such quantum leaps in scale they can no longer be as informal and flexible as before, but they can remain poverty oriented and participatory. (Carroll, 1992:177)

Bebbington and Farrington, who have also done valuable empirical work on NGOs in agricultural development in Latin America, are more cautious in their conclusions:

> The agricultural development activities of NGOs acting alone and iso-
> lated from any influence on policy are highly constrained in the impact
> they can achieve. To achieve greater impact seems to require some
> form of relationship with government. Yet the terms on which such
> relationships have been offered by government and donors have hith-
> erto been unattractive to many NGOs. Whether and, if so, at what level
> NGOs should enter relationships with governments are ultimately deci-
> sions that only they can take. We would though note that some NGOs
> appear to have found a room for manoeuvre within this impasse, and
> have been able to gain space to influence government – but at a cost to
> the NGOs' identity and autonomy. (Bebbington and Farrington,
> 1993:215)

Arellano-Lopez and Petras, on the other hand, in their study of Bolivia, are unequivocal in concluding that NGOs cannot compensate for a policy environment dominated by neo-liberalism which by its very nature will increase inequality and absolute poverty no matter how efficient they are: 'For international donors and national governments to assign NGOs the responsibility for poverty alleviation, and for NGOs to accept that responsibility in the absence of the necessary policy environment is to indulge in mutual self-deception' (Arellano-López and Petras, 1994:560). They also conclude that the strengthening of NGOs has gone hand in hand with the weakening of state agencies and grass roots organisations and undermined both the institutional capacity of Latin American countries to develop alternative development agendas to those of the international financial community and the ability of opposition voices to call for such an alternative. Far from fostering democracy, these authors conclude, that in Bolivia NGOs may have undermined and weakened it.

Such a conclusion at least draws our attention to the fact that the claims made about NGOs were allowed to go unchallenged for too long. While they can fulfil the potential expected of them, equally they can fail and even contribute to the perpetuation of the elitist and unequal societies many were established to change. We need new tools for assessing precisely when and how NGOs can fulfil that potential.

BETWEEN CO-OPTION OR IRRELEVANCY: A FALSE DICHOTOMY?

The previous section has emphasised that NGOs like other organisations are faced today with a number of different political paths and choices. There have been and will continue to be a variety of responses within the NGO community. But even those NGOs who refuse to become part of the dominant political project, that of the New Policy Agenda, have to face important questions about what kind of role they will play if they are not to be marginalised in the development process.

Perhaps there is a third way for these NGOs between the dangers of co-option and irrelevancy, involving a great deal more reflection and analysis of what gives them a legitimate role in social processes and who they should be accountable to. If they accept that their role is not as protagonists in those processes but as 'empowerers', advocates and lobbyists, they must clearly seek legitimacy from the social groups they serve and claim to represent. Such legitimacy must rest on visible mechanisms of accountability. Research on such mechanisms is needed, but the Social Audit methodology developed by the New Economics Foundation in England would be one way of ensuring that NGOs respond to the needs of those they claim to work for (Zadek and Gatward, 1995). Research is also needed on criteria for measuring social processes such as 'empowerment' which can be accepted alongside more obvious outcomes and measures of achievement, such as services provided, people trained and credit disbursed. International NGOs will also have to make choices in terms of what kind of local NGOs in the South they wish to fund and why. By seeking an open dialogue with local counterparts so that there is basic agreement on the objectives and purpose of the funds, the difficult question of how accountability to funders can be distinguished from that to beneficiaries could be addressed.

A final conclusion of this chapter would rather go against the concern with NGO–state–donor relations, and focus much more on NGO–beneficiary relations. Who do NGOs work for, how and why? Social change will only come about when those excluded from access to wealth and power are able to make their own claims to justice, equality, rights, services and technical support. The role of the state is central to these concerns. Whether NGOs help them to do this or simply strengthen their own institutional capacity and relationship with the state must be investigated. In this conclusion, I would support that of the Human Development Report of 1993:

> In eradicating poverty and providing social services, NGOs are unlikely ever to play more than a complementary role...their importance lies in making the point that poverty can be tackled rather than tackling it to any large extent... Encouraging participation means responding sensitively to the felt needs of people and communities – and responding in ways that meet those needs without 'taking over'. There is always the risk of placing too much emphasis on effective delivery and too little on nurturing and strengthening participation. This tendency is likely to be heightened as NGOs open themselves up as channels for government funds. (UNDP, 1993:98–9)

18 Conclusion: Too Close to the Powerful, Too Far from the Powerless?

David Hulme and Michael Edwards

INTRODUCTION

The contributors to this volume have presented a wealth of experiences, data, concepts and competing analyses of what is happening in the relationships between NGOs, states and donors. Clearly, simple generalisations about the nature of these relationships are not feasible. The empirical accounts reveal that different things are happening in different places and that institutional histories and national and local contexts shape events as much as more generalised, indeed globalised, factors. Secondly, there are the inevitable questions of causality: if an NGO suddenly allies itself to donor policies how do we disentangle the influences of donor finance, from recently liberalised state policies, from a change in leadership of the NGO? This is particularly difficult to do when, as in this case, developments are still in their early stages and experience is recent and still poorly documented. Thirdly, there is the issue of which analytical frameworks are most appropriate. From a neo-liberal perspective, more NGOs and GROs (regardless of their quality) are beneficial, since automatically they contribute to economic efficiency and political pluralism (and, if low quality, they will simply become redundant!). From a radical perspective, once such organisations accept donor funds they are co-opted and are unlikely to contribute to progressive social change. In practice, neither position is tenable without detailed empirical analysis: once such analysis is undertaken then ideological 'black' and 'whites' reappear as shades of grey. While Bebbington and Riddell, Commins and Mawer (this volume) and Cannon (forthcoming) have described positive interactions, others (Hodson, Pearce, Perera, Wanigaratne and Wood) have raised serious grounds for concern.

It is clear from this collection, however, that the 'associational revolution' (Salamon, 1993:1) in developing countries is significantly influenced by external factors including donor enthusiasms for NGOs as agents of economic and political change (see Chapter 1). NNGOs and SNGOs have expanded in number and scale through donor support. For GROs the picture is more complicated: many have been catalysed (though that term may be challenged) by donors and SNGOs, but others have their origins and continuance based in endogenous factors. While the role played by supply-side factors (the availability of donor finance and the influences of aid agencies and states) in the recent rise of NGOs and GROs can be contested, there can be no doubt that recent years have seen a rise in the influence of supply on 'association' and 'collective action' and a corresponding decrease in the significance of demand factors (the felt needs of the poor and disadvantaged) on group formation and mobilisation. John Clark's paper (Chapter 3) makes this point forcefully and Tom Dichter (Chapter 8) comments on the way in which the donor prioritisation of financial sustainability has led many NNGOs into credit programmes that offer cost recovery possibilities. Recent detailed research by Richard Montgomery (1995) describes how supply-side factors have shaped the ways in which the Bangladesh Rural Advancement Committee (BRAC) mobilises and operates village organisations (VOs). In effect, rather than being member organisations that articulate member needs and preferences, the VOs operate as sub-branches of BRAC's organisational structure. Effective group formation for the achievement of project objectives clearly does not equate with strengthening civil society. Farrington and Bebbington's (1993:177) prognostication is certainly being borne out in many cases: 'while they [NGOs] generally profess a closer affinity to the poor than to the state, they bear more resemblance to the state than they do to the poor – and in most of their activities they operate in a manner that is more akin to the state than to any organisation of the poor'.

NGOs AND THE MYTHS OF DEVELOPMENT

Underpinning the rise of NGOs and GROs have been recent shifts in the myths of development, beloved of official agencies who require easily fundable answers to messy and complex problems, and motivated more often than not by ideology and fashion rather than experience and empirical validation. In the 1970s the 'myth of the state' – that the state can provide for all the needs of all citizens – was burst. This opened up some ground for NGOs and GROs as the 'myth of the market' – that the private sector can provide for all the consumption needs of all consumers – took control in the 1980s. As this unravelled in the late 1980s then a new myth was needed: 'the myth of the market plus civil society'. This still holds centre stage, although problems obviously arise when civil societies are weak or fragmented and markets are non-competitive and poorly-regulated. These (real-world) conditions create much more significant challenges to the current myth than donors are wont to admit, and take us back to more searching, and as-yet unanswered, questions about the public/private mix and what roles are appropriate for governments, markets and civic institutions in successful societies. There are no universal answers to such questions, and there never will be.

When contrasted with 'successful' experience in western Europe, east Asia, and elsewhere, these myths are all gross oversimplifications. Complex and changing relations between elements of the state, the private sector and civil society underpin both economic growth and enhanced capacities to meet social needs. Contexts and historical timing are of key importance, especially in an area so culturally sensitive as this. The dangers of imposing foreign models (economic or political) on other societies have been well documented in the development literature (Lehmann, 1990; Brautigam, 1992; Bebbington and Thiele, 1993). With increasing funding from Northern governments, NGOs are now in danger of being used in precisely this way, especially where large numbers of new organisations are being formed on the back of readily available donor funds, with weak social roots and no independent supporter base (as in the case of Nepal). This may be particularly problematic in countries in transition from a centrally planned economy, where NGOs are very new and huge areas of state–society relations are being rapidly redefined, under great pressure from outside interests to conform to Western models. Is this really strengthening civil society, or merely an attempt to shape civil society in ways that external actors believe is desirable? Will it promote sustainable forms of democracy or call forth a backlash against foreign interference (both Howell and Wanigaratne in this volume point to the indigenous resentments sparked off by externally controlled interventions)? Successful civil societies develop their own systems and structures, norms and sanctions, over hundreds of years: by and large, they take care of their own strengthening (as Robert Puttnam, 1993, has argued for Italy).

Nevertheless, the 'market plus civil society will yield development' myth has clearly favoured NGOs and GROs, and (for the time being at least) this myth seems here to stay. The key question for this Conclusion is: what implications does this have for NGOs and GROs themselves, and for wider questions of political economy such as overcoming poverty and state–society relations? What do the chapters in this book tell us about the impact of current trends in NGO–state–donor relations in these crucial areas?

TOO CLOSE FOR COMFORT: MYTH OR REALITY?

If NGOs have indeed moved too close to donors, the danger is that in so doing they will have helped external interests to promulgate a myth of development which, like all the others before it, will not only fail to resolve the problems of poverty and injustice in the world but will in important respects make long-term, sustainable progress more difficult to achieve. These 'side-effects' include the erosion of government capacity to care for the mass of its citizens, the distortion of civil society as NGOs and GROs become less independent, and the disenfranchisment of citizens as state provision is privatised and accountability is reduced further (*see* Wood, Chapter 5).

The evidence in this volume shows that there have been a variety of experiences. While Bangladesh appears to be pursuing the current myth and state functions are 'franchised' out (Wood) the international picture reveals little documentary evidence of NGOs converting wholesale into public sector contractors as Korten (1990) warned (see Robinson in this volume). What does seem to be happening, however, is a more gradual and less visible process in which a significant proportion of NGOs move closer and closer to donors and to the support of donor interests. It commences with the agreement to use aid monies: progresses with the adoption of donor techniques for programming, implementing, monitoring and accounting for performance (see Edwards and Hulme, 1995, for detailed accounts of this); subsequently it moves on to shaping the nature of appointments and the internal structures of NGOs with the recruitment of English speaking, logical framework experts and information departments which function as public relations units; eventually, the organisational culture is attuned to donors – and the local, indigenous and informal features that have underpinned NGO and GRO activity are lost (Pratten and Ali Baldo, 1995). Rather than a rapid deterioration in the patient's condition, we are witnessing a gradual hardening of the arteries in the NGO world as organisations become more bureaucratic and less prone to take risks or bear the costs of listening to those who they seek to assist. Vision becomes just another agenda item in an endless series of meetings, sandwiched somewhere between Matters Arising and Any Other Business. 'In the absence of vision, pettiness prevails.' Many readers (especially staff from the large international and southern NGOs) will be familiar with this depressing story.

We identify this process as a gradual, but potentially catastrophic, weakening of NGO roots – both in the North (supporters) and in the South (members and beneficiaries) and in relation to an NGO's stated mission and values, vision and inspiration, independent voice and perspective.

NGOs IN THE NORTH

NNGOs have moved closer to donors in terms of both using donor funds and analysing and criticising donor policies. They have singularly failed, however, to persuade their supporters to become active citizens prepared to demand that their governments spend more on aid and spend it more effectively. NNGO lobbying and advocacy may even have backfired, fuelling the right-wing agenda of reducing aid flows by generating evidence that some aid-financed projects (for example, the Pergau Dam) are 'bad investments', and that some aid-financed policies (for example, structural adjustment) are bad for poor people. In the absence of a much more determined effort in public education, NNGOs cannot be surprised when a relatively disinterested northern electorate continues to see foreign aid as a low priority. The prospective cuts in World Bank IDA funds and in the UK's Overseas Development Administration (5.4 per cent in 1995/96) might well indicate a need for NNGOs to be part of a 'charm offensive' to rehabilitate the image of aid agencies in North America and Europe and strengthen public support for foreign aid expenditures, suitably reformed. Could it be that NNGOs with development interests are entering a period during which they need to get *closer* to aid agencies, to defend their role in development, while parting company with their 'colleagues' in some environmental NGOs (particularly in the USA) whose highly effective lobbying is often more concerned about the prospects of non-human species?

At a deeper level, NGO constituencies in the North seem no more willing now to make the personal sacrifices and changes in behaviour on which the future of the world depends (Commins, this volume). How much attention have NNGOs paid to lifestyle changes, nurturing attitudes of service among their supporters, solidifying an ethic of global solidarity, and so on – all things which started out at the core of their mission but are now rarely talked about, let alone properly resourced? Experience shows how difficult it is for even well-resourced NGOs in the North to achieve sustainable changes in their own civil societies (though no doubt with more effort, more could have been done) and large NGOs, such as OXFAM, admit that they avoid raising the issue of lowering levels of personal consumption with their supporters. How much more difficult it must be, then, to achieve such changes in *other* peoples' societies!

Addressing fundamental inequalities of power and resources by speaking out in favour of particular groups, organising to defend the interests of poor people, and lobbying governments for policy change, has always been central to the NGO mission. Many of the largest and most respected international NGOs of today (such as Save the Children and OXFAM) were born and raised in opposition to government policy and vested interests at the time. But can this role continue when NNGOs are becoming more and more dependent on government support? Increasing reliance on government contracts is already hindering the campaigning work of the larger NGOs in the USA and UK (Smith, 1990; Salamon and Anheier, 1993; Smith and Lipsky, 1993; Edwards, 1993). A context in which NGOs compete with each other for official support seems unlikely to foster the collaborative relationships on which successful policy alliances are built (Covey, 1995).

NGOs IN THE SOUTH

For SNGOs a similar process of convergence seems to be under way, in terms of finances, methods and concepts, as direct relationships with northern donors intensify. Upward accountability is becoming a norm, often in cultural contexts where all large organisations are already predisposed to operate in this fashion (Edwards and Hulme, 1995). The poor and disadvantaged become customers rather than members; participation becomes instrumentalist; and village groups become branches of the NGO rather than autonomous organisations (Montgomery, 1995). Strategic issues, such as what the state is doing for the poor (that is, all the poor people in the country), wither as the agency concentrates on its own cohort of the poor (that is, a tiny fraction of those in poverty). Good relations with donors are emphasised. The concern with the 'big picture' (of what the NGO, with donor assistance, can do) squeezes out the 'little picture' – the daily struggles of thousands of beneficiaries and millions of other poor people. Tragically, such convergence transmits through to the next generation of NGOs. A little under ten years ago Charles Elliott (1987) wrote of NGO personnel informed by Freire and Alinsky: talk with field managers nowadays and you are much less likely to hear of ideas of mobilising the poor. North American management gurus such as Stephen Covey and Peters and Waterman are more likely sources of inspiration, despite the fact that their writings are more about making profits and organisational survival. But that, perhaps, is what NGOs are about nowadays!

In this process, the popularity of certain forms of NGO (large, able to absorb donor funding, quiescent) with donors may lead to a widening rift between well-resourced service providers and poorly-funded social mobilisation agencies, a danger already identified by Pearce (1993) in Chile and Central America. The availability of large amounts of donor funding under 'social funds' intended to mitigate the effects of structural adjustment has refocused Bolivian NGOs (to take just one documented example) away from their traditional role in facilitating the activities of GROs towards implementation of welfare projects. This rift is exacerbated by governments fearful of social movements and advocacy NGOs, yet willing to accommodate service providers for the material benefits and political advantages they bring (Thomas-Slayter, 1994).

TOO CLOSE FOR COMFORT: OR HOW TO MANAGE CHANGE?

The chapters in this book show that predictions about the damage done to donor-funded NGOs and GROs are not inevitable, though there is certainly a temptation to suggest that all external interveners – states, donors, NNGOs and SNGOs – should leave GROs alone and let them get on with development themselves! GROs are by far the most vulnerable of the actors under discussion, and the potential damage done to them by insensitive outsiders is particularly worrying (as one of us witnessed in Sri Lanka with a Dutch NGO promoting unproven 'organic' agricultural practices). However, a case can be made that any problems which do arise when NGOs and GROs get closer to states and donors can be managed in such a way as to take advantage of the opportunities provided by collaboration, while minimising the threats. As the chapters by Bosch, Mawer and others in this volume show (and also Cannon, forthcoming), different actors can work together successfully when certain conditions are satisfied. Chief among these conditions are a favourable national context (for NGO/GRO activity); good-quality and long established relationships between governments, NGOs and donors (flexible rather than instrumental); and NGOs/GROs which are strong and independent (that is which, like the Thrift and Credit Cooperative Movement in Sri Lanka, can say 'no' to assistance if they judge it to be inappropriate). Nevertheless, it must be recognised that in the real world of international aid and national development, such conditions are rare.

By their very nature, NGOs are problematic organisations (Edwards and Hulme, 1995): raising money in one country and spending it in others, responsible to multiple stakeholders and constituencies, and working simultaneously in different (and sometimes conflicting) sectors and activities. These problems cannot be wished away, and they would be present whether or not NGOs were growing closer to donors and governments. However, it is clear that the closer identification of NGOs and GROs with external interests may make it more difficult for them to establish longer-term relationships with national governments and domestic sources of support. Yet it is on these relationships that the legitimacy of NGOs and GROs ultimately depends, at least if the organisations concerned see themselves as more than service-providers on contract to governments and donors.

All NGOs and GROs would therefore be wise to prioritise 'putting their houses in order' in these areas, before it is too late. This means raising more funds locally, becoming less dependent on government grants, strengthening links with grassroots constituencies, improving performance measurement and accountability systems, and encouraging learning. With these things in place, NGOs and GROs will be better able to identify problems and trade-offs as they arise, and raise the likelihood of taking the appropriate action (Edwards and Hulme, 1995). Above all, it means being clear about the role of the organisation in society and its direction and vision for the future. All this requires conscious action and a long-term strategy which may run counter to the short-term interests of those who see organisational growth (or even survival) as the goal of an NGO. As is happening today in the large NGOs of both North and South, the focus of attention has shifted away from empowering others for independent action, towards empowering NGO leaderships and serving the organisation and its own ends. The future, particularly for NGOs based in the North, will turn on how this fundamental challenge is resolved. As we have argued elsewhere (*ibid.*), the successful NGOs of the twenty-first century are likely to be those that maintain a clear and independent focus and specialisation, within networks and alliances that work synergistically to achieve broad but common goals.

CONCLUSION

In conclusion, we present not a set of answers but a set of strategic questions that arise from the volume in its entirety. For donors, the key questions must be: why are we exaggerating the role that NGOs play within civil society? Would not a more realistic analysis of what they can contribute help us to work with NGOs? In addition they should also ponder why their citizens (for bilaterals) and constituents (for multilaterals) do not provide them with support: have they an educational function in the north which they have singularly failed to achieve to date?

For those who control state power the questions are complex, given their great diversity, the short term pressures they face and the fact that some lack genuine legitimacy. The obvious question, though, is whether NGOs constitute a threat to state power or whether a more laissez-faire stance to their activities (except on the issue of probity) might not be likely to generate more benefits to them than costs.

NGOs and their staff – if they are prepared to seize the initiative, ask difficult questions and act strategically – have the greatest room for manoeuvre about the nature of NGO–state–donor relationships. NNGOs need to analyse carefully their current situations and ask whether it is not time to scale down, refocus and concentrate on a smaller number of objectives. Prime among these must be action in their own societies where they can be most effective. This could mean 'alternative trading', specialist advice and support to southern partners, participation in global alliances for lobbying and advocacy, domestic development work, and greater attention to encouraging values and attitudes of service, voluntarism and sustainable living. It certainly means more attention to development education: raising the awareness and knowledge of northern publics so that they appreciate the consequences of not demanding that their governments assist poorer people in poorer countries more effectively. This is an old debate among NNGOs, but not a sterile one: the growing strength of NGOs in the South provides a new context in which to return to old but crucial questions with renewed vigour.

For SNGOs, perhaps the time has come for a re-evaluation of the role of exogenous and endogenous factors in their programming and future direction. There would be no single answer to the questions raised by such a re-evaluation, but for many SNGOs it would surely mean returning to their roots: their ultimate achievements are not their scale, budgets or reputation, but their capacity to support effective association at the local level.

Embarrassing those in positions of power has always been a hallmark of NGO activity; the problem is that many NGOs themselves have now become the powerful, with depressing consequences for their ability to be self-critical, honest and courageous about the future. Perhaps now is the time to turn the spotlight on NGOs themselves; after all, there is nothing predetermined about the trends outlined in this book – NGOs have choices about what they do, how they do it and how it is financed. There is no inherent benefit in size or growth, nor is there one model of NGO activity which all must follow. Of course NGOs must work constructively and creatively with sources of funding, centres of influence, and those in political authority. But if they grow 'too close for comfort', NGOs, like Icarus before them, may plummet to the ground when the heat of the donors melts the wax in their wings.

Bibliography

Acosta, G., Flores, M., and Silva, G. (1994) 'Los Servicios Legales y las Campānas de Fin de Siglo: Preguntas y Propuestas', *El Otro Derecho*, vol. 5(3), pp. 75–88.

Aga Khan Foundation (1988) *The Enabling Environment*, report of Nairobi conference, London: Aga Khan Foundation.

Ainscow, M. (1993) *Special Needs in the Classroom: a Teacher Education Guide*, London: Jessica Kingsley/UNESCO.

Ainscow, M. (1994) 'Supporting International Innovation in Teacher Education', in H. Bradley (ed.), *Developing Teachers, Developing Schools*, London: David Fulton.

AKF/NOVIB (1993) *Going to Scale: the BRAC Experience 1972–1992 and Beyond*, The Hague: Aga Khan/NOVIB.

Anangwe, A. (1995) 'NGO–State Relations in Kenya', mimeo, University of Nairobi.

ANGOC (1988), 'NGOs and International Development Cooperation', *Lok Niti, Journal of the Asian NGO Coalition*, vol. 5(4), Manila: Asian NGO Coalition.

Annis, S. (1987) 'Can Small-Scale Development be a Large-Scale Policy? The Case of Latin America', *World Development*, vol. 15, Supplement, pp. 129–34.

Antonios, R. (1994) 'Strategies for Action for NGOs and the Notion of Civil Society', paper presented to the Conference on Egyptian Society in the Light of the New World Order, Cairo: University of Cairo, May.

APSA (American Political Science Association) (1995) 'Preliminary Program: 1995 Annual Meeting', *PS: Political Science and Politics*, vol. 28(2) (June), pp. 295–406.

Arellano-López, S. and Petras, J. (1994) 'NGOs and Poverty Alleviation in Bolivia', *Development and Change*, vol. 25(3), pp. 555–68.

ARTI (1991) *Approaches to Development: The NGO Experience in Sri Lanka*, Colombo: ARTI.

Australian Council for Overseas Aid (1992) *Aid for Change*, Canberra: ACFOA.

Babadji, R. (1991) 'The Associative Phenomenon in Algeria', in M. Camau (ed.), *Changements Politiques au Maghreb*, Paris: Centre National de la Recherche Scientifique.

Bebbington, A. and Farrington, J. (1993) 'Government, NGOs and Agricultural Development: Perspectives on Changing Inter-Organisational Relationships', *Journal of Development Studies*, vol. 29(2), pp. 199–219.

Bebbington, A. and Farrington, J. (1992) *Private Voluntary Initiatives and Governments, NGOs and Agricultural Development*, London: ODI.

Bebbington, A. and Kopp, A. (1995) *Bolivia Case Study: Evaluation of the Swedish NGO Support Programme*, Stockholm: SIDA.

Bebbington, A. and Riddell, R. (1994) 'New Agendas and Old Problems: issues, options and challenges in direct funding of southern NGOs', paper presented at

285

the Workshop on 'NGOs and Development: Performance and Accountability', University of Manchester, 27–9 June.

Bebbington, A. and Thiele, G. (eds) with Davies, P., Prager, M. Riveros (1993) *NGOs and the State in Latin America: Rethinking Roles in Sustainable Agricultural Development*, London: Routledge.

Bebbington, A., Domingo, T., Kopp, A. and Quisbert, J. (1995) *Peasant Federations, Food Systems and Rural Politics in Bolivia*, London: IIED.

Bebbington, A. *et al.* (1991) *Evaluacion Del Impacto De Los Proyectos Auspiciados Por La Fundacion InterAmericana Con Organizaciones Indigenas En El Ecuador*, Washington: Inter-American Foundation.

Bernstein, S. R. (1991) *Managing Contracted Services in the Non-profit Agency: Administrative, Ethical and Political Issues*, Philadelphia: Temple University Press.

Bhatnagar, B. and Williams, A. (1992) *Participatory Development and the World Bank: Potential Directions for Change*, Washington, DC: World Bank.

Biekart, K. (1995) 'European NGOs and Democratisation in Central America: Assessing Performance in the Light of Changing Priorities', in M. Edwards and D. Hulme (eds), *NGO Performance and Accountability: Beyond the Magic Bullet*, London: Earthscan and West Hartford: Kumarian Press.

Blair, Harry (1993) 'Doing Democracy in the Third World: Developing an Applied Theory of Democracy', paper for the annual meeting of the American Political Science Association, Washington, 2–5 September.

Blair, Harry (1994) 'Civil Society and Democratic Development: A CDIE Evaluation Paper', Washington: USAID, PPC/CDIE/E/POA, 24 February.

Blair, Harry (1995) 'Civil Society and Building Democracy: Lessons from International Donor Experience', paper for the annual meeting of the American Political Science Association, Chicago, 31 August–3 September.

Blair, Harry and Gary Hansen (1994) *Weighing in on the Scales of Justice: Strategic Approaches for Donor-supported Rule of Law Programs*, USAID Program and Operations Assessment Report No. 7, Washington: USAID, Center for Development Information and Evaluation, February.

Boularès, N. (1993) 'Associative Life in Tunisia', paper presented to the Conference of Tunisian NGOs on the Challenges of the Future, Tunis, July.

Bratton, Michael (1989) 'The Politics of Government–NGO Relations in Africa', *World Development*, vol. 17(4), pp. 569–87.

Bratton, Michael (1986) 'Beyond the State: Civil Society and Associational Life in Africa', *World Politics*, vol. 41(3), pp. 407–30.

Bratton, Michael (1990) 'NGOs in Africa: Can They Influence Public Policy?' *Development and Change*, vol. 21(1), pp. 87–118.

Brautigam, D. (1992) 'Governance, Economy and Foreign Aid', *Studies in Comparative International Development*, vol. 27(3), pp. 3–25.

Brautigam, Deborah (1991) 'Development, Institutional Pluralism and the Voluntary Sector', Washington D.C.: World Bank.

Brodhead, Tim and Herbert-Copley, Brent (1988) *Bridges of Hope? Canadian Voluntary Agencies and the Third World*, Ottawa: North-South Institute.

Brown, L. David (1988) 'Organizational Barriers to NGO Strategic Action', *Lok Niti Journal of the Asian NGO Coalition*, vol. 5(4), Manila: ANGOC.

Brown, L. David (1990) 'Policy Impacts on the NGO Sector', Washington D.C.: World Bank.

Brown, David L. and Korten, D. C. (1991) 'Working More Efficiently with Non-governmental Organizations', in Paul and Israel (eds), pp. 44–93.

Burgos, G. (1994) 'Los Servicios Legales Alternativos: Preguntas Indiscretas Ante el Nuevo Contexto Político-Economico', *Portavoz*, vol. 38, pp. 18–26.

Cannon-Lorgan, C. (forthcoming) 'Dancing with the State: the Role of NGOs in Health Care and Health Policy', *Journal of International Development*.

Carroll, T. (1992) *Intermediary NGOs: the Supporting Link in Grassroots Development*, West Hartford: Kumarian Press.

Carroll, T., Humphreys, D. and Scurrah, M. (1991) 'Grassroots Support Organisations in Peru', *Development in Practice*, vol. 1(2), pp. 97–108.

Cernea, Michael (1988) *NGOs and Local Development*, Washington, DC: World Bank.

Chambers, R. (1992) 'Spreading and Self-Improving: a Strategy for Scaling-up', in M. Edwards and D. Hulme (eds), *Making a Difference: NGOs and Development in a Changing World*, London: Earthscan.

Chambers, R. (1995) 'Poverty and Vulnerability: Whose Reality Counts?', *IDS Discussion Paper* 347, Brighton: Institute for Development Studies.

Chambers, Robert (1983) *Rural Development: Putting the Last First*, Harlow: Longman.

CIVICUS (1994) *Citizens Strengthening Global Civil Society*, Washington, DC: Civicus.

Clark, John (1991) *Democratizing Development: The Role of Voluntary Organizations*, West Hartford: Kumarian Press.

Clark, J. (1993) *The State and the Voluntary Sector*, Human Resources Development and Operations Policy Working Paper No. 12, Washington, DC: World Bank.

Cohen, Joshua and Rogers, Joel (1992) 'Secondary Associations and Democratic Governance', *Politics and Society*, vol. 20(4) (December), 393–472. (Also the responses in this special issue of the journal).

Colclough, C. and Manor, J. (1991) *States or Markets? Neo-Liberalism and the Development Policy Debate*, Oxford: Clarendon Press.

Commission on Global Governance (1995) *Our Common Neighbourhood: the Report of the Commission on Global Governance*, Oxford: Oxford University Press.

Covey, J. (1995) 'Accountability and Effectiveness in NGO Policy Alliances', in M. Edurads and D. Hulme (eds.) *NGO Performance and Accontability: Beyond the Magic Bullet*, London: Earthscan and West Hartford: Kumarian Press, 167–181.

DAC (Development Advisory Committee of the Organization for Economic Co-operation and Development) (1995) *Participatory Development and Good Governance*, Development Co-operation and Guidelines Series, Paris: OECD.

De Coninck, J., with Riddell, R. C. (1992) 'Evaluating The Impact of NGOs in Rural Poverty Alleviation: Uganda Country Study', *Working Paper 51*, London: Overseas Development Institute.

de Silva, K. M. (1981) *A History of Sri Lanka*, Colombo: University Press.

Diamond, Larry (1992) 'Introduction: Civil Society and the Struggle for Democracy', in Larry Diamond (ed.), *The Democratic Revolution: Struggles for Freedom and Democracy in the Developing World*, New York: Freedom House, pp. 1–27.

Diamond, Larry (1994) 'Toward Democratic Consolidation: Rethinking Civil Society', *Journal of Democracy*, vol. 5(3) (July), pp. 4–17.

Echenique, J. (1994) 'NGOs and Pro-Democracy Movements in Latin America', in A. Clayton (ed.), *Governance, Democracy and Conditionality: What Role for NGOs?* Oxford: INTRAC.

Economist Intelligence Unit (1994) *Thailand Country Report, Third Quarter, 1994*, London: EIU.

Edwards, M. (1991) *Strengthening Government Capacity for National Development and International Negotiation*, London: Save the Children Fund.

Edwards, M. (1993) 'Does the Doormat Influence the Boot? Critical Thoughts on UK NGOs and International Advocacy', *Development in Practice*, vol. 3(3), pp. 163–75.

Edwards, M. (1994a) 'NGOs in the age of information', *IDS Bulletin*, vol. 25(2), pp. 117–24.

Edwards, M. (1994b) 'International Non-Governmental Organisations, "Good Government" and the "New Policy Agenda": Lessons of Experience at the Programme Level', *Democratization*, vol. 1(3), pp. 504–515.

Edwards, M. (1994c) 'NGO Performance and Accountability in the New World Order: a Personal Summary of the Manchester Conference', mimeo, SCF-UK, London.

Edwards, M. and Hulme, D. (1992) *Making a Difference: NGOs and Development in a Changing World*, London: Earthscan.

Edwards, M. and Hulme, D. (1994) 'NGOs and Development: Performance and Accountability in the "New World Order"', mimeo, London: Save the Children Fund (UK) and Manchester: Institute for Development Policy and Management.

Edwards, M. and Hulme, D. (eds) (1995) *NGO Performance and Accountability: Beyond the Magic Bullet*, London: Earthscan and West Hartford: Kumarian Press.

El Taller (1995) *NGOs and Civil Society in the Arab World*, Tunis: El Taller.

Elliott, Charles (1987) 'Some aspects of relations between North and South in the NGO sector', *World Development*, vol. 15(supplement), pp. 57–68.

Farrington, J., and Bebbington, A., (1993) *Reluctant Partners? Non-governmental Organisations, the State and Sustainable Agricultural Development*, London: Routledge.

Fernandez, A. P. (1987) 'NGOs in South Asia', *World Development*, vol. 15 (supplement), pp. 39–49.

Fernandes, R. (1985) 'Sem Fins Lucrativos', *Comunicacoes ISER*, vol. 4(5), July, Rio de Janeiro: ISER.

Fernando, Edgar (ed.) (1982) *Rural Development in Sri Lanka*, Ministry of Plan Implementation.

Fernando, Sunimal (1991) *Development of NGOs of Sri Lanka. A Directory*, Colombo: IRED – Development Innovations and Networks.

Fisher, J. (1993) *The Road from Rio*, New York: Praeger.

Fowler, A. (1988) 'NGOs in Africa: Achieving Comparative Advantage in Relief and Micro-Development', *IDS Discussion Paper* 249, Brighton: Institute for Development Studies.

Fowler, A. (1992) 'Distant Obligations: Speculations on NGO Funding and the Global Market', *Review of African Political Economy*, 55.

Fowler, A. (1993) 'Non-Governmental Organizations as Agents of Democratization: an African Perspective', *Journal of International Development*, vol. 5(3), May–June, pp. 325–39.

Fowler, A. (1992) 'NGOs as Agents of Democratization: An African Perspective', mimeo, (draft), May, Sussex: IDS.

Fox, J. (1992) 'Leadership accountability in a regional peasant organization', *Development and Change*, vol. 23(2), pp. 1–36.

Freire, P. (1972) *Pedagogy of the Oppressed*, London: Penguin, New York: Herder and Herder.

Friedmann, J. (1992) *Empowerment: The Politics of Alternative Development*, Oxford: Basil Blackwell.

Gamage, Willie and Dias, Richard (1990) *Some Aspects of Government–NGO Relations in Sri Lanka*, Colombo: IRED – Development Innovations and Networks.

GAO (United States General Accounting Office) (1994) *Promoting Democracy: Foreign Affairs and Defense Agencies Funds and Activities – 1991 to 1993*, Washington: GAO.

Garforth, C. (1993) 'Rural People's Organizations and Agricultural Extension in the Upper North of Thailand: Who Benefits?', mimeo, University of Reading.

Garilao, E. D. (1987) 'Indigenous NGOs as strategic institutions: managing the relationship with government and resource agencies', *World Development*, vol. 15(supplement), pp. 113–120.

German, T. and Randel, J. (1995) *The Reality of Aid 1995*, London: Earthscan.

Ghazali, A. (1991) 'A Contribution to the Analysis of the Associative Phenomenon in Morocco', in M. Camau (ed.), *Changements Politiques au Maghreb*, Paris: Centre National de Recherche Scientifique.

Gilson, L., Sen, P. D., Mohammed, S. and Mukinja, P. (1993) 'Assessing the Potential of Health Sector Non-Governmental Organizations: Policy Options', *Health Policy and Planning*, vol. 9(1), March, pp. 14–24.

Good, A. (1994) 'Paying the Piper, Calling the Tune? Present and Future Relationships among Northern NGOs, Southern NGOs and the ODA', paper presented at the International Workshop on NGOs and Development: Performance and Accountability in the New World Order, Manchester: Save the Children Fund (UK) and Institute for Development Policy and Management.

Granovetter, M. (1985) 'Economic Action and Social Structure: The Problem of Embeddedness', *American Journal of Sociology*, vol. 91(3), pp. 481–510.

Hanlon, Joseph (1990) 'New Missionaries in Mozambique', mimeo, London.

Hansen, Gary (1995) 'Constituencies for Reform: Strategic Approaches for Donor-supported Civic Advocacy Programs', fourth draft (revised), Washington, DC: USAID/PPC/CDIE/POA.

Hashemi, S. (1995) 'NGO Accountability in Bangladesh: Beneficiaries, Donors and the State', in M. Edwards and D. Hulme (eds), *NGO Performance and Accountability: Beyond the Magic Bullet*, London: Earthscan and West Hartford: Kumarian Press.

Hawley, K. (1992) *From Grants to Contracts: A Practical Guide for Voluntary Organisations*, London: NCVO/Directory of Social Change.

Hirschman, A. O. (1970) *Exit, Voice and Loyalty*, Cambridge, Mass.: Harvard University Press.

Hirsh, P. (1994) 'The Thai Countryside in the 1990s', *South-East Asian Affairs*.

Hojman, D. (1993) 'Non-Governmental Organisations (NGOs) and the Chilean Transition to Democracy', *European Review of Latin American and Caribbean Studies*, vol. 54, pp. 7–24.

Howell, J. (1993a) *China Opens its Doors: the Politics of Economic Transition*, Hemel Hempstead: Harvester Wheatsheaf and Boulder, Col: Lynne Rienner Publishers.

Howell, J. (1993b) 'The Poverty of Civil Society: Insights from China', *Discussion Paper*, no. 240, School of Development Studies, University of East Anglia.

Howell, J. (1994) 'Refashioning State–Society Relations in China', *The European Journal of Development Research*, vol. 6(1), pp. 197–215.

Howes, M. and Sattar, M. G. (1992) 'Bigger and Better? Scaling-up Strategies Pursued by BRAC 1972–1991', in M. Edwards and D. Hulme (eds), *Making a Difference: NGOs and Development in a Changing World*, London: Earthscan.

Hulme, D. (1994) 'Does the World Bank have a Learning Disability? A Reply to Venkatesan', *Public Administration and Development*, vol. 14(1), pp. 93–7.

Hulme, D. and Edwards, M. (eds) (1996) *NGOs, States and Donors: Too Close for Comfort?* London: Macmillan.

Hulme, D. and Mosley, P. (1996) *Finance Against Poverty*, two vols, London: Routledge.

Huntington, Samuel P. (1968) *Political Order in Changing Societies*, New Haven: Yale University Press.

Hyden, Goran (1995) 'Assisting the Growth of Civil Society: How Might It Be Improved?', paper for Workshop on Civil Society and Democracy, arranged by the Development Assistance Committee of the OECD, Uppsala University, Sweden, 12–13 June.

Irvine, G. (1987) *The World Bank and World Vision: A Status Report*, World Vision International Staff Paper.

Isenman, Paul (1980) 'Basic Needs: the Case of Sri Lanka', *World Development*, vol. 8, pp. 247–9.

Jorgensen, H., Larsen, J. and Udsholt, L. (1993) *The Role of Danish Development NGOs: Challenges for the Future*, Copenhagen: Danish Volunteer Service.

Kandil, A. (1994) *The Status of the Third Sector in the Arab Region*, Tunis: El Taller.

Karp, A. W. (1992) 'Contracting NGOs to Implement Rural Water and Sanitation Projects in Bolivia', *Waterlines*, vol. 11(1), July, pp. 23–5.

Kendall, J. and Perri 6 (1994) 'Government and the Voluntary Sector in the United Kingdom', in Perri 6, S. K. E. Saxon-Harold and J. Kendall (eds), pp. 16–40.

Klinmahorm, S. and Ireland, K. (1992) 'Government–NGO Collaboration in Bangkok', in M. Edwards and D. Hulme (eds), *Making a Difference: NGOs and Development in a Changing World*, London: Earthscan.

Korten, D. (1987) 'Third Generation NGO Strategies: A Key to People-Centred Development', *World Development*, vol. 15, supplement, pp. 145–59.

Korten, David C. (1990) *Getting to the 21st Century: Voluntary Action and the Global Agenda*, West Hartford: Kumarian Press.

LaFond, A. (1995) *Sustaining Primary Health Care*, London: Earthscan/Save the Children Fund.

Landim, L. (1993) *Para além do Mercado e do Estado? Filantropia e Cidadania no Brasil*, Rio de Janeiro: ISER.

Lateef, K. Sarwar (1992) *Governance and Development*, Washington, DC: World Bank.

Lawson, C. and Kaluwa, B. (1992) *Seven Malawian Parastatals: An Appraisal of Performance and Policy*, CDS Occasional Paper 01/92, Bath.

Lefort, C. (1983) *A Invencao Democratica – Os Limites do Totalitarismo*, São Paulo: Editora Brasilense.

Lehmann, D. (1990) *Democracy and Development in Latin America*, Cambridge: Polity.

Levinson, M. and Wehrfritz, G. (1994) 'Some Cracks in the Wall of the Miracle Economy', *Newsweek*, 16 May.

Lewis, D., Sobhan, B. and Jonsson, G. (1994) *Routes of Funding, Roots of Trust? Swedish Assistance to Non-Governmental Organizations in Bangladesh*, Stockholm: SIDA.

MacDonald, Laura (1992) 'Turning to the NGOs: Competing Conceptions of Civil Society in Latin America', paper presented to the Annual Meeting of the Latin American Studies Association, Los Angeles, 24–7 September.

Makabenta, L. (1995) 'Thailand', *Jakarta Post*, 13 January.

Manila (1989) 'Asian NGO Coalition', *The Manila Declaration on People's Participation and Sustainable Development*, Manila, June.

Marc, Alexandre (1992) 'NGOs in Kyrghyzstan', mimeo, Washington, DC: World Bank.

Meyer, C. (1992) 'A Step Back as Donors Shift Institution Building from the Public to the "Private" Sector', *World Development*, vol. 20(8), pp. 1115–26.

Michels, Robert (1915) *Political Parties*, reprint, New York: Dover, 1959.

Ministry of Finance and Planning (1981) *Public Expenditure Programme*, Colombo: Government Printer.

Montgomery, R. (1995) 'Disciplining or Protecting the Poor? Avoiding the Social Costs of Peer Pressure in Solidarity Group Micro-Credit Schemes', *Papers in Development*, 12, Swansea: Centre for Development Studies.

Montgomery, R., Bhattacharya, D. and Hulme, D. (1996) 'Credit for the Poor in Bangladesh: The BRAC Rural Development Programme and the Government Thana Resource Development and Employment Programme', in D. Hulme and P. Mosley (eds) *Finance Against Poverty*, vol. 2, London: Routledge.

Moore, B. (1996) *The Social Origins of Dictatorship and Democracy*, Boston: Beacon Press.

Moore, M. (1993) 'Good Government? Introduction', *IDS Bulletin*, vol. 24(1), pp. 1–6.

Mosher, S. (1991) 'Cynicism Evident in Aid to China Flood Victims: Give and Let Live', *Far Eastern Economic Review*, vol. 153, 8 August, p. 10.

Muir, A., with Riddell, R. C. (1992) 'Evaluating the Impact of NGOs in Rural Poverty Alleviation: Zimbabwe Country Study', *Working Paper 52*, London: Overseas Development Institute.

Mushi, S. S., Semboja, J. and Therkilsden, O. (1992) 'Issues of Service Provision in the 1990s in Eastern Africa', paper presented at a Seminar on 'State and Non-State Provision of Services in Eastern Africa and South Asia', Copenhagen, June.

NCARRD NGO Committee Sri Lanka (1980) *Report of the National NGO Workshop on Follow-up to WCARRD*: 5–6 September.

Nerfin, M. (1987) 'Neither Prince nor Merchant: Citizen', *IFDA Dossier*, Geneva: IFDA.

Norway (1995) Royal Norwegian Ministry of Foreign Affairs, 'Support for Democratic Development', Oslo: Royal Norwegian Ministry of Foreign Affairs, May.

OECD (1994) *Development Cooperation*, Paris: OECD.

Olson, Mancur (1993) 'Dictatorship, Democracy and Development', *American Political Science Review*, vol. 87(3) (September), pp. 567–76.

Organization for Economic Cooperation and Development (1988) *Voluntary Aid for Development: The Role of NGOs*, Paris: OECD.

Overseas Development Administration (1995) *A Guide to the Social Analysis of Projects*, London: HMSO.

Overseas Development Institute (1990, 1991) various papers on NGOs in the Agricultural Sector by John Farrington and Anthony Bebbington, including 'The Scope for NGO–Government Interaction in Agricultural Technology Development' and 'Private Voluntary Initiatives', London: ODI.

Overseas Development Institute (1995) 'The Funding of NGOs', *ODI Briefing Note*, London: ODI.

Paul, S. and Israel, A. (eds) (1991) *Nongovernmental Organizations and the World Bank: Cooperation for Development*, Washington, DC: World Bank.

Pearce, J. (1993) 'NGOs and Social Change: Agents or Facilitators?', *Development in Practice*, vol. 3(3), pp. 222–7.

Politics and Society (1992) 'Special Issue: Secondary Associations and Democracy', vol. 20(4), December.

Powell, W. W. (ed.) (1987) *The Non-profit Sector – A Research Handbook*, New Haven, Corr.: Yale University Press.

Pratten, D. and Ali Baldo, S. (1995) 'Return to the Roots: Processes of Legitimacy in Sudanese Migrant Associations' in M. Edwards and D. Hulme (eds.) *NGO Performance and Accountability: Beyond the Magic Bullet*, London: Earthscan.

Przeworski, A. (1991) *Democracy and the Market, Political and Economic Reforms in Eastern Europe and Latin America*, Cambridge: Cambridge University Press.

Puttnam, R. (1993) *Making Democracy Work: Civic Traditions in Modern Italy*, Princeton: Princeton University Press.

Qureshi, Moeen (1990) 'The World Bank and NGOs: New Approaches', speech to the Washington Chapter of the Society for International Development, Washington, DC: World Bank, 22 April.

Rademacher, A. and Tamang, D. (1993) *Democracy, Development and NGOs*, Kathmandu: SEARCH.

Ramesh, J. (1995) 'NGO Accountability in India: the Working Womens' Forum Model', in M. Edwards and D. Hulme (eds) *Beyond the Magic Bullet: NGO Performance and Accountability in the Post Cold War World*, London: Earthscan and West Hartford: Kumarian Press.

Randel, J. (1992) 'Scaling-up and Community Capacity: Some Experiences of ActionAid Uganda', paper presented at a Workshop on 'Scaling-up NGO Impact', University of Manchester/SCF-UK.

Rausch, Jonathan (1994) *Demosclerosis: The Silent Killer of American Government*, New York: Times Books, Random House.

Riddell, R., Bebbington, A. and Peck, L. (1995) *Development By Proxy. An Evaluation of the Swedish NGO Support Programme*, Stockholm: SIDA.

Riddell, R. and Robinson, M. (1996) *NGOs and Rural Poverty Alleviation*, Oxford: Oxford University Press.

Riddell, R. C. and Bebbington, A. J., with Davis, D. (1994) *Developing Country NGOs and Donor Governments*, London: Overseas Development Institute.

Ritchie-Vance, M. (1991) *The Art of Association: NGOs and Civil Society in Colombia*, Rosslyn, VA: Inter-American Foundation.

Robinson, M. (1993) 'Governance, Democracy and Conditionality: NGOs and the New Policy Agenda' in A. Clayton (ed.), *Governance, Democracy and Conditionality: What Role for NGOs?*, Oxford: INTRAC.

Rosenberg, Richard (1994) 'Beyond Self-Sufficiency: Licensed Leverage and Microfinance Strategy', Washington, DC: USAID, 4/26/94. Draft of a paper later given at the Brookings Institute conference, autumn.

Roth, G. (1987) *The Private Provision of Public Services in Developing Countries*, Washington, DC: World Bank and Oxford University Press.

Rousseau, M. and Sissons, C. (1992) *A Study of Canadian Coalitions of Non-Governmental Organizations*, Ottawa: CCIC/CIDA.

Rutherford, S. (1995) *ASA: The Biography of an NGO*, Dhaka: University Press.

Salamon, L. M. (1993) 'The Global Associational Revolution: the Rise of the Third Sector on the World Scene', *Occasional Papers*, no. 15, Baltimore: Institute for Policy Studies, Johns Hopkins University.

Salamon, L. M. and Anheier, H. K. (1993) *The Third Route: Subsidiarity, Third-Party Government and the Provision of Social Services in the United States and Germany*, report to OECD, Paris.

Salamon, L. M. (1987) 'Partners in Public Service: The Scope and Theory of Government–Non-profit Relations', in Powell (ed.), pp. 99–117.

Salamon, L. M., and Anheier, H. K. (1991) 'Towards an Understanding of the International Non-Profit Sector', project outline, Johns Hopkins University Institute for Policy Studies, December.

Salamon, L. M. and Anheier, H. K. (1992) *In Search of the Non-Profit Sector: The Question of Definitions*, Baltimore, MD: Johns Hopkins University.

Salmen, L. F. and Eaves, A. P. (1989) *World Bank Work with NGOs*, Country Economics Department, WPS 305.

Salmen, L. F. and Eaves, A. P. (1991) 'Interactions between Nongovernmental Organizations and the World Bank: Evidence from Bank Projects', in Paul and Israel (eds), pp. 94–133.

Samaraweera, Vijaya (1973) 'The Development of the Administrative System from 1802 to 1932', in K. M. de Silva (ed.), *History of Ceylon*, vol. III, University of Ceylon, Peradeniya.

Santos, B. (1994) 'Subjetividade, Ciudadania y Emancipación', *El Otro Derecho*, vol. 5(3), pp. 7–60.

Save the Children Fund (1993) *Report on the Integrated Education Workshop for South-East Asia*, Bangkok: Save the Children Fund (UK).

Saxon-Harold, S. K. E. and Kendall, J. (eds) (1994), *Researching the Voluntary Sector: A National, Local and International Perspective*, 2nd edn, London: Charities Aid Foundation.

Schaffer, B. B. (1969) 'Deadlock in Development Administration' in C. Leys (ed.), *Politics of Developing Countries*, Cambridge: Cambridge University Press.

Serrano, I. (1994) *Civil Society in the Asia–Pacific Region*, Washington, DC: CIVICUS (World Alliance for Citizen Participation).

Smillie, I. (1993) 'Introduction', in I. Smillie and H. Helmich (eds), *Non-Governmental Organisations and Governments:Stakeholders for Development*, Paris: OECD.

Smillie, I. (1995) 'Painting Canadian Roses Red', in M. Edwards and D. Hulme (eds), *Beyond the Magic Bullet: NGO Performance and Accountability in the Post Cold War World*, London: Earthscan and West Hartford: Kumarian Press.

Smillie, I. (1995) *The Alms Bazaar*, London: IT Publications.

Smillie, I. and Helmich, H. (1993) *Non-Governmental Organisations and Governments: Stakeholders for Development*, Paris: OECD.

Smith, B. (1990) *More than Altruism: the Politics of Private Foreign Aid*, Princeton: Princeton University Press.

Smith, S. and Lipsky, M. (1993) *Non Profits for Hire: the Welfare State in the Age of Contracting*, Cambridge, Mass.: Harvard University Press.

Sollis, P. (1992) 'Multilateral Agencies, NGOs and Policy Reform', *Development in Practice*, vol. 2(3), October, pp. 163–78.

Tandon, Rajesh (1987) 'The Relationship between NGOs and Government', mimeo, paper presented to the Conference on the Promotion of Autonomous Development, New Delhi: PRIA.

Tandon, Rajesh (1991) *NGO–Government Relations: A Source of Life or a Kiss of Death?* New Delhi: Society for Participatory Research in Asia.

Tandon, Rajesh (1992) *NGOs and Civil Society*, Boston: Institute for Development Research.

Tendler, Judith (1982) *Turning Private Voluntary Organizations Into Development Agencies: Questions for Evaluation*, Program Evaluation Discussion Paper no. 12, Washington, DC: US Agency for International Development, April.

Thai Development Newsletter (1994) 'Public Forum Urged on Charter Changes', *Thai Development Newsletter*, p. 24.

Thomas-Slayter, B. (1994) 'Structural Change, Power Politics and Community Organisations in Africa: Challenging the Patterns, Puzzles and Paradoxes', *World Development*, vol. 22(10), pp. 1479–90.

Tilakaratne, S. (1992) *Status Paper on the NGO Involvement in Rural Development of Sri Lanka*, Colombo: IRED.

Tolfree, D. (1995) *Roofs and Roots: the Care of Separated Children in the Third World*, London: Arena/Save the Children.

UNDP (1993) *Human Development Report 1993*, Oxford: Oxford University Press.

UNESCO (1993) *Special Needs in the Classroom: a Teacher Education Resource Pack*, Paris: UNESCO.

UNESCO (1994) *Making it Happen: examples of good practice in special needs education and community-based programmes*, Paris: UNESCO.

Uphoff, N. (1986) *Local Institutional Development*, West Hartford: Kumarian Press.

Uphoff, N. (1987) '*Relations between Government and NGOs and the Promotion of Autonomous Development*', paper presented to the Conference on the Promotion of Autonomous Development, Ithaca: Cornell University.

Uphoff, N. (1995) 'Why NGOs are not a Third Sector', in M. Edwards and D. Hulme (eds.) *NGO Performance and Accountability: Beyond the Magic Bullet*, London: Earthscan, pp. 17–30.

USAID, Directorate for Policy (1991) 'Democracy and Governance: USAID Policy', Washington, DC: USAID.

USAID (1994) *Strategies for Sustainable Development*, Washington, DC: USAID, March.

Van Tuijl, P. (1994) 'Conditionality for whom? Indonesia and the experience of the IGGI: the NGO experience', in A. Clayton (ed.), *Governance, Democracy and Conditionality: what role for NGOs?*, Oxford: INTRAC.

Voorhies, S. J. (1993) 'Working with Government Using World Bank Funds: Lessons from the Uganda Orphans and Health Rehabilitation Program', *World Vision Staff Working Paper* No. 16, Monrovia: World Vision International.

Wapenhans, W. (1992) *Effective Implementation: Key to Development Impact*, Report of the Task Force, Washington, DC: World Bank.

White, G. (1994) 'Civil Society, Democratization and Development (1) Clearing the Analytical Ground', *Democratization*, vol. 1(3), pp. 375–90.

Wiarda, Howard J. and Kline, Harvey F. (1993) 'The Latin American Tradition and Process of Development', in Wiarda and Kline (eds), *Latin American Politics and Development*, 3rd edn, Boulder, Col.: Westview Press, pp. 1–125.

Wils, F. (1995) 'Scaling-up, Mainstreaming and Accountability: the Challenge for NGOs', in M. Edwards and D. Hulme (eds), *NGO Performance and Accountability: Beyond the Magic Bullet*, London: Earthscan and West Hartford: Kumarian Press.

Wood, G. D. (1994) *Bangladesh: Whose Ideas, Whose Interests?*, London: IT Publications and Dhaka: University Press.

World Bank (1980) *World Development Report 1980*, Washington, DC: World Bank.

World Bank (1990) *World Development Report 1990*, Oxford: Oxford University Press.

World Bank (1992) *Terms of Reference for Study on the NGO Sector in Uganda and Tanzania: NGO Sector Study Issues Paper*. Washington, DC: World Bank.

Zadek, S. and Gatward, M. (1995) 'Transforming the Transnational NGOs: Social Auditing or Bust?', in M. Edwards and D. Hulme (eds), *Beyond the Magic Bullet: NGO Performance and Accountability in the Post Cold War World*, London: Earthscan and West Hartford: Kumarian Press.

Zadek, S. and Szabo, S. (1994) *Valuing Organisation: The Case of Sarvodaya*, NEF Working Paper No. 1, London: New Economics Foundation.

Index